Inclusive and Accessible Secondary $

Drawing on extensive professional experience and detailed empirical evidence, this resource sets out an insightful, highly practical approach to teaching science to secondary-aged students with learning difficulties and other special educational or additional support needs (SEND/ASN).

The book explores the barriers that the secondary school science curriculum currently presents to those who do not learn in the expected way, before providing a wealth of practical strategies to help teachers, in both specialist and mainstream settings, to make science more accessible. Multiple science topics are covered in depth, including living and non-living matter, the periodic table, electrical energy, the solar system, the environment and more. Each topic is supported by extensive teachers' notes outlining activities that will allow educational practitioners to enact the principles of accessibility in the classroom.

With rich field notes and practical takeaways included to accompany key insights, this accessible book will provide science teachers at the secondary school level, as well as support staff and anyone aspiring to teach science to SEN/ASN learners, with the guidance and resources they need to make science education meaningfully inclusive.

Jane Essex is an educator with a professional and research interest in science education for diverse learners. She has pioneered inclusive and accessible STEM outreach events. Her work was recognised with the Royal Society of Chemistry's Inclusion and Diversity Award in 2019.

Inclusive and Accessible Science for Students with Additional or Special Needs: How to Teach Science Effectively to Diverse Learners in Secondary Schools
Jane Essex
2023/pb: 978-0-367-76627-6

True Partnerships in SEND: Working Together to Give Children, Families and Professionals a Voice
Heather Green and Becky Edwards
2023/pb: 978-0-367-54494-2

Teaching Reading to All Learners Including those with Complex Needs
Sarah Moseley
2023/pb: 978-1-032-11475-0

The SENCO Survival Guide: The Nuts and Bolts of Everything You Need to Know, 3ed
Sylvia Edwards
2023/pb: 978-1-032-21947-9

Cultural Inclusion for Young People with SEND: Practical Strategies for Meaningful Inclusion in Arts and Culture
Paul Morrow
2023/pb: 978-0-367-64123-8

Providing Relationships and Sex Education for Special Learners
Paul Bray
2021/pb: 978-1-138-48747-5

Inclusion: A Principled Guide for School Leaders
Nicola Crossley and Des Hewitt
2021/pb: 978-0-367-34528-0

Leading on Inclusion: The Role of the SENCO
Mhairi Beaton, Geraldene Codina and Julie Wharton
2021/pb: 978-0-367-42050-5

The Governance Handbook for SEND and Inclusion: Schools that Work for All Learners
Adam Boddison
2020/pb: 978-0-367-37003-9

Inclusive and Accessible Secondary Science

How to Teach Science Effectively to Students with Additional or Special Needs

Jane Essex

Routledge
Taylor & Francis Group

LONDON AND NEW YORK

Designed cover image: Photograph by Gaston Welisch

First published 2024
by Routledge
4 Park Square, Milton Park, Abingdon, Oxon OX14 4RN

and by Routledge
605 Third Avenue, New York, NY 10158

Routledge is an imprint of the Taylor & Francis Group, an informa business

British Library Cataloguing-in-Publication Data
A catalogue record for this book is available from the British Library

ISBN: 9780367766283 (hbk)
ISBN: 9780367766276 (pbk)
ISBN: 9781003167815 (ebk)

DOI: 10.4324/9781003167815

Typeset in Helvetica
by KnowledgeWorks Global Ltd.

This book is dedicated to my neuro-diverse family, especially my very special sister, Emma. The book owes much to many generous colleagues, at Strathclyde University and elsewhere, who have supported my vision for inclusive science. A special mention must go to Margaret Minns from whom I have learned so much.

Contents

List of figures

Introduction

There is a widespread trend towards inclusive education across the globe. In some places, this represents an increasing presence of children with disabilities who had previously not been in education at all, whilst in other parts of the world it is associated with a reduction in separate specialist provision in favour of attendance at the schools attended by their peers. These converging pressures have driven local policies and this makes the provision of opportunities to access a broad curriculum a question of compliance, as well as a matter of educational justice. If you have been teaching for more than a short time, you may well have observed a change in the profiles of the learners just in your own school or workplace. The pressures bringing this about are both moral, as a response to our changed understanding of the rights of children, including disabled children, socially beneficial as a mechanism for promoting social cohesion and economic, in being an efficient use of expensive resources such as buildings and teachers. Having taught for almost 40 years, in mainstream schools in England and then as a teacher educator visiting placement schools, I have certainly observed a shift. Pupils who might well have attended a special school being placed in mainstream school, initially in an attached unit and, more recently, in classrooms alongside their peers. At a personal level, my sister was classed as ineducable as a small child but was rendered educable by a change in the law in 1970.

Reflective question:

Consider your own local context. Are you aware of any structural rearrangement of provision for pupils with special/additional support needs that has taken place, such as the closure of specialist provision or a change in the way in which a child's school is determined? If not, do you think it is policy or pragmatism that has provided greater leverage for inclusion in your locality?

Given the multiplicity of 'pushes and pulls' for educational inclusion, it will come as no surprise that inclusion has multiple definitions. For the purposes of this book, it will be used to mean that all pupils have shared experiences, here of learning science, and equivalent learning opportunities. I make no assumption about the organisation of education and simply record that my aspiration of inclusive education is one in which all pupils are enabled to be present, participating and achieving (Scottish Government, 2019, p. 6) in a science class, whether or not it is a lab and whether or not the teacher is a science specialist or a teacher of multiple subjects.

Despite the increasing diversity of pupils in schools who are expected to follow a standard science curriculum, there remains surprisingly little advice on how to teach rigorous science inclusively. The limited evidence available suggests that science teaching and inclusive teaching are understood as distinct professional orientations and that teachers do not widely see them as intersecting (Swanson & Bianchini, 2015). This was certainly my experience when I started my first university-based job and began to run inclusive and accessible science events. A number of people thought it was either pointless or impossible, so it has been very satisfying to prove them wrong on both counts and on numerous occasions. The sharp demarcation of science from inclusion is reinforced by the fact that science is a high status, academic subject, meaning that specialist teachers should be engaging primarily in the nurturing of the next generation of highly able scientists (Select Committee on Science and Technology, 2002; Wellington, 2001). Paradoxically, the same high status of the subject is also what makes non-specialist staff working with exceptional learners want their students to have access to it (Essex, 2018). In this apparent tension between excellent science teaching and inclusion of pupils with SEND, it is notable that some researchers suggest that disability is the least considered marker of diversity when science teachers are prepared to teach inclusively (Pugach et al., 2020). Exacerbating the difficulties faced by science teachers is the dearth of published classroom support materials and

DOI: 10.4324/9781003167815-1

very limited information about science education for students with special/additional support needs (Brooke & Solomon, 2001).

Reflective question:

Do you think that inclusion is especially hard to implement in some subject areas, such as science, or do you think that every subject area faces its own distinctive challenges when it comes to inclusion?

It is partly to challenge the widely held assumptions about the incompatibility of full inclusion and excellent science learning that I offer in this book. In it, my primary focus in this book is those with a learning difficulty, learning disability developmental delay or global learning delay. Their development is substantial and delayed across wide areas of development, and the difference exists throughout the individual's life. People with learning difficulties (LD) are likely to need support of various kinds in order to live their life to the full (Scottish Commission for Learning Disability, n.d.). By contrast, people with specific LD, such as Dyslexia, Dyspraxia and Autism, experience difficulties with very specific aspects of daily life, often to do with processing information, and these may affect the person less over time as their brain develops further.

Learners with LD (and they **are** all, in the right circumstances, learners) are thought by the charity Mencap to number about 2.5% of all children in the UK. However, children rarely sit tidily in their assigned 'pigeonhole' so some of these young people will also exhibit specific LD (Autistic Spectrum Condition, Dyslexia, Dyspraxia, Dyscalculia) in addition to their difficulties in learning more generally. Others will have concomitant difficulties in terms of health conditions, mobility or sensory impairments and these are all important to factor in to planning the best science learning experience. Whilst these conditions are all important in considering a young person's learning, there are specialist providers of support for difficulties relating to needs that might be viewed as 'medical' in nature and I defer both to their expertise and the battery of assistive technologies that they can offer. Equally, many of the functional difficulties associated with specific learning conditions, and in which those pupils perform less well than their global attainment would lead us to expect, are shared by those with LD. I hope those who are primarily teaching those with specific LD will free to 'cherry pick' through the ideas here and find things that will work in their teaching situation.

I am not clinically qualified so do not adopt a medicalised view of diversity. It is not the place of teachers to view diversity as something to be 'diagnosed', 'treated' or 'cured'. Instead, I consider functional difficulties and opportunities that pupils with LD commonly face when they come to science lessons. I also note that they come with as many positive attributes and interests as their neuro-typical peers and that these are as much of an asset as anybody else's. Good science teaching will enable them to maximise on these strengths whilst finding 'workarounds' for their difficulties and is liable to make them rewarding and pleasurable to teach!

No book could possibly address all the possible combinations of opportunities and barriers, subject matter and pupil profiles that may arise, but I hope that it will highlight some important principles upon which individual teachers can base their own pedagogic choices. The single most important characteristic of inclusive teachers, regardless of age phase or specialism, is that they are observant, reflective and open to making changes that will enhance learning. By remaining constantly alert to how their teaching impacts on the pupils, demonstrating what is known as 'responsive teaching', you will be able to tailor the material in this book to your individual teaching situation.

The question of why science teachers should be actively teaching all pupils, irrespective of their characteristics or previous attainment, has a number of answers. These are explored in Section 1. However, the most pressing argument is that all pupils **can** learn science and benefit from doing so. The range of benefits is explored more fully in Section 1. When they are not learning science or not benefiting from their learning, teachers need to consider whether the science teaching is right for the learners in question. Whilst many individual teachers have little choice over what they teach, we all have choices about how to teach it. This book is intended primarily for teachers who are following an externally prescribed curriculum with diverse learners. The aim of this book is to help such teachers of science to recognise the many barriers to inclusive science education, which are discussed in Section 2, so that they can anticipate and mitigate against them in lessons. It is also intended to help them to be more critically aware of how their practice can support learners who face additional barriers to engagement in science. Examples of adjustments for commonly taught topic are illustrated in Section 3, whilst Section 4 considers how to assess learning in ways that capture the true extent of learners' understanding. In the hope that the contents of the book, and trials with some of the suggested strategies, will whet your appetite for further ideas, Section 5 suggests further ways to extend your inclusive science network and resource base.

Finally, a comment on where the evidence in this book comes from. It is not only drawn from extensive, and deeply rewarding, experience of teaching those with LD but also rests on published research as far as possible. As might be expected on the grounds of demographics, there is more published evidence on this topic from larger populations than the UK, most specifically in North America. Nevertheless, it is painfully obvious that the shortfall in evidence is not simply down to different population size but that there is a massive shortfall in academic and professional publications about science learning by people with LD, relative to publications about science education for other specified groups. This is because research funders fail to see the purpose of such research and are prone to the assumption that science is inevitably a 'hard' subject, not suited to learners who find learning difficult.

The current absence of a wide literature about inclusive science teaching is also mirrored by the absence of recent literature addressing what might be termed the technicalities of teaching in other areas, such as literacy. This is the rationale for the inclusion of some references that might be considered quite dated and which refer to some of the practical strategies for scaffolding learning. The debate on inclusion as a general approach has left such literature by the professional wayside. Some of these I share here because they still speak to skills that will enhance inclusive teaching, both in science and elsewhere, and it would be a shame for their insights to be lost. Being aware of these 'hacks' is not a soulless alternative to manifesting the attitudes that underpin inclusion but may help us better to turn our intentions into a practical reality on our classrooms.

Another cause of the lack of evidence to counter the assumed incompatibility of excellence in science and inclusion of LD pupils is that there is a shortage of staff who are both good teachers of science and good teachers of diverse learners. This gap permits the assumptions about incompatibility or futility to remain unchallenged by a lack of evidence to the contrary. As the astronaut Sally Ride observed, 'You can't be what you can't see'. I hope that this book will encourage teachers to share more widely their experiences of teaching science to pupils with LD, both their successes and failures, using the professional groups and publications set out in Section 6. In this way, we can all, to some extent, 'Be the change you want to see'.

References

Brooke, H., & Solomon, J. (2001). Passive visitors or independent explorers: Responses of pupils with severe learning difficulties at an interactive science centre. *International Journal of Science Education*, *23*(9), 941–953. https://doi.org/10.1080/09500690010016094

Essex, J. (2018). Why 'science for all' is only an aspiration: staff views of science for learners with Special Educational Needs and Disabilities. Support for Learning, *33*(1), 52–72.

Pugach, M. C., Matewos, A. M., & Gomez-Najarro, J. (2020). Disability and the meaning of social justice in teacher education research: A precarious guest at the table? *Journal of Teacher Education*, *72*(2). https://doi.org/10.1177/0022487120929623

Scottish Commission for Learning Disability. (n.d.). https://www.scld.org.uk/what-is-a-learning-disability/

Scottish Government. (2019). *Guidance on the presumption to provide education in a mainstream setting*. 2 key features of inclusion and developing inclusive practice – Presumption to provide education in a mainstream setting: Guidance. gov.scot (www.gov.scot)

Select Committee on Science and Technology. (2002). *Second report (HC)*. https://publications.parliament. uk//pa/cm200203/cmselect/cmsctech/260/26002.htm

Swanson, L., & Bianchini, J. A. (2015). Co-planning among science and special education teachers: How do different conceptual lenses help to make sense of the process? *Cultural Studies of Science Education*, *10*(4), 1123–1153.

Wellington, J. (2001). What is science education for? *Canadian Journal for Science, Mathematics and Technology Education*, *1*(1), 23–38.

1 Why teach science to all learners?

In this section, the potential benefits of learning science, specifically by learners with learning and other associated difficulties, will be considered. There are numerous benefits to these learners of learning science but, despite these, neuro-divergent learners and science education are commonly seen as a poor match.

'The fossils of old thoughts'

Science has been, historically, an exclusionary discipline (Reid & Hodson, 1987) and the notion that all learners should have access to it is not deeply embedded within its culture. Despite this, there is a growing body of evidence that learning science by a wide range of learners is both possible and beneficial (Essex, 2020), as I will show in further detail in this book. A subject that began as an offshoot of a classical education in ancient universities and the hobby of rich men has been increasingly taken up by a more representative cross section of the population, for instance through adult education initiatives (Cooter & Pumfrey, 1994). However, this popularisation of science has only slowly led to it being considered (almost) universally beneficial.

Science has been on the school curriculum since the middle of the nineteenth century for a succession of different reasons (Jenkins, 2013). These have varied from 'humanisation' and moral education of students, the development of cognitive functions such as observation, deduction and recall, to meeting post-war economic imperatives and, most recently, scientific literacy for citizenship (Jenkins, 2013). Several of these purposes continue to be held to be pertinent by science teachers (Essex, 2018; Essex & Melham, 2019) but the standard format of the curriculum still appears to be largely shaped by the need for specialists, of the sort who will engage in the high-value research and development, rather than for the ordinary citizen. However, some authors have made great efforts to encourage a more encompassing view of science education, for instance Harlen (2010, pp. 6–7) maintains that the purpose of science education is

> … to develop and sustain learners' curiosity about the world, enjoyment of scientific activity and understanding of how natural phenomena can be explained. … The main purpose of science education should be to enable every individual to take an informed part in decisions, and to take appropriate actions, that affect their own wellbeing and the wellbeing of society and the environment.

Much of the shift in the practice in science education has been driven not so much by evolving ideas about the discipline of science but by educational reforms. These changes, in response to shifting societal values, have led to increasingly diverse learners entering a school system in which science is taught. The phrase 'science for all' became a byline for the aspirations of educationalists over the following decade which, in England and Wales, culminated in the introduction of a science national curriculum. This common curriculum made explicit the expectation of universal access to all subject areas, including science. It is part of reform that was intended to standardise equality of curriculum opportunity and should mark the end of ideas of a 'ghetto education', in which education becomes deterministic (Reid & Hodson, 1987).

Thus, the expectation that all pupils would learn science was borne of policy drivers and shifting patterns of school recruitment, rather than any educationally informed considerations. Despite this rather dubious inception, the practice of inclusive science has yielded data that show that is of genuine benefit to diverse learners. Nevertheless, much more research is still needed on the benefits that are of inclusive science teaching (Özgüç & Cavkaytar, 2015). Whilst some teachers, possibly informed by its more elitist traditions, continue to assume that disability is a barrier to participation in science. However, others have discovered many benefits to pupils of learning science (Essex, 2020; Librea-Carden et al., 2021). All of these functions are reflected

DOI: 10.4324/9781003167815-2

to varying degrees in teachers' reasons for teaching it to pupils with SEND (Special Educational Needs and Disabilities).

Purposes of the science curriculum

Although the presentation of the science curriculum is commonly a body of knowledge to be learnt, so-called declarative knowledge, it is capable of being and doing much more. Reid and Hodson (1987) identify three distinct clusters of purposes for science education: learner-centred, society-centred and science-centred. Although the curriculum tends to focus on science-centred aims, amongst the aims of science education, there are still a number of society-centred and learner-centred aims that are emphatically relevant to all learners, including those with learning disabilities (LD). These include:

- To enhance their awareness and understanding of the world in which they live (Librea-Carden et al., 2021)
- To show them one of the ways in which knowledge can be created, specifically the use of physical evidence to test and refine ideas (procedural knowledge?)
- To equip them with the skills to make decisions in a scientific way, for example about possible lifestyle choices
- Skills rehearsal or development, such as data processing, communication, manipulative skills, analysis, evaluation and problem-solving (Belland et al., 2009)
- To facilitate their access to science-based jobs and those jobs which require the skills that science develops

Some people would add to this list that learning science can:

- Foster personal attributes such as motivation or creativity or tenacity
- Induct pupils into important elements of modern culture, for example scientific accounts of climate change or health care

In addition to these outcomes, I would argue for the inclusion of three very important affective outcomes that can arise from learning science:

- The pleasure of succeeding in a high status subject area
- Opportunities to work socially and collaboratively (Belland et al., 2009)
- Enjoyment, especially of practical work

Reflective questions:

Of all the reasons for teaching science to pupils with LD given above, which ones do you value most highly?

Do you think that any of the different reasons listed are more relevant to pupils with LD than pupils who are typically attaining?

These reasons hold good for all children, regardless of the ways in which these aspirations are achieved and despite varying levels of prior attainment. In fact, some authors have noted that doing science specifically enhances pupils' attainment in those areas in which their profile indicates they have especial difficulties. This may happen because science can help to form links between pupils' interests and experiences, with the formal curriculum (Librea-Carden et al., 2021). The potential difficulties that the subject matter presents to pupils who learn in an atypical way, and the high demands that many curricula place upon learners in considered in detail in Section 2. Here, I want to consider the evidence we have of success that can be achieved in science by learners with Special Educational Needs (also termed Additional Support Needs [ASN], or 'exceptional' or 'special' learners). Much of the evidence comes from the evaluation of the effect of an intervention of interest to the researcher, which may introduce bias to the evaluation and we have to recognise that almost any change can bring about positive change, regardless of whether it directly causes the change. This is the so-called Hawthorn effect. Nevertheless, each of these studies contributes to a picture of learners with LD being able to participate and achieve in science, often considerably better than is anticipated. They also point to professional development benefits to science teachers of engaging with teaching science to neuro-diverse pupils.

Reasons why all pupils should be taught science

The benefits of inclusive science to the school community are now considered under eight headings.

Learning benefits for pupils

There is a significant body of published evidence to substantiate the belief that pupils with SEND can demonstrate academic attainment and progress, including those with very severe learning difficulties (Essex, 2020). A study by Brooke and Solomon (2001), two researchers who lacked experience of learners with learning difficulties, showed that visitors with severe LD who came to an interactive science centre were far from 'passive visitors' but were 'independent explorers'. After working with the interactive exhibits, members of the group were noted to be able to manipulate apparatus purposefully, showed sustained engagement with the exhibits and explored the causation of phenomenon, irrespective of their ability to communicate their intentions or findings. The issue of whether the demonstration of verifiable attainment is impeded by the adherence to standard curriculum and assessment tools is considered further in Section 4.

The learning of pupils with LD can be divided into three main areas.

1. The learning of scientific content, such as facts about scientific topics, technical words. Özgüç and Cavkaytar (2015) gathered evidence showing that pupils can learn, remember and generalise ideas they have learnt in science. There is clear evidence that pupils can retain concepts in the medium-term, and that this may be facilitated by the selection of suitable pedagogic strategies (Aydeniz & Kotowski, 2012). Learners who cannot talk about what they recall may still demonstrate that they have learnt by physically replicating an experiment (Brooke & Solomon, 2001). There is plenty of evidence, both anecdotal and formal research data, supporting the idea that this population can assimilate academic content. For example,

    > Today I videoed Class e) studying solids and liquids. Teacher G touched their hands and lips with solid chocolate, then melted chocolate, each time repeating the words and signing 'solid' or 'liquid'. The assessment was to show them a plain biscuit and ask them whether he should use liquid or solid chocolate, if he wanted to make a chocolate biscuit. Every student pointed or eye gazed to the sign for liquid. It was amazing to see that they had understood the properties and were then able to apply their insight to the task.

    > (Essex, 2020, pp. 553–554)

2. Developing a deep understanding of science and its processes, through being able to connect ideas and evidence to each other, and to connect different scientific ideas together. The importance of understanding science extends far beyond school success, as it can be viewed as a way of understanding the world more generally. To show the ways in which scientific knowledge is created (epistemology). Learning about the processes of science and the ways in which science generates and uses evidence, also known as 'scientific literacy'. Driver, Newton, and Osborne (2000) argue that science shouldn't exclude anyone, *everybody* should be helped to develop scientific literacy because of its centrality in helping people to make sense of their everyday lives.

    It is important to recognise that whilst literacy and numeracy can render making sense of scientific material science additionally difficult (Villanueva et al., 2012), the evidence is that these barriers are not insurmountable. Comprehensive reviews of the literature considering the development of reading skills (Browder et al., 2006) and mathematics (Browder et al., 2008) provide multiple examples of students successfully acquiring the academic skills.

As an example of developing a deeper understanding of science and its processes, a pupil with LD demonstrated an understanding of the use of models in science in the following incident,

> A group of pupils were describing an activity in which a mint was dropped into a bottle of cola and a plume of carbon dioxide and cola erupted from the bottle. They told the visitor, as they had been told, that this was a model of how volcanoes can contribute to climate change. They described burying the bottom half of the bottle in sand on the beach; the visitor asked why they had done that. This hadn't been discussed but I expected them to say that it had been to limit the chance of the bottle falling over and spraying us all with cola. However, one of the pupils suggested that it was because the eruptions start underground so if we want to understand what happens, we have to make it as like a real volcano as we can.
>
> (Field notes, November 2021)

3. Developing an understanding of how science can contribute to the wider world and our understanding of it, such as why immunisation is an important way of combatting infectious diseases or how to limit climate change. As an example,

> So exploring all of this (Electricity), I can see the results now in class, now the students who would never tell me that the iPad needs to be charged, will now ask me to go and charge it.
>
> (Teacher quoted in Essex, 2020, p. 10)

Reflective question:

In your experience, how much does the current approach to assessment prevent pupils with LD demonstrating the full extent of their learning in the three domains described above?

Pupils' enjoyment

The key role of motivation in successful learning (Reid & Hodson, 1987) is a reminder that, whatever sort of science curriculum or approach to pedagogy that is adopted, it should be enjoyable enough to keep pupils motivated. Hands-on work has been observed to enhance motivation (Therrien et al., 2014). Many pupils are very enthusiastic about experimental and other practical work in science (Essex, 2020; Scruggs & Mastropieri, 2007), but this category covers quite a wide range of activity, some of it not clearly explicitly linked to the development of scientific concepts. The potential disconnection between fun and understanding is illustrated by the following incident,

> As students discussed what they would do for a school science fair that was being planned, Mark was very excited about doing the coke and Mentos fizz, until someone reminded him that he would have to explain the science behind what happened. He then said he wasn't sure about doing it.
>
> (Observation of lower secondary pupil with Learning Disability)

To be clear, there is no doubt that play-based learning is learning. However, this book is about teaching and learning in a curriculum area, so assumes that a primary purpose of any activity is to learn science and to learn about science. This means that science lessons need to be more than simply 'messy play' but can beneficially offer opportunities for relatively undirected exploration. This type of hands-on activity can be important, and for some learners, an essential component of their learning (Pyle & Danniels, 2017) but for the purposes of this book needs to align to learning. There is much evidence the experimental work is enjoyed by many, but without having associated understanding this is simply 'cook book' recipe following or messy play with scientific equipment. The sequential shift in the locus of control as a learner moves from unstructured play to a formal investigation is brought about by increasing levels of teacher direction.

There is a balance to be struck between enjoyment without extrinsic purpose and enjoyment that is intended to promote learning. Although pupils often ask for 'fun' lessons, we should not forget that an important source of enjoyment is the intrinsic satisfaction of learning, and the consequent success that goes with it. Although it is documented that learners with LD are quite quickly discouraged when they do not succeed at a task (Villanueva et al., 2012), equally they get great satisfaction from their achievements. Paradoxically, the fact that science is seen as 'hard', for reasons that are set out in Section 2, success in the subject is highly valued and enhances self-esteem hugely.

Reflective question:

Do you think that focusing on pupils' enjoyment risks turning learning opportunities into purposeless messy play? Or do you think that pupils, especially those with LD, can learn through play if offered the guidance they need to make wider sense of their experiences?

Pupils' personal development

Studying science can instil and nurture characteristics that will be important in adult life, including psycho-social development. This is an area which has not been documented in science-specific contexts but has been noted to be a common manifestation of developmental delay (Gresham et al., 2004; Steele, 2004). This can present particular problems in science because its pedagogy rests so largely on social interaction, resting on evidence of the centrality of social constructivism to optimal learning in science. However, the learning gains associated with the promotion of social interaction–focused science learning, for example peer tutoring and/or cooperative learning, are appreciable as are the psycho-social gains. These include an increase both engagement and motivation (Scruggs & Mastropieri, 2007). Alongside this, there is a widespread and largely uncritiqued custom of doing practical work in groups, often to ensure access to scarce experimental resources. For these reasons, delayed social development may present management challenges in lessons and interaction require much monitoring, but nevertheless science offers an excellent opportunity for the development of social skills.

Another benefit associated with effective science learning is the associated attitudinal gain, pupils feel more confident about themselves and their capacities (Librea-Carden et al., 2021). This may seem paradoxical, since science has a reputation as a hard subject and the barriers that it commonly presents are set out in considerable detail in Section 2. Nevertheless teaching it to all pupils can signal high expectations and thus enhance attainment (Villanueva et al., 2012).

Development of pupils' transferable skills

There is a widely held perception that science is 'for very clever people' and that its purpose is to develop specialist skills in the future science workforce. However, researchers have found that transferable skills are retained by all learners after their practical application (Aydeniz & Kotowski, 2012). Such skills include observing, communicating, offering explanations and evaluating possible explanations. There is tantalising evidence that indicates that learning science, specifically the 'nature of science' and developing the associated skills, can bring about enhanced attainment in the skills that characterise their disability (Librea-Carden et al., 2021). This possibility holds out the prospect of science education being a key part of a school's efforts to promote pupil development. The combination of experiential learning, the modelling of how knowledge is created (known epistemology) and the use of core skills, such as literacy and numeracy, makes the subject a powerful vehicle for promoting skills development (Essex, 2018; Villanueva et al., 2012). This finding makes a very strong argument for learning science by all pupils, on the basis of the skills development that it facilitates. The fact that the greatest development occurs in those skills which pupils have the greatest difficulty and which are the most disabling for them surely makes active participation in science education an imperative. Some of these skills are the generic or transferable skills that employers often say they seek in including procedural knowledge, or how to do things, and also problem-solving, sometimes called 'knowing what to do when you don't know what to do'. Because learners with LD commonly find it difficult to approach scientific problems using accepted scientific thinking processes, they may think of creative alternative ways to achieve the desired outcomes (Essex, 2020; Librea-Carden et al., 2021). This laterality may not be intentional, rather borne of necessity, but it can be very effective and open up new lines of thinking and practice. One of the major assets that pupils with LD bring is a lower level of prior formal knowledge, which makes them much more open to alternative possibilities.

Enhancing pupils' cultural participation

As stated earlier in this section, science is an important element of our cultural life, whether that is media stories that involve science, to making everyday decisions informed by science ideas or through going to visitor sites where science is communicated. For example, Park et al. (2019, p. 2) published a report on taking pupils with 'special education' students to a science festival and talk about the pupils who attend benefit from being given the chance to share 'the heritage of a culture'. The shared understanding and values associated with acculturation provide is vital for mutual understanding and social cohesion, which is what inclusion is intended to bring about. This is the aspect of education that (Biesta, 2020) calls 'socialization'. Without having access to the science component of wider culture, pupils will be partially excluded.

> **Reflective question:**
>
> Do you feel that the content of the science curriculum 'crowds out' serious consideration of wider personal development of the sort considered under the sections 'Pupils' personal development', 'Development of pupils' transferable skills' and 'Enhancing pupils' cultural participation'?

Empowerment of pupils

The sociologist, Pierre Bourdieu (1986), considered how culture could confer privilege and give people greater opportunities, a notion that he termed 'cultural capital'. By this, he meant the extent to which they have power and are able to make choices. Researchers have drawn on Bourdieu's ideas to describe the way in which engaging specifically with science can enhance a young person's future involvement in science and their life chances. They call this 'engagement, aspirations, and achievement/attainment' in science (Archer et al., 2012, p. 883) 'science capital' and appropriate science education is pivotal in the development of this capacity. Note that science capital is a concept that encompasses knowledge, attitudes and future intentions to do science, as well as understanding how science contributes to our culture. This means that is far more than simply about knowing science but is about how doing science can enrich and empower pupils in a way that is comparable to the benefits of engaging in other aspects of culture.

All young people, regardless of their characteristics, can develop greater science capital and doing so increases their willingness to engage with further science and their development of the associated transferable skills. Bourdieu originally proposed that capital is created by the interaction amongst three factors:

- An individual's 'habitus', which is their habitual practices and assumptions with which they are surrounded, such as the ways in which science is usually taught
- The resources an individual possesses, including economic, cultural and social resources
- The individual's 'field', which is the wider social contexts in which an individual operates.

The research evidence suggests that science capital is similar to cultural capital but is created by equivalent factors specifically in the science domain. This analysis also points to key aspects of science education that need to be considered. So, science lessons can enhance the pupils' science capital if they,

- Create a suitable 'habitus', meaning an environment in which positive expectations are displayed towards all learners, a willingness to change from usual practices if doing so will make the science more accessible and meaningful.
- Expand the learners' cultural resources by offering them access to the cultural aspects of science, rather than just knowledge. It is also important to pay attention to the very diverse cultures in which science has been carried out and ensuring that diverse practitioners of science are recognised and valued (see Section 3 for some examples).
- Ensure that pupils have a chance to work like a scientist, and to gain experience of some of the ways in which professional scientists work (Aydeniz & Kotowski, 2012).
- Enhance the pupils' social resources within the class by facilitating group work and social learning, with support if they find this difficult.

- Enlarging a pupil's 'field' can be achieved by the purposeful development of new social resources. Social links beyond the class can be widened by arranging science visits, by bringing in outside presenters, arranging on-line involvement with science activities beyond the school (see Section 6 for suggestions as to how this might be done).

In order to develop pupils' science capital, teachers need to recognise that this requires a distinctive approach to science education, and that this has implications for both individual teachers and schools. The development of science capital is not just a question of studying recommended resources or engaging with certain scientific content. It is important to note that the approach to science as a form of cultural capital does not privilege and specific science curriculum and does not pre-suppose that the purpose of science is to produce a future science workforce. It is as much about understanding that science is a social practice and needs to be portrayed as such. This can be unnerving for teachers raised on notions of science as an objective truth. Anyone aiming to enhance their pupils' science capital is cautioned away from using in public a mug bearing the Neil deGrasse Tyson quote, '*The good thing about science is that it's true, whether or not you believe in it*'. Only by portraying science as a human activity will pupils see that they have a contribution to make to it. At the heart of the science capital approach to science education is intended to challenge structural inequalities in opportunities and so must centre on building enthusiastic and engaged science learners, in partnership with families and communities over a long timescale. It envisages science as meeting diverse needs in diverse ways and so is an important notion for anyone who wishes to teach science in a genuinely inclusive way.

> **Reflective question:**
>
> In what ways do practices in your school perpetuate ideas about the 'deficiency' or needs of LD pupils and in what ways are they encouraged to take agency in their learning?

To facilitate professional growth in teachers

Although an analysis of the impact of inclusive science teaching tends to focus on how it affects pupils, it must be stated that teaching science to diverse learners, including those with LD, benefits teachers. Although it may feel as if it adds to their work load, it is hugely beneficial to both their understanding of learning and their teaching. Lest this sounds as if learners with SEND are being unwitting test subjects, I would say that I believe that all lessons should involve reciprocity between teacher and learners but that exceptional learners can teach and learn in new and especially striking ways. I have observed that the benefits extend across the whole range of teaching backgrounds and all categories of pupils with LD. Consider the following quotations, which illustrate this point. The first is by a senior teacher at a school working with pupils described as having 'profound and moderate learning difficulties' which decided to include science on its curriculum,

> In quite a few experiments, because the practicality of it and because it was shared ideas, the teachers would plan an activity and all the classes would join this particular class, so that it was really a good sharing of ideas. It's not just that you are thinking about your students, it is how it can be planned and how your pupils respond to other people's experiments.

Just as teachers working in a special education environment described themselves as gaining valuable professional development from learning to teach science, so science specialists describe how teaching diverse learners sheds new light on the process of science learning and science teaching. This extends beyond gaining the pedagogic skills required to work with an unfamiliar population but extends to a fundamental re-evaluation of current practice. For example, an academic, who teaches engineering to post-graduate students and described their teaching as 'logical' and 'quite boring', then attended a STEM summer school for pupils attending special schools and delivered a workshop. In their subsequent reflection, they said,

> From this experience I think I actually thought of education at different levels. There is always room to improve your teaching quality and the learning experience.

These experiences illustrate the more general point that teaching inclusively does not only rest on the possession of a suite of technical capacities but rather on a set of dispositions including, more importantly, that of being open-minded. International research (European Agency for Development in Special Needs Education, 2012) indicates that inclusive teachers are, above all else, those who are reflective, observant, analytical and reflexive, that is aware of how they influence the events they are observing and attempting to understand. Contrary to some of ideas that are found in policy, teacher discourse and teachers' professional identity, 'special education', teachers do not differ in their technical abilities to respond to learner diversity. What inclusive teachers all share is a belief in learners being the key resource in their classroom because of their diversity, not despite it. Whilst adjustments may be required to meet individual pupil needs, some of them requiring very specific skills development, many more of the techniques that support LD learners will, incidentally, benefit others too. This focus on pedagogy and learner response may be more immediately evident in the discussion of teaching by those experienced in creating an inclusive classroom (Swanson & Bianchini, 2015) but it comes not from being trained to work with pupils with LD, but rather from having a disposition that is open to the development opportunities that teaching these pupils offers. A university academic and a researcher who contributed to a programme of inclusive and accessible STEM outreach described their decision to participate in these terms,

> I could see the value of that. It's about how you can make (science) research accessible it's about how you can make concepts accessible. … I thought I had a lot to learn from the process and I have.
>
> (Evaluation interview, 2021)

To provide teachers with further evidence on teaching and learning

Courtade et al. (2007) carried out an extensive literature review of published articles on teaching science to U.S. pupils with significant learning difficulties over a 20 year period. Given both the size of the U.S. school population and repeated policy and curriculum initiatives to offer a balanced curriculum to all, it is shocking that only 11 such studies were located, most of these considered only a single pupil. This deficit means that school staff working with this population have very little reliable evidence on which to base decisions about teaching science to this population. The situation is not much better now, nor is it significantly better for pupils with mild LD. For this reason, it is important that teachers trial different teaching strategies and share their experiences (failures as well as successes, ideally!). In the absence of substantial evidence, we are all action researchers, investigating our own practice. To expand the body of evidence, anyone who is teaching science to diverse learners is warmly encouraged to find mechanisms for disseminating their findings, through professional gatherings of different types and journals. Section 6 suggests some mechanisms for sharing experiences of science learning by diverse pupils.

Reflective question:

Can you recall instances where working with diverse pupils has helped you to understand your role better or to teach better? How has your ability to reflect and respond constructively to unexpected incidents in lessons changed over your time as a teacher?

Conclusion

We are not achieving genuine inclusion if we do not offer all our learners the best opportunities for development that we can. This requires us to suspend any prejudiced assumptions that we may hold about who science is for. Beyond moral and political arguments, however, there are very practical educational reasons to embrace the notion of 'science for all'. As has been shown, there are multiple advantages to having an appropriate science education. These extend far beyond the usually cited reasons of creating the future STEM workforce, though it would be excellent to think that learning science could help to reduce the huge level of under-employment found in adults with LD. Many research studies and extensive teacher experience concur that science can make a valuable contribution to a young person's development, regardless of their perceived 'disabilities' (sic). Indeed, some authors suggest that science has an especially valuable role to play in the development of those whose development is not typical and can even help to accelerate development in those areas in which they struggle most.

References

Archer, L., DeWitt, J., Osborne, J., Dillon, J., Willis, B., & Wong, B. (2012). Science aspirations, capital, and family habitus: How families shape children's engagement and identification with science. *American Educational Research Journal, 49*(5), 881–908. https://doi.org/10.3102/0002831211433290

Aydeniz, M., & Kotowski, E. L. (2012). What do middle and high school students know about the particulate nature of matter after instruction? Implications for practice. *School Science and Mathematics, 112*(2), 59–65. https://doi.org/10.1111/j.1949-8594.2011.00120.x

Belland, B. R., Glazewski, K. D., & Ertmer, P. A. (2009). Inclusion and problem-based learning: Roles of students in a mixed-ability group. *RMLE Online: Research in Middle Level Education, 32*(9), 1–19.

Biesta, G. (2020). Risking ourselves in education: Qualification, socialization, and subjectification revisited. *Educational Theory, 70*(1). https://doi.org/10.1111/edth.12411

Bourdieu, P. (1986). The forms of capital. In J. Richardson (Ed.), *Handbook of theory and research for the sociology of education* (pp. 241–58). Greenwood.

Brooke, H., & Solomon, J. (2001). Passive visitors or independent explorers: Responses of pupils with severe learning difficulties at an Interactive Science Centre. *International Journal of Science Education, 23*(9), 941–953.

Browder, D. M., Spooner, F., Ahlgrim-Delzell, L., Harris, A. A., & Wakemanxya, S. (2008). A meta-analysis on teaching mathematics to students with significant cognitive disabilities. *Exceptional Children, 74*(4), 407–432.

Browder, D. M., Wakeman, S. Y., Spooner, F., Ahlgrim-Delzell, L., & Algozzinexya, B. (2006). Research on reading instruction for individuals with significant cognitive disabilities. *Exceptional Children, 72*(4), 392–408.

Cooter, R., & Pumfrey, S. (1994). Separate spheres and public places: Reflections on the history of science popularization and science in popular culture. *History of Science, 32*(3), 237–267.

Courtade, G. R., Spooner, F., & Browder, D. M. (2007). Review of studies with students with significant cognitive disabilities which link to science standards. *Research and Practice for Persons with Severe Disabilities, 32*(1), 43–49. https://doi.org/10.2511/rpsd.32.1.43

Driver, R., Newton, P., & Osborne, J. (2000). Establishing the norms of scientific argumentation in classrooms. *Science Education, 84*(3), 287–312.

Essex, J. (2018). Why 'science for all' is only an aspiration: Staff views of science for learners with special educational needs and disabilities. *Support for Learning, 33*(1), 52–72.

Essex, J. (2020). Towards truly inclusive science education: A case study of successful curriculum innovation in a special school. *Support for Learning, 35*(4), 542–558.

Essex, J., & Melham, P. (2019). Experiences of educational transition: Young women with ASD, and the staff supporting them, speak. *Support for Learning, 34*(1), 86–111.

European Agency for Development in Special Needs Education. (2012). *Teacher education for inclusion (TE41)*. https://www.unicef.org/albania/reports/teacher-education-inclusion-te41

Gresham, F. M., McIntyre, L. L., Olson-Tinker, H., Dolstra, L., McLaughlin, V., & Van, M. (2004). Relevance of functional behavioral assessment research for school-based interventions and positive behavioral support. *Research in Developmental Disabilities, 25*(1), 19–37. https://doi.org/10.1016/J.RIDD.2003.04.003

Harlen, W. (2010). *Principles and big ideas of science education.* https://www.ase.org.uk/bigideas

Jenkins, E. W. (2013). The 'nature of science' in the school curriculum: The great survivor. *Journal of Curriculum Studies, 45*(2), 132–151. https://doi.org/10.1080/00220272.2012.741264

Librea-Carden, M. R., Mulvey, B. K., Borgerding, L. A., Wiley, A. L., & Ferdous, T. (2021). "Science is accessible for everyone": Preservice special education teachers' nature of science perceptions and instructional practices. *International Journal of Science Education, 43*(6), 949–968.

Özgüç, C. S., & Cavkaytar, A. (2015). Science education for students with intellectual disability: A case study. *Journal of Baltic Science Education, 14*(6), 804–820.

Park, H., Kim, Y., & Jeong, S. (2019). The effect of a science festival for special education students on communicating science. *Asia-Pacific Science Education, 5*(1). https://doi.org/10.1186/S41029-018-0029-0

Pyle, A., & Danniels, E. (2017). A continuum of play-based learning: The role of the teacher in play-based pedagogy and the fear of hijacking play. *Early Education and Development, 28*(3), 274–289.

Reid, D. J., & Hodson, D. (1987). *Science for all: Teaching science in the secondary school.* Cassell.

Scruggs, T. E., & Mastropieri, M. A. (2007). Science learning in special education: The case for constructed versus instructed learning. *Exceptionality : The Official Journal of the Division for Research of the Council for Exceptional Children, 15*(2), 57–74.

Steele, M. M. (2004). Making the case for early identification and intervention for young children at risk for learning disabilities. *Early Childhood Education Journal, 32*(2). https://doi.org/10.1007/s10643-004-1072-x

Swanson, L. H., & Bianchini, J. A. (2015). Co-planning among science and special education teachers: How do different conceptual lenses help to make sense of the process? *Cultural Studies of Science Education, 10*(4). https://doi.org/10.1007/s11422-014-9582-3

Therrien, W. J., Taylor, J. C., Watt, S., & Kaldenberg, E. R. (2014). Science instruction for students with emotional and behavioral disorders. *Remedial and Special Education, 35*(1), 15–27. https://doi.org/10.1177/0741932513503557

Villanueva, M. G., Taylor, J., Therrien, W., & Hand, B. (2012). Science education for students with special needs. *Studies in Science Education, 48*(2), 187–215.

2 Why do pupils with learning difficulties underachieve in science and how can teachers mitigate this?

Introduction

Having established the fact that all learners benefit from being taught science in Section 1, I will go on to look at some of the major barriers that are embodied in standard presentations of the school science curriculum. These may look like an impenetrable combination of obstacles and they seem to be deeply entrenched in the content and pedagogic tradition of school science. Reid and Hodson (1987, p. viii) ask, *Can schools cause special needs?* and, in the case of learning disabilities (LD), the analysis below may lead you to conclude that they do. Long-term endeavours to ensure that everyone has access to science will doubtless require major curriculum reform so that different facets of the subject are available to diverse learners (Osborne & Dillon, 2008).

I am conscious of the fact that many teachers reading this book will not feel able to modify *what* they teach. Despite this, they can still adapt the way in which they teach it and their decision-making about modification needs to be underpinned by a secure knowledge of the curriculum. As a major international study notes in its recommendations (European Agency for Development in Special Needs Education [2012, p. 14]),

> The essential knowledge and understanding underpinning this area of competence [inclusion] includes ... using the curriculum as a tool for inclusion that supports access to learning.

My hope is that even by being aware of the pitfalls, they may be helped to better anticipate likely difficulties and to plan accordingly. This section links the documented barriers to corresponding mitigation strategies that teachers can use to minimise these difficulties and so maximise learning. By using these strategies to meet the needs of individual pupils, it is possible to make science less difficult for all learners and starts to challenge widely held assumptions about the inevitable difficulty of the subject.

What different theories tell us about learning science

The extent to which science is understood as the process by which new knowledge is derived, and the extent to which it is about the approach to knowledge construction that is adopted, is a perennial debate and lies outside the scope of this book. However, the issue of understanding where knowledge comes from is more than a device to promote effective learning. It is also considered to be a crucial element of educational justice (Stroupe et al., 2019) and so is an important consideration for anyone concerned about genuine inclusion. What does bear comment about the debate in the context of this book is the fact that the tendency to present science as a body of received knowledge gives rise to assessment that rests heavily on recall. This immediately disadvantages a population of learners who commonly have problems with retrieval of previously learnt material from their memory, both short term and long term. They have been found to benefit from courses that focus on scientific processes (Villanueva et al., 2012). Current science curricula are usually very 'content rich' (Hirsch, 2016). We need to acknowledge that this, so-called Sputnik Curriculum (Bybee, 1997; Rudolph, 2002) intended for the most highly performing individuals who will become professional scientists and whose work will bring economic, political and military power to their country, is exclusionary of those who cannot access a very elitist curriculum. Nevertheless, the role of science qualifications as a 'gate keeper' to many high status careers for students higher up in the secondary school presently 'hijacks' the curriculum lower down the school (Essex et al., 2019). Meanwhile, performativity pressures may lead some schools to enrol LD pupils on to courses for which they are not well suited, and in which their poor achievement further fuels the notion that science is not suited to them.

DOI: 10.4324/9781003167815-3

The discrepancy between curriculum and many learners is made worse by the fact that many teachers feel the need to cover a lot of content from the very start of secondary school, when the formal curriculum doesn't require it. The perceived impact of the assessment imperatives that dominate the later years of secondary school prevents science teachers from taking advantage of the flexibility they have to make major changes to the early secondary science curriculum (Dunne et al., 2007). Pressures upon teachers to ensure the highest possible outcomes by pupils when they take important external exams, such as GCSE (General Certificate of Secondary Education) or National 5, have changed how they view science lower down the school and teachers often treat lower secondary science as the 'pre-preparation' for external assessment. One of the consequences of this is that teachers may feel reluctant to sacrifice content even though that would improve accessibility for learners with LD (Dunne et al., 2007; Essex et al., 2019). There is a counterargument that introducing key content to start with, and ensuring as good a grasp of it as possible, enables further factual content and more complicated concepts later. This approach, which I think of as being like a ramp for learning, can smooth progression. However, it requires judgement about what is core and what could be deferred without serious less of meaning. There are examples of this approach modelled in Section 3.

It may also be a form of 'future proofing' of students, who are thought to be capable of later development that will enable them to enter a class where they will be taking standard external examinations in what is viewed as a 'gate keeper' qualification (Hodson, 2003). Because the science curriculum is so very sequential in nature, students who have missed material are heavily disadvantaged in their later studies (Villanueva et al., 2012) that teachers may feel, possibly sub-consciously, that following a similar, albeit 'thinned' version of the curriculum protects students' future mobility (Dunne et al., 2007).

Reflective question:

Based on your experience, in what ways do you think that the learning of pupils with LD is different to learning by their peers? Is it the speed at which they learn or the ways in which they learn or are there other aspects of their learning that is distinctive?

Piaget's ideas about concrete and abstract thinking

One of the major difficulties in the science curriculum is that the concepts rapidly become abstract, whereas we know that progression from concrete to abstract thought frequently does not take place until pupils reach upper secondary school age. The extent to which this premature move into the world of the intangible, or sub-microscopic as Alex Johnstone (1991) called it in his reflective account of the difficulties that are unwittingly embedded in accepted approaches to science, is far from inevitable. The 'father (sic) of modern chemistry', Antoine Lavoisier, did not understand elements as being made of just a single type of atom. Whilst this was for historic reasons, rather than because he had LD, the point is that you can be a perfectly good scientist without grasping the idea of atoms.

A measure of the extent of this problem can be seen if we use an established tool, Piaget's model of the stages of cognitive development. Jean Piaget developed a taxonomy, or hierarchical list, of conceptual processes, based on his observations of a socially selective group of young people. There are certainly criticisms that can be made of his methodology, and also of the way in which people are inclined to interpret his level (or 'ladder') model as an accurate description of expected development. It can also be misinterpreted as meaning that development progresses in a uniform, linear and unidirectional fashion for all pupils. In fact, much anecdotal evidence suggests that pupils frequently seem to move between stages in both directions lesson by lesson and show variable stages of development depending on the content and context of the lesson. It may be helpful to re-think progress and see it not in terms of steady incremental growth in one strand of knowledge and understanding, but rather a 'spreading out' of learning so that individual chunks become connected and consolidated and their understanding of a whole concept or topic becomes more complete. Harlen (2010) likens this to completing a jigsaw puzzle in that there are several different approaches that can ultimately lead to success.

Nevertheless, the levels that he described (Inhelder & Piaget, 2013) provide a useful framework against which the capacity of learners and the demand of their work can be audited. They also help you to identify teaching and learning strategies that will support secure understanding of material at the lower levels of cognitive development, upon which further understanding can

Level	Expected age according to Piaget	% of 16 year-olds attaining level	Characteristics of thinking
3B Late formal	By 16	13	Learners demonstrate reliable use of most, or all, of the operations. Able to use inverse proportionality & multi-factorial variables
3A Early formal	12 onwards	32	Can think formally about hypothetical or intangible phenomena. Operations include controlling & excluding variables, ratio and proportionality, compensation, equilibrium, correlation. Capable of deductive reasoning.
2B Late concrete	By 11	88	Learners demonstrate reliable use of most, or all, of the operations.
2A Early concrete & below	7	100	Learners demonstrate some of the following: logical thought about concrete phenomena. Understand concepts of reversibility, conservation, less egocentric & so able to adopt multiple positions, intentional de-centring (seeing more than one aspect of a phenomenon at once), can sequence things e.g. understand that instructions need to happen in a certain order. Can carry out inductive reasoning but not deductive reasoning.
[Pre-operational]	6 and below	100	Represent phenomena e.g. by drawing or imaginary play. Understand cause and effect. Start to be able to monitor their own thought processes (meta-cognition).

Figure 2.1 Table showing the levels of cognitive development identified by Piaget and the ways of thinking that characterise each level, plus the ages at which he thought each level was typically obtained and the proportion of pupils achieving each level in later, large-scale surveys (Shayer & Adey, 2002).

be built in due course. The second from left-hand column shows the typical ages at which he observed his study population achieved the various levels. The third column from the left in Figure 2.1 shows the proportion of 16-year-old pupils in a mainstream school who were later assessed as being at the different Piagetian levels (Shayer & Adey, 2002). Around two thirds do not become able to think reliably in an abstract, or formal, way by the age of 16. The data we have refer to pupils in mainstream schools, the vast majority of whom would have been neuro-typical and so this situation can only be more of a problem for those with LD.

The full extent of this problem becomes clear when we consider an analysis of the science curriculum, using Piagetian levels to describe the different levels of demand, indicated that learners need to be functioning at the formal operational stage of development to take an interest in, let alone understand, large sections of the science curriculum. The researchers found that the levels of conceptual development demonstrated by pupils in mainstream secondary schools were not anything like what Piaget's original work would have led them to expect (Shayer & Adey, 1981). Indicative figures, based on numerous studies, are shown in the middle column of Figure 2.1. The discrepancy is striking and would be expected to be even wider for pupils with LD. Students with a mild to moderate learning difficulty are frequently observed to operate in the concrete and pre-operational Piagetian stages (Klein & Safford, 1977). This sizeable discrepancy renders much of the standard curriculum meaningless to those with learning difficulties and developmental delays (Brigham et al., 2011).

The early push towards abstract thinking penalises pupils who do not achieve this later, or not at all. This was brought home to me when I supervised a 16-year-old pupil who had been permanently excluded from her other science lessons for disruptive behaviour.

> She asked if she could do the dissolving sugar practical, which she had done aged 11 or 12. As she stirred in the icing sugar, caster sugar, granulated sugar and coffee sugar crystals and noticed that the larger surface area the faster they dissolved, she elbowed her neighbour in excitement and exclaimed, 'It's them particles! Them particles they were telling us about!' She had, evidently matured cognitively to the point where you could really understand a concept that she had encountered some five years previously. I had to wonder then how much of her disruptive behaviour was created by the mismatch between her understanding and the curriculum she was obliged to follow.
>
> (Field note, April 2002)

The difficulties are further compounded by the highly sequential nature of the curriculum, in which learning often builds upon prior classroom learning (Villanueva et al., 2012). The idea that some ideas are foundational to the nature of the subject, and without being able to grasp them the subject does not make coherent sense, is termed a threshold concept (Land, 2008). Science learning depends on several threshold concepts, for example that living things are made of cells and substances are made of particles, and subsequent learning depends on pupils grasping these at the point they are introduced in the curriculum. Whilst cells are something that can be shown to exist under a microscope (although seeing them and accepting that they are the smallest units of life may not be the same thing), physics relies on an understanding of the concept of forces whose effects can be felt even if they cannot be discerned directly, chemistry relies on threshold concepts that relate to intangible phenomena. The abstract nature of many threshold concepts means that those who do not (and cannot) grasp them, such as the pupil described in the account of the pupils who understood particles aged 16, rather than 12 when they were first introduced, are doomed to enduring a curriculum that becomes ever less comprehensible to them.

Adey and Shayer looked at the mismatch between learners and curriculum demands by exploring ways to accelerate pupils' development of formal thinking. Their work with the CASE (Cognitive Acceleration in Science Education) project provides strong evidence that it is possible to enhance young people's cognitive development (Shayer & Adey, 2002). This shift was achieved by supporting the development of target understandings (schemata) in the long-term memory, which is described further in the section on cognitive load theory (CLT). The project team showed that pupils aged 11–13 made much faster progress towards abstract thinking if their lessons if they incorporated five elements, including engagement at the concrete, or tangible, level (Shayer, 2003). This approach can be used successfully with all pupils, whether or not they achieve thinking at the highest level (Simon & Richardson, 2009). We should, however, remain sceptical about the fitness of purpose of a curriculum which requires such additional interventions to make it accessible to the majority of learners.

The CASE project suggested that the elements of lessons that promote development towards formal thinking were as follows. Whilst these were presented in a series of lessons that had been constructed with the intention of improving scientific thinking, they can also be incorporated into regular, curriculum-driven lessons to promote pupils' construction of meaning (Bächtold, 2013).

1. *Concrete preparation*. This involves 'hands-on' learning, and the acquisition of essential vocabulary. This could be an experiment or a demonstration or considering a model or something else experiential. This is the 'doing' part of the lesson.
2. *Cognitive conflict*. This requires learners to work through something that 'isn't right', but that can be resolved with further deliberation or guidance. Cognitive conflict may be something that the teacher deliberately introduces but can be spontaneous when pupils encounter something unexpected. One example of this is when pupils were asked to predict whether everyday items would float or sink in water and then test their predictions. One pupil predicted that the banana, which had indeed floated previously, would float but, in fact, it sank. He memorably exclaimed, 'B&**$y hell. The b*$%*&d!'s gone and sunk!' It was, however, the start of a memorable discussion about what turns a floating banana into a sinking one that extended his understanding of the phenomenon.
3. *Social construction* involves working with others to extend their understanding of the earlier work. This might have involved asking them why the banana that had floated earlier no longer did so.
4. *Meta-cognition* means 'changing thinking' and, in practice, involves conscious reflection on their own, and each other's, thought processes. This commonly takes place when pupils talk to each other.
5. *Bridging* is when the ideas developed during the CASE intervention are applied to the pupils' science learning and to their everyday experiences. So the floating and sinking discussion could be used to consider the separation by density of waste materials, such as plastics, for recycling.

Although these ideas were originally incorporated into a series of 'Think Science' lessons, I have used them in lessons that were focused on delivery of the standard science curriculum. Although they may seem quite time-consuming, my own experience suggests that it enhances learning and, by helping pupils to understand key concepts in a transferable way, they make subsequent learning easier and more secure. So ensuring deeper thinking about both subject matter and their own learning can end up being a shrewd investment of the teacher's time in the medium term.

The second aspect of cognitive development that Piaget described is the shift from working inductively, which involves identifying patterns and generating ideas based on multiple observations, to deductive working, in which they use a general theory and apply it to a specific context. Younger pupils, or those with greater degrees of developmental delay, may need varying levels of support in identifying general patterns (McGinnis, 2013; Therrien et al., 2017). Pupils who are working at a concrete or inductive level will struggle to carry out investigations in the approved way because they cannot yet use theory to inform their predictions (Scruggs & Mastropieri, 2007). Some pupils will only be able to describe a general inductive pattern if they are given very structured questioning and exposition of ideas. This is one of the advantages of devices such as the ever popular concept cartoons, in which a limited range of possibilities is advanced for evaluation without pupils having to take personal responsibilities for the suggestions, thus saving them from having a 'wrong idea' (Naylor, 2014). Many will explore the phenomenon empirically and derive their findings from a series of apparently random trials and then infer patterns. Based on their inferences, they may then be able to explain what has happened using theory. From an assessment perspective, this approach is not judged to be successful, because it is not theory driven. Nevertheless, it **is** an investigation and one with notable historic precedents so not to be dismissed! It is worth remembering that the roots of science were in those early practitioners who made the first experimental observations and created tentative theories that others went on to refine.

Reflective question:

What is the role, if any, of theories in your approach to teaching? Do you tend to focus on 'what works' in your classroom or are there any theories or frameworks that you currently use to guide your work?

Making the abstract more concrete

Before concluding this section on difficulties with science teaching as they can be understood using Piaget's taxonomy, I want to reiterate the importance of concrete experience in learning. Concrete learning through activities, whether this is experiments or simply seeing, smelling and handling objects and substances, in line with any risk assessment, increases both the enjoyment and motivation of Pupils with LD as well as attainment (Mastropieri et al., 2015; McGinnis, 2013; Westwood, 2007). Similarly, experimentation and practical investigation, which is considered in further detail later in the section, has been found to have multiple benefits, including an increase in pupils' engagement, recall, understanding and confidence in science (Mulvey et al., 2016). This means that experiments, if well taught and with support in place, provide crucial insights for SEN learners, as many of the anecdotes in this section demonstrate. The importance of experimental work is considered in more detail in the section headed *Experimental skills*.

Modelling, specifically physical modelling, is another important tool for aiding comprehension because they can render abstract or intangible phenomena accessible but only if well used. It is important that the model is comprehensible to the learners and that pupils are clear about their purpose, namely to explain scientific ideas or to make predictions(Tregidgo & Ratcliffe, 2000). It is also important to consider the qualities of the teaching model's 'source', the idea, object or process being represented. In Tregidgo and Ratcliffe's study, which looked at learning about cells by two parallel classes, the learning associated with looking at 3-D models of very small but 3-D objects was noticeably more effective. This raises the questions as to whether 3-D models were more effective because there was a correspondence between the qualities of the source, the scientifically accepted understanding of the structure and function of cells.

Evaluation of the impact of using modelling with a mixed attainment group indicated significant benefits to learning, which was more pronounced for pupils who used 3-D models as opposed to 2-D models. Given what is known about the greater need for concrete experience by pupils with LD, I would expect the benefits to be greater for this group and this was indeed the case. Pupils with low prior attainment who made and used 3-D models, as well as 2-D models, in discussing the content matter (cells) were found to outperform their counterparts who had high prior attainment levels but who had only made and used 2-D models in several key areas:

- They did better in a test on the subject matter because they were more able to recall the accepted scientific ideas taught.
- They appeared to have learnt more new content to recall it and be able to communicate it more successfully.
- Could apply what they knew to novel situations more often and were more frequently correct.
- Exhibited fewer misconceptions
- Used newly taught technical vocabulary more often and correctly
- Retained the acquired understanding more securely over a longer period (ten weeks)
- Were able to answer questions in much greater detail and with a higher level of specificity. This was the aspect of their progress that was most pronounced.

As is so often seen in education, and especially in learning by those for whom it is harder than their peers, the additional time taken to make and use 3-D models paid dividends in terms of both short-term and medium recall, understanding and ability to apply the knowledge (Harrison & Coll, 2008).

Where possible, pupils should be actively involved in devising, analysing or evaluating the models used, rather than simply being shown someone else's representation. They can also raise engagement, including digital models, which can be used to make intangible or invisible phenomena visible or audible (Sola Özgüç & Cavkaytar, 2015). Models can be useful to show what happens, or to explain why things happen or to help predict what is going to happen, especially when they relate to things that can't be directly experienced. The definition of a model that I will use is a 'simplified representation constructed for a purpose' and it is crucial that both teacher and pupil are clear about the specific purpose for which any model is constructed. To be used effectively, the teacher needs to identify the key aspects of the target phenomenon or that the model represents. For example, the particle model explains why solids have a fixed shape and don't flow, whereas the particles in liquids and gases are mobile, so don't have a fixed shape. After establishing the ways in which the model represents the key features of what is being taught, for example that each ball represents one particle of matter, it is also important to be clear with pupils what simplifications have been made. This is not to demean the value of educational models, the simplifications are made in order to render the representation comprehensible and what, therefore, the limitations of the model are (van Driel & Verloop, 1999). For example, the particles are usually shown as spheres but may have a myriad of other shapes. The connection between the 'real thing' (the source) and the model needs to be articulated repeatedly so that the equivalence is securely established. Models lend themselves very usefully to active learning through which their use can be made effective. For example, pupils can be asked to match the feature of the source to the feature of the model, or they can be asked to evaluate the model.

For example, when using polystyrene balls in a box to illustrate states of matter, pupils should be encouraged to focus on the way that the balls are arranged (close together or far apart) and how fast they are moving. Pupils can be encouraged to think up other ways of showing these two features. Once the descriptions of the two features have been clearly established for the model solid, model liquid and model gas, pupils can then be encouraged to critique the models. Whether they know the answers to the questions are irrelevant, what they are learning that models are constructs have limitations and so are open to critical evaluation. Suitable questions (and a suitable response, based on consensus understanding) might include:

- Do they think all particles are, in reality, perfectly round? (They are not.)
- Are all particles the same? (No.)
- What do they think is between the polystyrene balls? (Air)
- What is between the minute particles that matter is made of? (Nothing at all, a vacuum).
- Are groups of particles kept together in real life by a box? (They stay together because they are pulled together by forces of attraction, these get weaker as the material gets hotter and particles move faster.)
- Do they think that things can ever get so cold that the particles don't move at all? (Yes, at $-273°C$).

Such an approach helps them to see that models in science are not just scaled up versions of reality, which is a common misapprehension (Grosslight et al., 1991). Despite evaluation being a higher order thinking skill, those with SEN can offer some very interesting insights, suggesting that they can develop a good appreciation of how scientists use models. This is likely to happen if the evaluation enables them to draw on their wider prior learning and experience, rather than requiring them only to recall specified content from previous lessons. To illustrate this, consider the observation of these pupils investigating the effect of temperature on the production of bubbles in a wafer biscuit,

> The pupils tested the baking powder when added to water at different temperatures. They observed that more bubbles were produced more quickly in very hot water but commented that this could be more dangerous in a biscuit factory.
>
> (Field notes, June 2020)

Reflective question:

Which models do you commonly use in school? Do you ask pupils to evaluate models or in some other way encourage pupils to understand the limitations of the model?

Bloom's taxonomy: Another way to assess demand

Lest this discussion of attainment as assessed by Piagetian levels seems rather pessimistic, it is useful to use a second account of learning, that of Benjamin Bloom. Bloom's taxonomy of cognitive processes (Krathwohl et al., 1965) sets out learning processes in a hierarchy according to the degree of cognitive processing that each one requires. (There are also Bloom's taxonomies in the affective domain and psycho-motor domain.) The levels of the taxonomy (or ordered list) are summarised in Figure 2.2. These processes are used by some assessment bodies to characterise attainment. A GCSE (the school leaving exam in England, Wales and Northern Ireland) is reckoned to base 40% of the assessment on recall, 40% on application and 20% by evaluation (OFQUAL, 2021). Bloom's taxonomy has been widely used, not least because it gives rise to associated learning intentions.

It should be noted that a similar taxonomy, the structure of learning outcomes, or SOLO (Biggs & Collis, 1982), has also achieved some traction in classrooms. One of the major attractions of SOLO is that it lends itself to visual representation and so may be accessible to some pupils. It is beyond the scope of this section to compare the two in detail but regardless of which system is used, it is important that learning intentions are formulated, shared with learners and are associated with observable and assessable outcomes.

From the data, it appears that, despite difficulties in processing multiple, abstract concepts, students with learning difficulties can demonstrate higher order approaches to processing content (so-called higher order thinking skills or HOTS [Miri et al., 2007]). The slight caveat here is that those with LD may not readily be able to recall newly acquired knowledge and apply or evaluate it simultaneously, so it may be advisable to provide a recap of the knowledge to be processed before they are asked to apply it or evaluate it. This observation fits well with CLT, and the notion that these learners may be able to process fewer concepts simultaneously. An example of successful evaluation was provided by the following example,

> Pupils, who had been attending a summer STEM scheme about sustainability, were describing their experiences afterwards. They were asked whether they would like to live in the castle near the activity centre where the scheme had been located. To our surprise, a chorus of negative responses was forthcoming, drawing on both what they had learnt during the workshop and wider experiences.
>
> All those walls make it too expensive to heat!
>
> It needs a lot more insulation to make it warm.
>
> The sea will wear away the cliffs next to it, it will fall down into the sea.
>
> You couldn't put solar panels on those rooves.
>
> (Field notes, November, 2021)

Level of learning	Associated learning processes	Notes	Examples of attainment at the level
Knowledge	List, recall, name, define	If learners engage with content using one of the higher levels, they can gain knowledge without rote learning	State whether cornflour is a liquid or a solid. Recalls what happens to the rocket when you add more fizzy tablets
Understanding	Explain, compare	Involves having a grasp of what lies behind the knowledge, for example being able to explain what happens, or recognise generalisable features of phenomena	Says why they think cornflour is a solid. Can describe how the distance travelled by the rocket would change if you put more tablets in.
Application	Choose, classify, design	Draws on knowledge and understanding and uses it in a new context	Is the cornflour and water mixture a solid or a liquid and why do you think that? Can decide what the best number of rockets to put in a fizzy rocket is and explain their selection.
Analysis	Compare, investigate, predict	Recognises the contribution of different factors to a phenomenon	Describe how the runniness of the cornflour 'gloop' changes as they add more water? Does adding more cornflour or does changing the hardness of your slap change the 'splat' more? Can suggest other materials that change when they are pushed. Can predict how the distance travelled by the rocket would change if they put four tablets in, instead of one?
Synthesis	Invent, improve, justify	Uses different bits of knowledge to create a substantial understanding of one thing	Can think of a way to explain why the mixture 'splats' when they slap it. Suggest how to build a fizzy rocket that would fly the furthest. Explain why the re-designed rocket would go further.
Evaluation	Assess, criticise, recommend judge,	Uses substantial understanding to assess an outcome	Decide what is the best 'recipe' for making 'gloop' and explain why it is the best. Decide which fizzy rocket is the best, thinking about its cost, the mess it makes and the distance it travels.

Figure 2.2 Bloom's taxonomy of learning with illustrative examples from science.

This observation that pupils with LD are indeed able to demonstrate HOTS is corroborated by earlier findings of enhanced attainment in science that was associated with programmes that purposively introduce higher order, or critical, thinking skills. For example, Taylor et al. (2012) found that a programme aimed at enhancing critical thinking skills produced similar, sizeable improvements in the Cornell Critical Thinking scores of previously low attaining groups, including those with moderate learning difficulties (MLD), as had been seen in their high achieving peers. In comparison, previously low attaining students who did not follow the course showed the same low score on both the occasions that they were tested. Similarly, another study showed pupils who were required to critique their peers' ideas as they interpreted results from an experiment, a process that requires analysis and evaluation, were able to do so if given some supplemental instruction (Villanueva et al., 2012).

Although pupils with LD may not be reliably confident about demonstrating the higher processes, there is ample evidence that they can do this, that building in support mechanisms such as prompt questions can assist and that rehearsing HOTS enables them to improve in their deployment of them. The benefits of enabling pupils to carry out higher order thinking skills, for instance in problem-based learning activities, are that they can increase the motivation and social confidence of students with LD (Belland et al., 2009).

To illustrate this, consider this example of a non-verbal pupil who demonstrated that they could execute both analysis and evaluation during a science lesson,

> The activity involved classifying materials (water, cornflour) as liquid or solid. Students then had to mix a small amount of each and decide whether the mixture was a liquid or solid. Learning support assistant Naima was seated between Callum and another student and was guiding the other student on how to put cornflour on to a laminated sheet, and, separately, a spoonful of water. The student was guided to use a small wooden spoon to mix the two and to try pushing it. Callum observed this and, when the pot of water was put on the table, reached over and looked at it. He then looked over again at his neighbour and appeared slightly puzzled. When the packet of cornflour was put back on the table, he reached for it and shook some into the pot of water. He glanced over at his neighbour again, then started to look across the table and under the table. He bent to retrieve a twig that he had brought in after break time and put under the table. He then used the twig in place of the spoon, to stir the water and cornflour together and make the 'gloop', as his neighbour had.
>
> (Essex, 2020, p. 553)

One of the unintended consequences of the content rich curriculum that science teachers are commonly required to deliver is that they focus on assessing content acquisition. Indeed, this was a common criticism levelled by teachers at the CASE approach, which intentionally developed HOTS. However, the over-focussing on content knowledge disproportionately disadvantages pupils with LD who are known commonly to have difficulties with memory.

However, it is possible to use pupils' capacity to use HOTS and to minimise the disadvantage caused by their difficulties in recalling previously taught content. One method for doing this is to get pupils to apply their learning to the classification of examples that the teacher provides, for instance living and non-living things or examples and non-examples of something (Apanasionok et al., 2020). The approach that does this is process-based science, in which the focus is on the way in which processes associated with science generate scientific knowledge and pupils' development of these skills. It should be noted that pupils with LD may need more explicit modelling of the thought processes that underpin scientific knowledge, but there is convincing evidence that they can succeed in acquiring a good grasp of scientific processes (Villanueva et al., 2012). It is also worth noting that by focusing on key skills which are considered in the context of different science topics, which gives learners the reassuring familiarity borne of repeated exposure to an idea or an organising principle. On account of the difficulties that pupils with LD experience with recall (Steele, 2004; Therrien et al., 2011), a major advantage of process-based science is that it can reduce the pressure that pupils feel, especially but not exclusively those with LD, to recall content. It is also commended for developing understanding and securing content acquisition that may have been missed earlier on, either because of a delay in ability to process the information (Villanueva et al., 2012). Perhaps more surprisingly, there is evidence that learning around the skills associated with science, commonly termed nature of science raises teachers' expectations of pupils with SEN (Mulvey et al., 2016). This in turn enhances attainment (Rosenthal & Jacobson, 1968a).

In the interest of balance, it must be said that process-based approach to science learning is not without its critics and has been termed 'content-free science' by some, although the familiarity of these critics with the approach has been questioned by others (Bybee, 1997; Osborne & Dillon, 2008; Reid & Hodson, 1987). Other critics claim that process-based courses teach pupils only about scientific processes rather than teaching them science itself. One of the counterarguments is that it lends itself readily to assessment of practical competences and so builds in early success, which we know that Pupils with LD benefit from even more than their neuro-typical peers (Villanueva et al., 2012).

Reflective question:

What have been your experiences of asking pupils with LD to deploy higher order thinking skills? Have you identified strategies that improve their demonstration of HOTS, such as modelling suitable responses or scaffolding pupils' answers?

A major factor is probably the anxiety on the part of teachers about whether it makes content more difficult to manage in a climate of high stakes assessment that focuses on content acquisition. However, such counterarguments have not been derived from data that considers the learning of LD pupils and so may be underpinned by the notion of science lessons as preparation for future science specialists, rather than an entitlement of all learners. For these reasons, it seems that embedding explicit awareness of process into science education can make science more accessible and so deserves consideration.

Harlen (2010) suggested that science be organised around what she termed the 'big ideas' of science, and this, like process-based science, is a framework that can be used to create coherence by the use of recurring organising principles to link different pieces of content. It considers school science to be more than the preparation of future professional scientists, instead presenting the 'big ideas' as those which,

> … together enable understanding of events and phenomena of relevance to students' lives during and beyond their school years.
>
> (Harlen, 2010, p. 2)

In contrast to process-based science, however, the 'big ideas' framework considers the conceptual links between content. This has the same benefits to learning of structuring material and key principles and reinforcing these through repeated use. However, the emphasis on creating a deeper understanding of content by helping pupils to see connections between different sections may help with the assimilation of material in the format that is likely to be assessed. The 10 'big ideas' are:

- All material in the Universe is made of very small particles.
- Objects can affect other objects at a distance.
- Changing the movement of an object requires a net force to be acting on it.
- The total amount of energy in the Universe is always the same but energy can be transformed when things change or are made to happen.
- The composition of the Earth and its atmosphere and the processes occurring within them shape the Earth's surface and its climate.
- The solar system is a very small part of one of millions of galaxies in the Universe.
- Organisms are organised on a cellular basis.
- Organisms require a supply of energy and materials for which they are often dependent on, or in competition with, other organisms.
- Genetic information is passed down from one generation of organisms to another.
- The diversity of organisms, living and extinct, is the result of evolution.

A similar approach was also adopted in the United States' *Next Generation Science Standards* (NGSS Lead States, 2017). In the context of the latter curriculum, the benefits of using connecting concepts so that pupils can clearly see the connections between sections of content that appear disparate have been shown to support science learning by those with LD (Therrien et al., 2017). These 'big ideas' are not so much organising principles for curriculum but 'markers' of the way in which scientific ideas permeate the whole curriculum; explicit reference to them as they are encountered in the disciplinary core ideas of different sections of the curriculum is advocated because it helps pupils to see the coherence of the apparently disparate sections of content (Therrien et al., 2017). Applying the thinking processes, which American science educators term 'cross-cutting concepts', to these 'big ideas', to specific content lets pupils see how ways of using these big ideas changes but that the idea stays consistent. For example, the particle model of states of matter, the ability of some materials to conduct an electric current and the composition of different planets in the solar system all consider the role of particles in the mass behaviour of substances, even though they would be found in three different sections of the science curriculum.

The notion of re-visiting a concept repeatedly so as to build up a more complete understanding is sometimes called the 'spiral curriculum' (Bruner, 1960) and is especially powerful as a way of enhancing recall by pupils with LD (Therrien et al., 2011). Sola Özgüç and Cavkaytar (2015) provided evidence that the greater the time that was spent on the subject matter, the greater the learning. It is important to note that this is not the same as simply repeating content, which is liable to cause boredom in both teacher and pupils (Sola Özgüç & Cavkaytar, 2015). I have observed that intentionally moving the structure away from a series of sequential inputs on a certain topic is especially possible with pupils with LD because they commonly bring less prior formal knowledge and so do not resist innovative presentations of material.

The final approach that draws upon thinking skills rather than the ability to recall content is that of arranging the scientific content around topics or problems and to deploy the science content to understand a specified topic, an approach known as problem-based learning. This enables pupils to see the importance of science in people's lives, what is termed 'knowing about science' and an aspect of the subject which may be less well recognised by SEND learners (Park et al., 2019). This context-driven approach does not detract from pupils' exposure to content, even though it may not be organised along traditional lines. It also makes the science relevant and often clearly related to the concrete experiences of pupils, which is considered important to the acquisition of new learning (Boyle et al., 2020). One final strength of this approach is that it may facilitate some individualisation of the curriculum, in that although the content may not change pupils can select from a given range, the context they prefer to look at the operation of the knowledge (McGinnis, 2013). For example, in a topic on chemical change, they could choose to find out about the changes when cake mix is made and baked or how to make herbal medicines from cinchona bark or what happens inside a car engine. Deploying individual interests is an excellent way to enhance pupils' science capital, which has been described in greater detail in Section 1. One study found that the SEND pupils who did best in science were those who did home experiments or watched popular science programmes on TV (Sola Özgüç & Cavkaytar, 2015). Another mechanism for initiating, or building upon, individual interests is to get pupils to participate in public engagement or university outreach initiatives (Park et al., 2019). Although staff working with pupils with SEND are often reluctant to take them to such events, fearing that the pupils may be ridiculed or humiliated (Essex, 2018), requesting adjustments of public engagement providers is likely to be met sympathetically. Indeed, many science visitor centres now actively encourage engagement from a wide range of visitors and positively welcome such approaches.

Reflective question:

To what extent do you feel constrained by the curriculum from allowing pupils to pursue individual interests? Are there any opportunities to engage further with pupils' science-related interests in your department's wider provision?

Ways in which those with learning difficulties may differ from their peers 1: Executive functions

Bronfenbrenner (1979) devised an ecological model of diversity, which considers the degree of 'fit' between learners and their learning environment. This notion of fit is important because it reminds teachers that our job is to create the optimal learning environment for each pupil. The preceding analysis of the curriculum has set out the ways in which it often creates a high or excessive challenge simply because of the inherent demands. However, there are things that we can do to support pupils to access a great deal of the curriculum, if not all of it.

It is slightly artificial to separate out the different aspects of learning which may present additional difficulty to pupils with special needs, but there are three skills, which (Therrien et al., 2011) term a 'triad of difficulties', that are widely required in science lessons. Steele (2004) writing in the basis of extensive practical experience concurs that these factors, along with social emotional problems, constitute the major barriers to learning science successfully. These are:

- Language, including reading and writing
- Core academic skills, which are the processes that enable a pupil to learn and includes organisational skills
- The acquisition and retention of information

However, it is not simply the content rich and abstract nature of the curriculum that causes difficulties to pupils with LD. It is the fact that pupils with LD are much more likely to have difficulties with various executive functions (sometimes termed the management systems of the brain) that make the standard curriculum more challenging to them than it is to their neuro-typical peers.

The intersection of these two factors amplifies the exclusionary effect of the standard science further. The executive functions that are commonly affected are:

- Planning
- Organisation
- Task initiation
- Sustain attention
- Goal-setting
- Decision-making
- Problem-solving

Other executive skills, when significantly lower than in neuro-typical peers, may contribute to slower curriculum progress in science. For children with LD or attention disorders, development in these areas frequently does not come naturally but needs active support and explicit attention from the teacher.

Attention span and self-regulation capacity

Difficulties with limited attention span can means the learners have appreciable difficulties in engaging with the lesson content for extended periods. This is thought to make a major contribution to the under-achievement of pupils with LD (Sola Özgüç & Cavkaytar, 2015; Steele, 2004). The problem is almost certainly exacerbated by the high demands of the curriculum. The best way to limit the deleterious effect of these difficulties is to have learning broken down into smaller 'chunks' so that there are frequent changes in activity, accompanied by a series of mini-plenaries that revise what has just been done and prepares pupils for their next activity. It is important, however, that the material is not simply broken down into small sections but that the sections are organised in an order that facilitates the development of an increasingly complex (and, arguably, complete) understanding of a topic. This is a key feature of the published 'Explicit Instruction' materials that have been shown to have a beneficial effect on science learning by pupils with LD (Apanasionok et al., 2020; Epistemic Insight website; Librea-Carden et al., 2021; Therrien et al., 2017). This does not, however, mean that the lesson undergoes a complete change every five or ten minutes but rather that the lesson is considered a succession of shorter related learning episodes.

For example, in a lesson on making red cabbage indicator and testing it, the teacher might divide up the 25 minutes for the experiment as follows:

- Five minutes to gather up equipment and to check that they have everything they need, shown on a list, followed by each group checking off the equipment collected by another group.
- Five minutes to light Bunsen burners and boil up the red cabbage. Teacher stops the heating and can check at a glance that everyone has some purple solution at a glance.
- Five minutes pupils watch the teacher testing a different indicator but using the testing protocol that the pupils will follow, for example putting a 1 cm depth each of a strong acid, weak acid, neutral solution, weak alkali and strong alkali into five test tubes, then adding three drops of indicator solution. The mechanism for recording the colour change can also be modelled at this point, for example a results chart, possibly along with colouring in with crayons to represent what is seen. Pupils are sent back to their work spaces.
- Ten minutes pupils carry out the experiment using their cooled cabbage extract, record their results and clear their apparatus away.

Short-term recall

This was cited earlier as one reason that a content rich curriculum is especially poorly suited to pupils with LD. The fact that the science curriculum is structured so that the learning of new material frequently rests upon successfully grasping previously taught content, makes problems with recall a great disadvantage to students for whom this is difficult (Villanueva et al., 2012). One approach to helping pupils to secure their learning is through repetition and re-visiting key ideas and facts (Apanasionok et al., 2020). Teacher's support, or scaffolding, is vital here in providing assistance that enables pupils to recall the desired information and has been shown to improve learning by Pupils with LD (Therrien et al., 2017). The scaffolding can involve both prompting the pupil and the explicit modelling of the desired outcome and could include briefly recapping the last lesson's content at the start of each lesson.

Two examples of both the difficulty and of effective scaffolding are given below:

1. *A pupil is asked what it is called when the water can't get any hotter. She can't remember. The teacher then prompts her, saying, 'It begins with a "b". It's when water is really bubbling'. The pupil then recalls the word 'boiling'.*
2. *The teacher shows the pupil that she is putting three drops on to the dimple tile using a dropper pipette. The teacher says, 'Not four or five. How many drops?' to which the pupil responds, 'Three'* (Field notes, February 2020).

To counter the recall demands of the formally structured curriculum, it is recommended that the material be structured around 'big ideas', to which the concepts, and associated vocabulary can be connected, giving the material coherence in a way that reinforces learning and enhances attainment (Gerstner & Bogner, 2010). In addition, much repetition of key words and ideas helps pupils to retain them. Similarly, teaching mnemonics (tricks to prompt the memory) has been shown to be powerful in aiding recall (Therrien et al., 2011).

Multi-sensory, also known as multi-modal, activities are especially powerful in enhancing learning, including higher order thinking, and recall by pupils with LD (McGinnis, 2013; Sola Özgüç & Cavkaytar, 2015) and the author has successfully used multi-sensory learning to assist memorisation, by teaching pupils a list of required properties of metals with accompanying sign language, which pupils proceeded to enact during their test as they tackled the relevant assessment questions! It should be noted that multi-modal teaching, which is the use of more than one form of input to convey the same concept, is very far from the now discredited notion of assigning pupils a VAK (visual, auditory or kinaesthetic) learner categorisation (White, 2005). The use of VAK can be used deterministically to impose restrictions upon the sensory opportunities for learners, whereas multi-modality offers diverse ways for all learners to access concepts. Think of it as a mixed 'diet' of input media that reinforces the core message with no-one forced to rely on inputs that they prefer not to. For instance, by saying the word, displaying the word and showing an object to illustrate, a concept offers three ways to access the concept and each input reinforces the teaching of the others. Many teachers have learnt empirically that this is a successful approach and have been using it before it had a formal name. The growth in digital technologies opens up new possibilities for exposing pupils to visual and audio inputs that would not be available in a classroom (Pellerin, 2014). There is significant evidence that techniques that purposively focus on memorisation and recall make a significant and positive difference, with active learning and peer teaching being especially powerful aid to recall (Brigham et al., 2011; Therrien et al., 2011, 2017). The other way to improve pupils' memorisation of material is frequent rehearsal and repetition (DeWitt, 2007) which may mean that less content can be covered but that which is taught is remembered. However, it should also be recognised that there is a 'trade-off' between the degree of difficulty of the material and the status that it affords, which boosts students' self-esteem when they achieve mastery of it (Essex, 2018). Facilitating access to some 'high status' can boost pupils' self-esteem and self-efficacy. One pupil I recall had very limited speech but was captivated when he overheard a staff member naming a plant that we had seen as 'glabrous rupture-wort'. For the rest of our week together, he pressed us to repeat it until he could say it too. Thereafter, he looked out assiduously for the plant so that he could shout out his newly acquired word.

Reduced processing capacity

We know that difficulties in processing several threads of information simultaneously are likely to cause greater difficulty for learning disabled students than their neuro-typical peers (Villanueva et al., 2012). Instructions with multiple steps can similarly exceed students' processing capacity but can helpfully be broken down into smaller segments. These difficulties can be understood in terms of 'cognitive load theory' (CLT), a model of learning that was based on experimental data and knowledge of the relationship between working memory, where information is attended to and sense made of it prior to storage in the long-term memory, where information is stored long term. The stored knowledge or understanding is known as a schema (Sweller et al., 2011).

CLT provides yet another way to think about the demands of the task, as Piaget and Bloom did, but unlike these, it quantifies demand. It describes three different forms of 'cognitive load' according to their part in the learning process:

- Intrinsic cognitive load is the work required by any learning task
- Extraneous cognitive load is the term for the way in which the information is presented to the learners
- Germane cognitive load refers to the effort needed to lay down information that has been processed in the short-term memory into the long-term memory; this permanent knowledge or understanding is known as a schema (plural schemata)

The load that a learner can process and store varies: those with LD usually have a reduced capacity, as do younger learners. It is important, therefore, not to overload the learners' capacity with unnecessary information or stimuli. The cognitive load that can be handled is also reduced at times of high emotional arousal which is why the learning environment is an important consideration. People with autism can be hyper-stimulated by routine stimuli and, again, this reduces the cognitive load they can handle (Doherty-Sneddon et al., 2012). When designing a task, it helps learners if the working memory is not required to process too much data at once, nor is it required to store data for very long. For this reason, it is important to limit the amount of information that the working memory is asked to process at any one time. By considering the learners' capacity in this way, CLT has been found to be useful in structuring lessons to optimise learning (Kirschner, 2002). (Note that, although this may seem to contradict the information on the suggestion that using multi-sensory inputs may assist learning, since this appears to double the load that the brain has to process. The important distinction is that all the sensory inputs are coding for the same concept.)

This can make consideration of multiple factors simultaneously very difficult, such as considering the various factors that may speed up a chemical reaction, or make recalling multiple bits of information, such as all the steps in multi-step sequence of instructions, hard to recall or put in the correct order if they are recalled. One pupil used to tell me that he could only deal with three instructions at a time, so he was duly only ever given three things to remember in one go. A number of colleagues advocate what they term 'slow practicals', in which the entire class carries out one step at a time and, once everyone has done this successfully, the next step is introduced.

Reflective question:

When you plan your lessons, how far do you feel able to take account of the limited attention span of some pupils? What strategies have you found successful in sustaining attention?

Teaching that reduces cognitive load

There are two teaching methods that have been devised, and for which published teaching resources exist, that deliberately structure the development of knowledge in such a way as to reduce cognitive load. Evaluation evidence shows that both directed instruction (DI) and explicit instruction (EI) promote learning (Hattie, 2012) and these two methods are described here. It is important to be clear that selection of any pedagogic approach needs to be done after due consideration of the learners and, importantly, of the sort of learning that is wanted. One source, written by authors who are very experienced in the field of science education for those with LD, suggests that, generally, this group of students develop understanding best from structured hands-on or active learning activities, whilst the memorisation of key vocabulary and general facts is best achieved by direct instruction and 'elaborative strategies'. Elaborative strategies are approaches that get learners to work actively in some way with the content to be learnt, for example constructing mnemonics or to prepare it for presentation to an audience (Scruggs & Mastropieri, 2007).

Evidence has shown that DI enhances both engagement and attainment (McGinnis, 2013). The teaching method involves breaking down content into small 'chunks' and then teaching these in an order that affords the opportunity for understanding to grow incrementally with incurring a high cognitive load at any point. The approach focuses on the structure of the content and sets out both the structure and the details of the content very clearly. It intentionally reduces cognitive load by limiting the amount of information that learners have to process at any one time, in a way that is consistent with the tenets of CLT. Its effectiveness is borne out by empirical evidence (Therrien et al., 2017) and it is for this reason that has been influential in shaping ideas about teaching and learning in practice, such as that described by McGill (2022). The lessons are supported by a highly structured teacher 'script'. Although many teachers might find the approach, especially DI, over-prescriptive it has to be borne in mind that out of mainstream settings non-specialist may be teaching science and may be supported by the degree of direction. For science teachers not needing this level of support, the impact of DI reminds them that the very careful and explicit structuring of content can help pupils considerably. In either case, the use of DI is not, despite the description given above, inherently incompatible with the notion of responsive teaching which is thought to enhance the inclusion of diverse learners (European Agency for Development in Special Needs Education, 2012). It is always important that staff monitor how pupils are receiving the content, be it from a script or not. Despite the highly structured form of DI lessons, the format is not always used simply to transmit content, and one of the strengths of DI, it has been found to work with a range of learning foci, for instance the development of understanding of scientific content or the acquisition of scientific vocabulary or the teaching of enquiry approaches (Aydeniz & Kotowski, 2012). It is also effective with a wide range of learners with a wide range of difficulties, including moderate and severe intellectual disabilities (Aydeniz & Kotowski, 2012).

EI builds upon the very structured approach to content introduction of DI, which it resembles in that lessons are highly planned in terms of intended content delivery. Similar to DI, EI pedagogy breaks the content down into smaller chunks in order to reduce cognitive load and has been shown to be very effective with pupils with LD, including those with significant learning difficulties (Apanasionok et al., 2020). The distinction between DI and EI is that emphasis is placed on the sequence of teaching and assessment strategies which are used to convey the content, as well as the content itself. During the course of the lesson, there is an intentional shift away from teacher-led to pupil-led activity. The shift in emphasis from content in DI to the teaching strategies that are used at each stage in EI enables the teacher to exercise more discretion about precisely how to impart the content knowledge. The phases of an EI learning episode are:

1. DI, in which the teacher leads the learning by showing how the new material to be covered links back to previous learning.
2. Demonstration and modelling. This involves pupils being engaged by the teacher to execute active thinking about the material, for instance by asking questions, or setting tasks for small group work. At this phase, the teacher is actively monitoring pupil learning and adjusting teaching and feedback in line with pupil performance.
3. Guided practice. During guided practice, pupils are asked to work more independently, possibly in groups. Teacher support is gradually withdrawn as pupil performance indicates that it is no longer needed or no longer needed to the same extent.
4. Corrective feedback/verification. During this phase of an EI lesson, the teacher is providing descriptive feedback, intervening with supplementary instruction where evidence indicates it is needed and encouraging pupils to analyse their own learning.
5. Independent practice is the phase during which the new learning is put into practice independently. Pupils are applying their learning independently whilst the teacher uses this phase to monitor pupil attainment and provide additional feedback.

Many teachers will recognise this general structure as one that is widely deployed in schools, possibly in response to policy but many times without conscious reference to any instructional technique. The fact that this is a widely used approach to organising teaching and learning reminds us that inclusive teaching is not a distinctive practice or one to be reserved for those with special needs but is simply effective teaching. However, it should be acknowledged that both DI and EI have been demonstrated to be highly effective in enhancing learning by those with LD. This suggests that, in a mainstream setting, reference to the EI structure meets the expectations of a 'universal (pedagogic) design for inclusion' which will benefit all pupils. In order to render the EI approach more universally applicable to different teaching contexts, it is useful to be aware of the characteristics of the EI approach (Archer & Hughes, 2011; Librea-Carden et al., 2021). The use of these characteristics is corroborated by earlier empirical observations of effective lessons, which have included maintaining pace, direct questioning and a succession of tasks that maintain pupil attention (Scruggs & Mastropieri, 2007). These features, which can beneficially be included in lessons, even if EI strategies and teaching materials are not being explicitly used, are:

- Having clearly defined learning intentions that are shared with the learners
- Reviewing relevant prior learning in preparation for learning new material
- The materials taught are carefully selected so that it is that which will impart the most important ideas that are relevant to what is being taught
- The knowledge is set out very clearly for the pupils, including the careful selection of vocabulary used to talk about the subject matter
- The material is presented in structured and logical ways
- The teaching helps pupils to make connections between knowledge as they acquire
- Actively seeking to identify and challenge misconceptions
- Offers as much scaffolding as individuals require to succeed
- Learning is reinforced by considering examples and non-examples of key concepts
- Ample opportunity for guided practice
- Careful monitoring of pupils' work
- Numerous opportunities to rehearse key ideas and to process the content by asking questions and receiving feedback
- Very explicit modelling of correct answers and the thinking associated with arriving at the correct answer, in other words demonstrating meta-cognition, as defined earlier
- Lessons are taught at a brisk pace

Reflective question:

Is it generally helpful to teachers to have a framework, such as the one described for Thinking Science or DI to use when planning their teaching? Are you concerned that these might detract from teachers' judgement and ability to make context-specific adjustments?

Another practical strategy that can reduce the load on both memory and processing capacity is an explicit adherence to consistent routines. For example, ensuring that lessons are in the same room, a consistent application of behaviour expectations and classroom routines. Other adjustments might include a deliberate reduction in the number of choices available to students, such as a more limited choice of reagents than might have been offered to neuro-typical peers. Pro-active management of the classroom in this way can achieve outcomes for pupils with LD who are equivalent to their neuro-typical peers (Canning et al., 1997). Similarly, the use of graphic organisers and other forms of visual representations (for example, integrated instructions for practical work) can assist with organisational problems (Steele, 2007).

Another suite of strategies that helps pupils with limited processing capacity to cope with substantial amounts of information is those that are collectively termed 'visual organisers' or graphic organisers. Dexter and Hughes (2011) found that graphic organisers, which are ways of showing visually how information is organised, are consistently helpful for learners with LD and help them both to grasp and to remember over the longer term the science content that is taught. Their findings are consistent with key learning theories. Representing how knowledge is organised and related promotes meta-cognition ('thinking about thinking') which Shayer and Adey (2002) showed to be a powerful tool to enhance learning. Similarly, the success of visual organisers can be explained in terms of the way that they direct the pupils' attention to how the knowledge is organised (Sola Özgüç & Cavkaytar, 2015). They thus help to ensure that the information is stored in the long-term memory, according to CLT. More than simply enhancing recall, visual organisers, along with other mechanisms for encouraging pupils to analyse the function of text, help to promote independent learning (Scruggs & Mastropieri, 2007). Practical ways of providing visual organisation of content include highlighting key text, by putting it in bold text or in a text box, and visual mechanisms for organising ideas, such as writing frameworks.

An example of a writing framework, here being used to organise information about an experiment, is shown in Figure 2.3. Figure 2.4 shows another visual organiser that was designed to help pupils to recall the information needed to answer exam questions that carried six points and were very difficult for pupils with limited processing capacity. Success in these questions had a large bearing on whether pupils passed the exam or not and use of the template was used to develop their ability to answer them confidently. Figure 2.5 shows an example of an approach

Title: SCAN ME	Title: SCAN ME	Title: SCAN ME	Title: SCAN ME
What is Thalidomide? What was it intended to be used for	What is Thalidomide? What was it intended to be used for	What is Thalidomide? What was it intended to be used for	What is Thalidomide? What was it intended to be used for
What else did doctors use thalidomide for?	What else did doctors use thalidomide for?	What else did doctors use thalidomide for?	What else did doctors use thalidomide for?
What happened next?	What happened next?	What happened next?	What happened next?
Why did this happen?	Why did this happen?	Why did this happen?	Why did this happen?
How did we change the way drugs are tested?	How did we change the way drugs are tested?	How did we change the way drugs are tested?	How did we change the way drugs are tested?

Figure 2.3 An example of a writing frame.

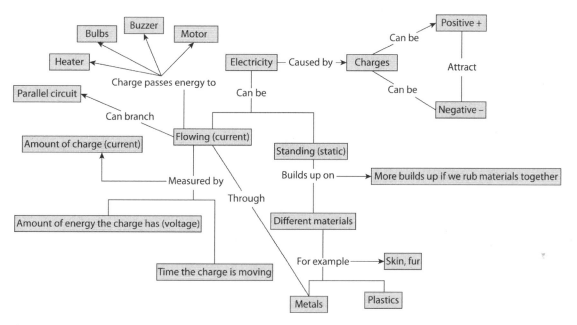

Figure 2.4 An example of a concept map.

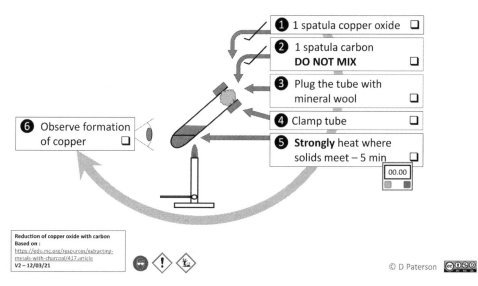

Figure 2.5 An example of integrated instructions (Paterson, 2018).

known as 'integrated instruction' in which the instructions for an experiment are shown next to the image of the relevant piece of apparatus which reduces the cognitive load and helps pupils to follow the sequence of instructions in the correct order. Figure 2.6 shows a set of photo instructions, which enables pupils to check that they have the correct equipment and reagents at each stage of the experiment.

Chromatography

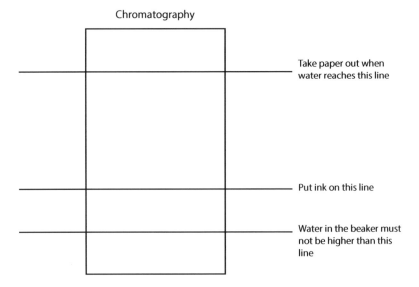

Take paper out when water reaches this line

Put ink on this line

Water in the beaker must not be higher than this line

1. Use the shape above to draw the three lines in pencil. Mark crosses at along the middle line. Mark them with different letters to show which ink is on each spot, for example S, U and P.

2. Dip a cocktail stick into the ink next to it. Put a spot of ink on the spot with the right code, for example Sheaffer ink on S, Unknown ink on U and Parker on P.

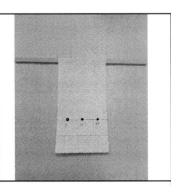

3. Attach the paper to the blue tack on the stick like that in the photo.

4. Put the water in the beaker. It should only be as high as the bottom line on the paper.

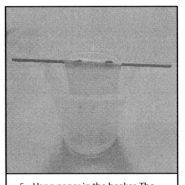

5. Hang paper in the beaker. The water should only reach the bottom line, not the middle one.

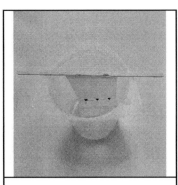

6. Allow the water to rise up the paper, taking the ink with it. Pull the stick away when the water gets up to the top line.

7. Compare the spots and see which ones match.

Sheet by Pam Tait, University of Strathclyde

Figure 2.6 An example of photographic instructions.

Teaching that enhances motivation

Although the role of pupils' motivation has long been intuitively understood by teachers and is documented in academic sources, this is not reliably reflected in the curriculum or approaches to teaching it. Benjamin Bloom, who is better known for the taxonomy that describes increasing demands of learning processes, also described a taxonomy of processes related to feeling, attitudes and values in the so-called affective domain (Krathwohl et al., 1965). At the highest level of emotional engagement, we can expect to find a young person who is keen to learn science and who makes personal decisions about engaging with it. Although this state might be expected to be seen in pupils who are learning well, this correlation is far from universal, and it is important not to assume that highly performing pupils are feeling highly motivated. Over decades of conducting inclusive and accessible science, I have often noted exceptional levels of enthusiasm for science of those with LD. For instance, I recall asking a group of young people, who had volunteered for a STEM summer school to pack up after lunch and go to the place where the next activity was being run. One leapt to her feet and said to the others, in an excited voice, 'Come on! Hurry up! We're going to do more <u>real</u> science!' Nevertheless, it is true that many pupils find the science curriculum irrelevant to their lived experience and this kills their interest, enthusiasm and motivation (Harlen, 2010). Many more are interested only inasmuch as a science qualification acts as a 'gatekeeper' to a job or course in which they are interested. Even this extrinsic motivation is not helpful to those who struggle with formal assessments (see Section 3 for more on assessment).

The way in which pupils feel about science inevitably affects how they respond to the cognitive demands of learning the subject. The relationship between affective response and cognitive attainment is poorly understood, but it seems self-evident that pupils are unlikely to have the motivation to persevere with a subject that they find hard if they do not enjoy at least some aspects of it. For science to be attractive to pupils who struggle with the cognitive element of science, it is important to create a sense of belonging, through participation and recognition for achievement and, arising from the sense of belonging, a sense of self-esteem. It should also be noted that we can only hope to meet these aims if pupils' basic physiological needs are met and they feel safe.

Reflective question:

Consider Bloom's affective taxonomy, shown in Figure 2.7, and the extent to which behaviours exhibited by pupils reflect their motivation. Are there other indicative behaviours that you would add to the list? For students showing low motivation, do you think that there may be other needs that are not yet being met and so inhibit pupils' engagement?

Level of feeling/valuing and features	*Some associated behaviours*	*Examples*
Characterisation. Acts independently and pro-actively based on how they value science	Discriminates, influences, modifies, selects	Chooses science as a subject option Chooses a science extra-curricular science activity from a range that they have found out about
Organisation. Plans a science activity independently or can formulate their own response to a contested science subject	Initiates, joins, justifies, suggests	Plans an investigation Forms a view on how serious a threat climate change is
Valuing. Values, and has confidence in, their understanding of science, shows consistently positive behaviours towards science	Works, reads, explains	Volunteers to answer questions about science Willing to explain something scientific to others
Responding. Responds positively to opportunities to engage in science that are directly presented to them	Replies, reacts, moves towards	Chooses science books to look at when given a free choice of books Accepts an invitation to attend extra-curricular science activities.
Receiving. Is willing to have science imparted to them, though does not engage actively and engagement not be sustained	Listens, watches, holds, touches	Attends some science lessons Listens to parts of the science lesson

Figure 2.7 Bloom's affective taxonomy.

Ways in which those with learning difficulties may differ from their peers 2: Functional skills

Pupils with LD also encounter other difficulties, specifically with functional skills; delays in these well may be secondary to pupils' atypical executive functions. Functional skills are those that enable pupils to deal with the requirement of learning and the workplace and are commonly listed as literacy, numeracy and IT skills. Of these, three skills are considered here as presenting additional difficulty for pupils with LD in science. These are organisation skills, literacy and numeracy.

Literacy and communication

Somewhat confusingly, the term 'scientific literacy' is used to denote the ability to understand the processes of science and how they are used to generate information, in this section however, I will restrict my analysis to the issues of using language for reading, writing and speech, including the use of scientific vocabulary. These problems not only impede both the development of understanding but also prevent pupils from gaining assessment credit for what they know and understand but cannot communicate (Canning et al., 1997; Mastropieri et al., 2006). It is also worth recalling the inhibitory effect of the 'hard' science curriculum on communication: Park et al. (2019, p. 11) quote a participant at a science fair reporting that '*Although I am not smart enough to explain science to the visitors, I asked my teacher to include me as a member. ...*'. For this reason, it is important that science teachers ensure that literacy development proceeds alongside a corresponding growth in scientific understanding.

Literacy is the functional skill that pupils with LD are most commonly seen to attain less well than their peers (Brigham et al., 2011). It is quite common for pupils to exhibit resistance to writing and teacher's requests to start writing are quite commonly met with reluctance, for instance pupils asking, 'Do I have to write this down?' or unsettled behaviour. Although science can be a useful 'vehicle for learning', helping to consolidate literacy and other functional skills (Villanueva et al., 2012, p. 189), it is important that science does not become a thinly veiled 'sweetener' for general literacy work. I would suggest that the literacy skills used in science should be those that are required to engage with the scientific ideas that are being taught. As in all matters of teaching, and even more so for inclusive teaching, the teacher's judgement, based on their knowledge of the pupils and the science content, is needed in deciding how to balance the demand and support of the lesson's literacy requirements in order to optimise literacy development and science learning (Hitchcock et al., 2002).

Technical words are deeply embedded feature of science and often convey rich meaning to those who understand them. Similarly, pupils who acquire and technical vocabulary are liable to pick up some of the scientific meaning associated with them. Nevertheless, technical terms present difficulties for many learners, most especially those whose reading, writing and spoken language fluency is significantly lower than would be expected from their chronological age (Boyle et al., 2020; Dougherty & Moran, 1983). Commonly observed difficulties are words with multiple meanings that appear to have a different meaning in science than in everyday use and that scientific words are perceived by pupils to be jargon, making sense to specialists but excluding them (Boyle et al., 2020).

Difficulties in comprehension of technical terms, combined with the likelihood of difficulties with memory, this means that strategic selection of vocabulary is important. Pupils are more confident in using technical terms that they may hear outside of the classroom and so have opportunities to rehearse (Sola Özgüç & Cavkaytar, 2015). For this reason, replacing technical words with everyday equivalents may be useful in supporting the acquisition of understanding of the concepts before pupils engage with the unfamiliar terminology (Canning et al., 1997). It also means that scientific vocabulary needs to be introduced and used repeatedly and explicitly, rather than relying on pupils 'just picking it up as they go' (Therrien et al., 2017). Practical strategies that have been used with success are the creating of displays with key terms accompanied by relevant illustrations and artefacts (Canning et al., 1997), or the loading of lists of target vocabulary words on to digital devices (McGinnis, 2013). Another adjustment to make in written sources is avoiding the passive voice, which was used to denote the supposed objectivity of science, a highly contestable claim anyway, and a literacy device that considerably raises the reading and processing demand of text (Bostian, 1983).

This balance cannot be achieved for most Pupils with LD by the use of traditional linguistically dense textbooks which stop pupils developing a secure understanding of the science and do not model language that the pupils can use effectively to express themselves and demonstrate their understanding (McGinnis, 2013; Parmar et al., 1994). Indeed, the problems that standard text formats present neuro-diverse learners may be a direct cause of under-attainment in LD learners (Pisha & Stahl, 2005). Unfortunately, there is a notable lack of suitable science resources adapted for students with below expected literacy or comprehension levels relative to the curriculum with which they are expected to engage, though this situation is slowly improving. There is also an unfortunate habit of publishing resources that will be used by these learners, such as revision guides for Foundation level science GCSE, until last. This means that those facing the biggest double obstacle, in terms of literacy and understanding of science, are given the least time to engage with the texts. The situation for learners with significant learning materials is even less promising, with texts in the United States for teachers working with this population not even mentioning the possibility of them studying science, despite initiatives intended to bring science education to all pupils, irrespective of their personal characteristics (Courtade et al., 2007).

Where undifferentiated materials (Piggott, 2002) are not available, it can be helpful to spend some time teaching pupils to engage with the text in a way that will assist them in making sense of the standard text. One study compared two different approaches to understanding and recalling standard text and found that a 'text-structure-based' approach was most effective strategy (Bakken et al., 1997). The approach involved asked pupils to identify different types of text, and the component parts of the text, such as a main idea, comparison or ordered list, as well as applying more general reading strategies such as predicting what might come next and identifying what a paragraph is about. Adoption of this active and analytical approach was compared to there being no specific intervention or a strategy of paragraph restatement (being asked to summarise what each paragraph says in a sentence). The findings suggest that investing time in helping pupils to engage more deeply with the purpose and structure of text helped pupils to remember the content of the text and that this gain persisted over the medium and long term.

Other possible solutions to literacy difficulties include greater use of digital devices to make resources readily available and easily editable, as needed (Sola Özgüç & Cavkaytar, 2015). The ability to intentionally use fonts that pupils find easier to make out is a great help. Key point to look out for is the spacing between letters, and this makes Arial or Comic Sans especially good fonts to use. Dyslexie is a font that has been created to make letters more easily distinguishable from each other and is intended, as the name suggests, to make it especially helpful for readers with dyslexia. Other helpful devices are the deployment of multi-modal representations of phenomena or concepts, such as pictures and words, speech as well as text (Boyle et al., 2020; Canning et al., 1997). A small but easy-to-implement adjustment to make to all teacher-prepared resources is to remove words that are spelled in block capital letters, sometimes for emphasis. In fact, text in block capitals slows reading by an estimated 20 per cent (Breland & Breland, 1944) due to it being less familiar as a format for reading and partly due to their letter shape. Instead, sentence case (capital and lower case letters) is recommended to for optimal reading speed shape (Poulton, 1967; Rickards & August, 1975). Besides this, spatial organisers (such as text boxes) and graphic illustrations have been found to be helpful ((Lovitt & Horton, 1994). Similarly, integrated instructions have the recommended characteristics to make instructions for experiment accessible (Paterson, 2018). Digital devices offer options to customise text, including e-books, to suit the learner's preferences. Pupils can also use handheld digital devises to prepare resources that can then be made available for subsequent classes. A good example of this is asking pupils to take photographs of an experiment and to put them into a digital book creator, alongside text describing what needs to be done at each stage of an experiment. Authors reporting on the evaluation of science festival noted that participants with SEND tended to provide less text and more photos in their evaluation, which suggests that they can provide a useful tool for communication for those who find writing more onerous (Park et al., 2019).

One fairly common response to pupils with low literacy is to provide abridged pre-written sheets or booklets with the key information provided. Some level of interactivity is then provided by asking pupils to fill in gaps in the text or to match up text, such as terms and definitions. This facilitates a fairly complete and largely accurate record of the subject matter, but at the expense of the learning that takes place when pupils actively engage with, and try out the use of, technical terms within their own writing and speech.

Reflective question:

Do you find literacy difficulties present a significant barrier in your lessons? Is it all literacy that is a problem or is it the technical vocabulary of science that causes most problems? What strategies have you found helpful in reducing such difficulties?

Assessing readability of resources

Whatever adjustments are made to enhance literacy, it is advisable to check the literacy demands of the text. Although these do not assess the conceptual demands of the material, they do give an indication of the level of difficulty in decoding the text that users face. Suitable tests include the reading age, Fry Readability Test (Fry, 1968) and the Flesch Reading Ease Test (Flesch, 1948), the latter two of which are quite easily carried out on a Word document (Microsoft, 2022).

The Fry Readability Test requires you to take 100 word samples of the text from the beginning, middle and end. Count the number of words in each sample of text. Next count sentences, including part sentences at the end of each sample. Finally, look at the number of syllables in each word, probably most easily done by keeping a tally chart of the number of syllables in each word. Count the total number of syllables. For example, the first 100 words of the text below have 6.9 sentences.

> Take 50 ml of water in a beaker, add 3 drops of washing up liquid and stir it gently. Then add a heaped teaspoon of baking powder. See how high the froth rises. Write down the greatest height it froths up to. Now repeat the experiment using 50 ml of warm water from the hot water tap and add the detergent and baking powder. Again, measure the height of the froth and write it down. Finally, ask your teacher to pour 50 ml of very hot water from a kettle, add washing up liquid and baking powder to the hot (100 words).

These two measurements (average sentence length [ASL] and number of syllables) can be read off a Fry Readability Graph. The one above falls on the boundary between U.S. Grade 6 and Grade 7, in other words it is considered suitable for typically attaining 11- or 12-year old. Working on a rule of thumb that to be read effortlessly the reading age of text should be about 2 years less than the reader's chronological age, this text should be easily accessible for a neuro-typical 13- or 14-year old. The analysis also points to ways to improve readability score. For example, it would be lower if the fifth sentence, a long list of instructions, were broken down into shorter sentences. Using the term 'washing up liquid' instead of 'detergent' drops the number of syllables in 100 words down to 132 and enhances readability slightly.

The Flesch (or Flesch-Kincaid) Grade Level Score is similar in that it calculates the grade of a pupil that would typically be expected to read it fluently and with understanding. It considers at the ASL, for which we use the same data as for the Fry Test, where in the example previously we knew that 100 words were divided into 6.9 sentences. This gives an average length of 14.5 words per sentence. We also need the average number of syllables per word (ASW), in the example above that is 137 syllables for 100 words, so the average is 1.37. These values are then put into an equation:

$$(0.39 \times ASL) + (11.8 \times ASW) - 15.59.$$

For the sample text analysed, this gives a Grade Level of Grade 6.23, slightly lower than the Fry Readability Test. Its huge advantage is that Word documents can calculate the Flesch Grade Level, once you have ticked the box under Proofing to do so. (If the document isn't in Word, it can be pasted into a Word document for checking.)

The Flesch Reading Ease score is also calculated by Word. This factors in the ASL and ASW and uses a different equation to give a score out of 100.

$$206.835 - (1.015 \times ASL) - (84.6 \times ASW) = \text{Flesch Reading Ease out of 100}$$

Number of syllables	Number of words	Total number of syllables
1	67	67
2	30	60
3	2	6
4	1	4
Total	100	137

Figure 2.8 The tally of words with different number of syllables.

Tier	Description of vocabulary	Examples from passage
1	Basic familiar words, used frequently in everyday conversation	And, in washing, gently, write
2	High frequency words that are used in different areas of study and life but which may convey multiple meanings. Also known as 'academic vocabulary' because they carry specific meaning in specific educational contexts	Froth, teaspoon, measure, baking powder, repeat, height
3	Low frequency words are low frequency words that have meaning in a specific context	detergent

Figure 2.9 The conceptual demands of different categories of words after Beck et al. (2013).

The higher your score, the easier the text is to read, the text above scores 76.4, so can definitely do with some of the adjustments considered above.

Tiers of vocabulary Analysing the types of words used in a document is an alternative approach to analysing text and one that is less mathematical but, more importantly, takes account of the conceptual demand of the language (Beck et al., 2013). For this reason, it is worthwhile to consider this way of considering text in conjunction, as shown in Figure 2.9 with one of the methods on measuring readability.

Handwriting is quite commonly unpopular with pupils who have SEND. This may be attributable to more general difficulties with literacy, for some pupils it may be associated with fine motor difficulties commonly observed to cause further problems than could be attributed solely to literacy difficulties. These can be reduced by the use of word processing, possibly combined with software that enables them to hear what they have written. There is also a role in the use of digital media as an adjunct to writing, for instance to record speech rather than writing things down, or to have an amanuensis or scribe to write down what is said. Voice-to-text software, such as the 'Dictate' function in recent versions of Word software, can be a huge help in generating a written record, whilst text-to-speech/read aloud software can scaffold the development of reading skills as well as assisting with engagement with the content conveyed by the text. The latter software is now available in pen devices that can record the speech, enabling it to be referred to again later.

Enhanced spelling

One frequent deterrent to literacy, most especially writing, is anxiety about spelling. This is exacerbated by unfamiliar or long words, of the sort that science commonly uses. There are two approaches to spelling that pupils will probably already have encountered in primary school, phonics and whole word recognition. Phonics (not only commonly synthetic systematic phonics but also analytic phonics and embedded phonics) is the approach that uses the sounds associated with single letters and then groups of letters. The approach has had significant policy backing and its advocates claim that it is powerful because it enables pupils to use a systemic approach to understanding the relationship amongst letters, sounds and many (but by no means all) words in the English language (Beck et al., 2013; Sullivan, 2018). However, some pupils find phonics challenging or impossible. For example, some pupils on the autistic spectrum, may process information very differently and so struggle to join individual letter symbols or sounds to form the whole word, are sometimes thought to have difficulties with the synthetic systematic phonics approach. However, evidence on the tendencies of groups of pupils with a shared special needs diagnosis, such as autism, is a far remove from prescribing a standard approach for any one group (Sermier Dessemontet et al., 2019). These pupils may prefer the 'whole word' approach to reading instead but this cannot be assumed. Recognising that very few science teachers will have received training in how to teach literacy, it is still appropriate for the teacher is to find out how an individual prefers to tackle literacy tasks and support them in doing so. Knowing that almost all pupils will have encountered phonics makes it appropriate to ask whether they have used a process of 'sounding out' words previously and how helpful they found it, also whether they prefer a different approach instead.

Two further approaches to spelling also merit consideration, especially for secondary age pupils. The first of these is the use of an aurally coded English (ACE) dictionary. This is available in two forms, one suitable for lower secondary aged pupils and one aged at older pupils and adults (Moseley, 2011, 2012). This helps the user to locate the correct spelling of words without needing to know anything at all about how to spell them in the first place! A standard dictionary quite often requires a certain level of spelling, for instance to spell science correctly, they need to know that there is a silent 'c' in it; similarly, chemistry has an 'h' that a weak speller would not expect to find. To find a word using the ACE dictionary, the user needs to identify three features of the spoken word. This is illustrated here by the process of looking up the word 'chemistry' in Figure 2.10:

1. The letter that they think the word starts with. For example, the hard 'c' sound may lead them to look for a word that begins with a 'k'
2. The first vowel sound: These correspond to the vowel sound in the names of animals that are depicted or, in the adult version, the names of colours
3. The number of syllables in the spoken word, which can be counted by clapping the word out, for example chem-ist-ry is a three clap word.

Step1. Find the page number, using the first letter and first vowel sound of the word, for example 'chemistry'.

Index

			A	B	C	D	E	F	G	H	I	J	K	L	M
	SHORT VOWEL	a	1	5	7	10	11	12	14	16	17	18	18	19	20
	SHORT VOWEL	e	31	32	33	34	36	39	39	40	41	42	42	43	44
	SHORT VOWEL	i	56	57	59	61	65	68	70	71	72	77	78	79	80
	SHORT VOWEL	o	94	95	96	99	99	100	101	102	102	103	103	104	105
	SHORT VOWELS	u oo	116	116	118	120	120	121	122	123	123	124	124	125	126

			A	B	C	D	E	F	G	H	I	J	K	L	M
	LONG VOWEL	ae	137	138	139	140	141	142	143	144	144	145	145	145	146
	LONG VOWEL	ee	153	154	155	156	157	158	159	160	161	162	162	163	164
	LONG VOWEL	ie	176	177	178	178	180	181	182	182	183	184	184	185	186
	LONG VOWEL	oe	195	195	196	197	197	198	199	200	200	201	201	201	202
	LONG VOWELS	ue oo	210	211	212	213	213	214	214	215	215	216	216	216	217

			A	B	C	D	E	F	G	H	I	J	K	L	M
	VOWEL SOUND	ar	225	226	227	228	228	229	229	230	230	230	231	231	232
	VOWEL SOUND	air	236	236	236	237	237	238	238	238	239	—	—	239	239
	VOWEL SOUND	er	242	243	244	245	245	246	246	247	247	248	248	248	249
	VOWEL SOUND	or	256	257	258	259	259	260	261	261	262	262	262	263	263
	VOWEL SOUND	oi	270	270	270	271	271	271	272	272	—	272	—	273	273
	VOWEL SOUND	ou	276	276	277	278	278	279	279	279	—	280	—	280	280

Note that if you are using the version of the ACE dictionary intended for young adults, the index (see below) indicates vowels sounds by the corresponding colour name. In this instance, the short 'e' is denoted by the sound in the word 'red'.

Figure 2.10 Illustration of how to use the ACE dictionary. *(Continued)*

Index

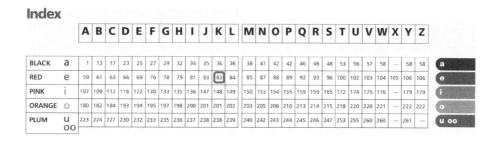

		A	B	C	D	E	F	G	H	I	J	K	L	M	N	O	P	Q	R	S	T	U	V	W	X	Y	Z		
BLACK	a	1	13	17	23	25	27	29	32	34	35	36	36		38	41	42	42	46	46	48	53	56	57	58	—	58	58	a
RED	e	59	61	63	66	69	76	78	79	81	83	83	84		85	87	88	89	92	93	96	100	102	103	104	105	106	106	e
PINK	i	107	109	112	116	122	130	133	135	136	147	148	149		150	153	154	155	159	159	165	172	174	175	176	—	179	179	i
ORANGE	o	180	182	184	193	194	195	197	198	200	201	201	202		203	205	206	210	213	214	215	218	220	220	221	—	222	222	o
PLUM	u oo	223	224	227	230	232	233	235	236	237	238	238	239		240	242	243	244	245	246	247	253	255	260	260	—	261	—	u oo

Step 2. Select the column that has the number of syllables on the page. These are shown as stars, often understood by pupils as the number of claps accompanying the word when they speak it. For chemistry, there are three claps or stars.

C   SHORT VOWEL **e**

*	**	***	***** **
*cell unit	cadet	celebrate	celebrated
Celt	caress es	celery	celebrating
*cent money /	caressed	celestial	celebration
hundred	cassette	cellophane	celebrity -ies
*cents money		cellular	celestial
	*cellar underground	celluloid	centenary -ies
*check ed stop / test	storage room	cellulose	centimetre
chef	cello s	Celsius	centrifugal ly
*cheque order to bank	Celtic	cemetery -ies	centurion
chess	cement	censorship	cerebellum
chest	*censer pan for	centigrade	ceremonial ly
	burning incense	centipede	ceremony -ies
cleanse d	*censor judge of what	centrally	
clef	may not be published	century -ies	chemically
cleft	*census es official count	cerebral	cholesterol
clench es	centaur	cerebrum	
clenched	central ly		collectively
	centre	chemical ly	commemorate
crèche / creche	centring	chemistry	commemoration
crêpe / crepe	*cession giving up		competitive
crept	ownership	cleanliness	competitiveness
cress es		clerical	competitor
crest	checking		complexity -ies

Step 3. If you can't see the word you are looking for, follow one of the suggestions to a different page. Repeat the process of looking in the column that corresponds to the number of stars or claps for the word.

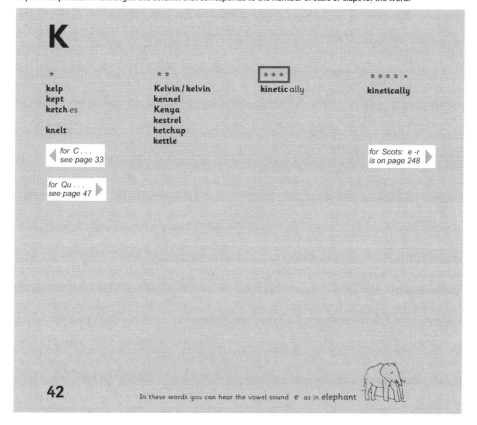

K

*	**	***	***** *
kelp	Kelvin / kelvin	kinetic ally	kinetically
kept	kennel		
ketch es	Kenya		
	kestrel		
knelt	ketchup		
	kettle		

◀ for C . . . see page 33

for Scots: e -r is on page 248 ▶

for Qu . . . see page 47 ▶

42   In these words you can hear the vowel sound **e** as in **e**lephant

Figure 2.10 (Continued)

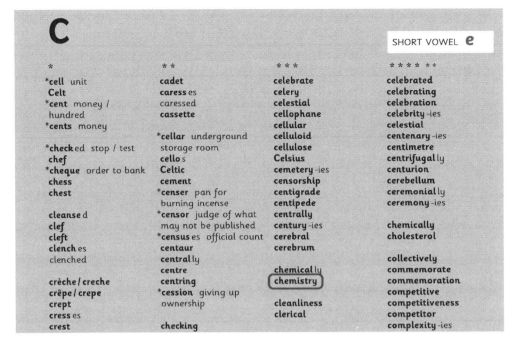

Figure 2.10 (Continued)

Morphographs are very useful in teaching both spelling and meaning in science, and many teachers use this approach instinctively. The morphographic course was written as a sequence of lessons that offers a systematic approach to spelling but, unlike phonics, considers 'word parts' rather than individual letters. It is also different from phonics in that these word parts are not simply a 'unit of sound' or phoneme, but a unit of meaning. These can be discovered by looking the words up in an English dictionary that gives etymology (word origins). This approach works well in science because so many of our technical terms are derived from Latin or Greek roots, which are compounded.

For example, the word *photosynthesis* is made of three morphographs:

$$photo(\text{light}) + syn(\text{with}) + thesis(\text{putting})$$

This example shows how knowing the word parts will enhance both spelling and understanding. Because the same word parts occur repeatedly, explicit rehearsal of them helps to make sense of many words. Knowing what 'photo' signifies helps learners to make sense of words like photograph and photovoltaic too. I found it useful to keep a working document to which staff and pupils can add as they encounter new words, possibly as an on-line document or perhaps as a poster on the wall. An example is shown in Figure 2.11.

Speech is closely associated with literacy, and, in a neuro-typical child, the development of speech precedes literacy by several years. However, the development of speech occurs atypically in around 5% of the population, often due to global or specific LD, such as some children with Autistic Spectrum Condition. There are also psychological reasons for reduced speech, such as shyness or elective mutism. Whatever the reason, promoting speech is an important part

Word part	Meaning	Example of use
Gen-	Make	Generate
Graph	Writing	Photograph
Hydro-	Water	Hydrogen
Ign-	Fire	Igneous
-lysis	Splitting	Hydrolysis
morph	Shape	Morphograph
Pro-	Before	Protein
-scope	See	Microscope

Figure 2.11 Examples of word parts (morphographs) found in scientific vocabulary.

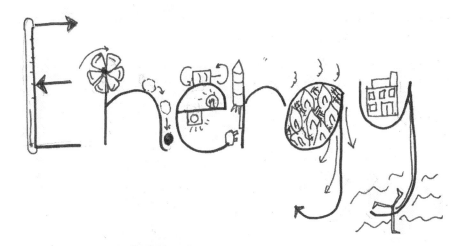

Figure 2.12 An example of a pictogram.

of a teacher's job and this is, arguably, even more true for science teachers than others. Whilst it used to be thought that speech was a manifestation of thought, Lev Vygotsky (1978) suggested that speech shapes thinking and learning. Any teacher who has ever said, 'I didn't fully understand that concept until I tried explaining it!' will recognise his point.

The fact that science conveys concepts that are hard to grasp means that the power of speech to promote understanding is a powerful tool for us. Many student teachers assume that science so commonly uses group work because it enables us to share scarce laboratory resources sound more effectively. This may, in part, be true, but there is also a wealth of evidence that shows that discussing concepts that are challenging helps pupils to grasp them more rapidly and securely (Stahl, 2005). However, pupils with delayed speech, or who choose not to speak, are being deprived of valuable opportunities to develop their understanding. For children who can write, non-verbal interactions can provide an equivalent alternative, for instance posting comments on sticky notes or annotating a group poster. For pupils who can't write, other forms of communication may be needed, such as drawing or asking them to choose an item from a selection or encouraging them to sign their ideas. Although there was a time when non-verbal communication was viewed as a lesser form of communication, modern neuroscience has shown that it can lead to the development of neural pathways in a similar way to those developed by talking about the same subject (Ramsden et al., 2011). In the light of this insight, we can be confident that encouraging conversation, whether spoken or not, is a valuable teaching strategy.

A final strategy that can be used occasionally to enhance communication and to reinforce both the spelling and meaning of words is the construction of pictograms (Clawson et al., 2012). A pictogram combines the letter construction of a word, other information, with image(s) that convey its meaning. Two examples are given in Figure 2.12

Reflective question:

The strategies outlined above all share the expectation that the language we use will be subject to analysis, either by the teacher or the pupils or both. In the light of the time pressures on both groups, can you identify one new strategy for enhancing literacy that you think merits the additional time it would take? Are there any additional barriers to using it, other than time?

Numeracy

Numeracy is an issue that besets learners at all levels of science and commonly undermines learners' confidence (Lenton & Stevens, 1999). For those with LD, it has been found to be a key determinant of attainment in science, meaning that difficulties with numeracy can impede progress with science (Olson et al., 2007; Villanueva et al., 2012). This is a very persistent difficulty, even when the numerical functions required have already been mastered in mathematics lessons, students may fail to see that they can transfer the same skills over to a different subject area. Some schools have a calculations policy to ensure that a common approach is used across the school and so pupils encounter consistency wherever in the curriculum they encounter numeracy. Students commonly lack confidence in their own ability to work successfully with numbers, which creates further anxiety about quantitative content in science (Elbaum & Vaughn, 2003). One key step that scaffolds the development of numeracy skills is to use qualitative descriptors before attempting to quantify the difference. For example, considering quantities in terms of least, more and most, or considering 'strong' and 'weak' acids and alkalis and their everyday uses, before considering pH numbers. Similarly, equations, where applicable, should be presented and used consistently. Although formula triangles are a superficially appealing way to solve equations, they also mask a lack of genuine understanding and only yield the correct answer if no errors are made during the process. Crucially, the lack of understanding denies students the chance to 'plausibility check' their answers (Southall, 2016).

Two strategies that experienced teachers use are to minimise the numeracy demands and ensure that it is clearly linked to the concepts addressed by the lessons. The other key factor to bear in mind is the complexity of the processing that is required to use the data and simultaneously make sense of it. So direct counting is far easier than calculating volume reacted by difference. Avoiding the use of decimal figures wherever possible also helps (Lortie-Forgues et al., 2015). Similarly, notion of direct proportionality (one factor gets bigger and causes a second factor to get bigger) is the most accessible type of proportionality for pupils to understand. For example, in an investigation to compare two indigestion remedies, pupils are asked to count how many drops of acid both of the two cures can neutralise. The greater the amount of acid that is neutralised, the stronger the alkali in the remedy. However, using a burette and asking pupils to calculate the volume of acid that has reacted adds another processing stage to the calculation. Compare these two observations of the same 12-year-old pupil, a week apart.

> In the first week, Brandon did the experiment to compare the different indigestion mixtures and found that 6 drops of acid neutralise the solution of tablet A whilst just 4 drops neutralise the solution of tablet B. He concluded that tablet A was stronger.
>
> The following week, the teacher reads a question in the end-of-unit test aloud, 'If I add 50 ml of water from one beaker to another beakers of 75 ml water, how much water would there be?' Brandon scowls and squirms. The teacher prompts, 'You need to add it'. The classroom support assistant models the finger method of addition to Brandon, If I had four fingers on this hand and no fingers on that one, how many would there be?' After four attempts, Brandon. correctly calculates the total volume of water.

(Field note, March 2020)

One useful tool to develop numerical processing skills for more demanding questions is to use concrete models. In the second instance, it may be helpful to model the problem, initially with beakers with volumes indicated on them. The same process can then be done using 'pencil and paper' models, either using a diagram of apparatus or using the so-called bar method (Morin et al., 2017), in which drawn boxes or strips of paper are used to represent quantities.

Reflective question:

Do you feel that our assumption that science is inherently mathematical is always justified? What compromises might you be making if you focused on qualitative and semi-quantitative descriptions?

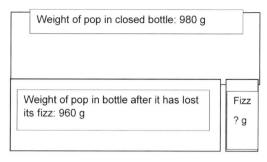

Figure 2.13 An example of the bar model being used to scaffold a calculation.

Ways in which those with learning difficulties may differ from their peers 3: Psycho-social characteristics

It is commonly observed that psycho-social factors can affect the conduct of lessons and this is very marked in a subject where group work is a staple organising principle. The reasons for doing this are partly practical, as it not only enables learners to share experimental resources but is also held to be of benefit to pupils' learning. Learning that is combined with social inter-action is likely to be more deeply understood and better remembered (Scruggs & Mastropieri, 2007; Stroupe et al., 2019). These benefits are strongest when pupils working collaboratively in a mixed group, in terms of attainment (McGinnis, 2013). However, effective group work does not happen without planning of the grouping arrangements and the nature of the tasks set and the difficulties in doing this are likely to be greater for learners with LD. One research paper specifi-cally documents how pupils with LD describe themselves as being afraid of taking on roles that are unfamiliar to them or appear to be of a greater level of difficulty than they believe they can respond to (Park et al., 2019).

In addition to the difficulties in learning that have been described above, there may also be communication difficulties to factor into the management of group work. Problems with recep-tive language (understanding) and expressive language (speaking) are common barriers and can make collaborative work more difficult than teachers expect (Boyle et al., 2020). It may be useful to provide tasks that can elicit discussion but where anyone with communication difficulties can make a meaningful contribution, for example matching pairs or rank ordering things. Note that these activities are asking the pupils to create visual organisers, whose usefulness has been discussed previously.

Despite its documented benefits, pupils with LD may struggle more than their peers to work collaboratively, either because they struggle to communicate clearly enough to negotiate the necessary inter-personal relationships, or because they have low self-esteem that inhibits their willingness to volunteer ideas within the group. Difficulties in forging inter-personal relationships seem to be commonly exacerbated by the low esteem that these pupils exhibit. This may arise from a history of low attainment and is liable to depress performance still further (Elbaum & Vaughn, 2003). The issue of low self-esteem certainly impedes the development of a suitable environment for learning when it results in defensive or even aggressive responses.

Problems with socialisation and communication may be even more pronounced in individual with autistic spectrum condition, who by definition are liable to have greater difficulties in social-ising and communicating. The is seems to be a generally under-recognised factor in science lessons, although learners with LD have been noted as having difficulties with social interactions and this has been considered a barrier to attainment by previous authors (Gresham et al., 2004; Steele, 2004). Indeed, the need for supporting those with LD to form and maintain friendships was explicitly considered in a 2001 white paper on their quality of life (Department of Health, 2001). Interestingly, this difficulty is not restricted to pupils with autistic traits, as some might think, and suggests that many of these pupils may experience delays in social as well as intellectual devel-opment. Because LD students face additional difficulties in forming and maintaining friendships (Meadan & Monda-Amaya, 2008), it is helpful to support the formation of positive relationships between individuals. This requires advance planning, for example of groups, with group structures clearly communicated in advance of the activity to avoid stresses caused by unpredictability.

There is also a need to assign roles in such a way that pupils are encouraged to work construc-tively with each other. One study indicated that pupils tended to adopt a distinctive role including group manager, task guidance provider and task performer and helped each other to overcome individual difficulties (Belland et al., 2009). My own observations indicate that this structure may well not emerge spontaneously and teacher direction is commonly needed. Mechanisms to foster this include the assigning of roles, for example 'safety monitor', 'observer', 'engineer' (to set up apparatus) and 'scribe'. Other useful devices are to arrange for pupils to be engaged in providing formative assessment to their peers, for example using a set of assessment criteria or asking them to provide EBI feedback ('even better if …'). These clear frameworks will be assisted by teacher monitoring and feedback whilst group work is being carried out.

For pupils who find group work especially difficult, whether because they have communication difficulties, are autistic or simply shy, additional adjustments may be needed, but these need not detract from the learning benefits of group work to the rest of the class. With all skills that are challenging, a gradualised approach is advisable so that pupils can experience a manageable level of challenge to help them to develop their ability to interact and collaboration. It may help them to work with one nominated partner to begin with, which could be a trusted support assistant or a friend in the group. Once this is done without difficulty, a third member, perhaps of the pupil's choosing, can join the group. Finally, the support assistant may be able to superintend the work without actively participating. This progress may take weeks or months but enables you to contribute to a pupil's wider development, as well as learning science. Sitting side-by-side reduces the expectation of eye contact which can be challenging for individual with ASC (Autistic Spectrum Condition). Asking pupils to work together to do tasks in which physical representations are constructed in such a way that facilitates involvement and response without a high level of social interaction may help. Suitable examples include have a small group of pupils matching, grouping or rank ordering cards with words or images on them.

Reflective question:

Do you recognise the potential difficulties in psycho-social aspects of learning? Are these difficulties recognised more widely, for instance in schemes of work, formal assessments? If so, what practical adjustments are made? If not, why do you think this is this generally overlooked?

Ways in which those with learning difficulties may differ from their peers 4: Experimental and investigative skills

As the previous section on the importance of concrete learning has set out, physical and sensory engagement with what is being learnt is very important for all learners but most important those who find learning difficult. There is a good body of evidence to show that hands-on experiences are not just popular (though they are) but can also enhance attainment (Scruggs & Mastropieri, 2007; Villanueva et al., 2012). Much of the policy discussion about pupil behaviour has tended to view behaviour as something distinct from learning, possibly a precursor to successful learning. Especially with neuro-diverse learners, it is far more helpful to view behaviour as communication, often about their learning. This means that pupils who understand what they are doing and enjoy what they are doing are far less likely to present challenging behaviour (Villanueva et al., 2012). I have observed myself that pupils who come to science outreach events with a reputation for very challenging behaviour conduct themselves in an exemplary manner when given work to do that they find interesting and challenging but achievable.

However, the expectation that science teachers hold that pupils will be able to make sense of their physical experiences and simultaneously making full scientific sense of their experiences can be problematic. This is likely to cause cognitive overload if it isn't managed carefully. This can be managed by doing a 'dry run' followed by a second attempt with an explicit focus on making scientific meaning. Unscheduled rehearsals can sometimes happen simply because the first attempt wasn't carried out correctly, or because pupils enjoy it so much that they ask to repeat it. When preparing an inclusive and accessible event, I always prepare twice as much kit as the number of pupils indicates should be needed for exactly this reason. Rehearsal of what is being learnt, whether intentional or purposive, is known to aid learning by pupils with LD (Librea-Carden et al., 2021). This could be done by demonstrating the experiment first then, having orientated the pupils as to what will happen, getting them to do the second run through themselves. Similarly, the use of virtual experiments can offer a chance to rehearse the steps and concepts before pupils carry out the experiment themselves (Therrien et al., 2017). Doing a demonstration is one widely used way of modelling how an experiment should be carried out and has been shown to be effective for learners with LD (Librea-Carden et al., 2021).

Another variation of this is the 'slow' or staged practical (Boxer, 2020). During this, the teacher shows one step of the practical at a time and then asks the class to carry out that step. Once everyone has completed that step, the teacher can demonstrate the next step before pupils carry it out themselves and so on. This approach facilitates ready monitoring of any pupil who has not followed the instructions and, for this reason, some teachers refer to it as a 'lock step' technique. Moving away from the standard model of class practicals done by pairs of pupils on a one-off basis will, inevitably have implications for technicians and their work so it is important that they are aware of the different approach you are adopting and the rationale. Commonly, once they understand the learning benefits of the alteration, they will be able to bring valuable expertise and insights to bear upon your changes.

There is quite often trepidation on the part of teachers around the risks associated with doing practical work in science. This is a great shame because this is many pupils' favourite aspect of the subject. Classroom observations suggest that the truth is the opposite of the common fears, in that pupils' difficulties with abstract concepts may lead them to struggle to assess risk inaccurately and so be unnecessarily cautious. We need to be very careful not to deprive pupils unjustifiably of the chance for hands-on learning, as it offers an opportunity to strengthen understanding (Sola Özgüç & Cavkaytar, 2015; Villanueva et al., 2012). One common cause of anxiety on the part of teachers is the perception that pupils' unpredictable behaviour may raise the risk of laboratory work to unacceptable levels (DfEE, 2004). It is true that many pupils exhibiting challenging behaviour also have learning difficulties, and one study found that as many as 50% of pupils exhibiting unpredictable behaviour (Department for Education, 2012) also had learning difficulties. Likewise, pupils with communication difficulties may appear defiant when they don't understand what to do. However, after 20 years of running inclusive and accessible science events, I have never encountered challenging behaviour when pupils were involved in experiments that they viewed as purposeful and possible. Likewise, Scruggs and Mastropieri (2007) note that teachers experience fewer problems than they anticipate when pupils are actively engaged in science activities, including experiments. This anecdotal evidence is in line with previous findings, such as that from a study, considering the rate of referrals for misbehaviour from a lab-based class, noted zero referrals which were far less than had been anticipated (Cawley et al., 2002).

Another important feature of experimental work is that it gives pupils a chance to explore by trial and error. Indeed, this concrete learning opportunity may help to explain why investigations increase pupils' engagement, recall, understanding and confidence in science (Mulvey et al., 2016). This is only possible when the risk assessment takes account of both the activities and reagents, plus the pupils doing the experiment. However, the use of small quantities or very dilute solutions of reagents, along with the choice of low hazard reagents, makes many experiments achievable in a safe manner. I have not observed instances of LD pupils knowingly taking risks, although they may forget safety warnings or become distracted and so deviate from safe practices. Quite often the reverse happens and pupils, finding it hard to assess the level of risk (Park et al., 2019), may be overly cautious about the risk of the experiment.

As with any other pupil (Abrahams et al., 2013), it is important that pupils are clear about what the learning intentions associated with experimental work are and that it degenerates into 'messy play'. Although this is still superficially attractive for students and may keep them happily occupied, it does not promote their learning and deprives them of the satisfaction of making progress. For this reason, it is not the way that I would choose to spend lesson time.

Enquiry-based learning & Investigation

Enquiry (or inquiry)-based learning is an approach that enables learners to

> Ask relevant questions, pose and define problems, plan what to do and how to research, predict outcomes and anticipate consequences, to test conclusions and improve ideas.
> (DFEE/QCA, 1999, pp. 23–24)

Enquiry-based learning places the learner at the centre of the process and promotes active discovery as the means of learning, as well as the motivation for learning. Teachers tasked with teaching a large body of content for assessment decry the approach, describing it as slow and prone to being hijacked by pupils who discover things that weren't intended by the teacher.

However, with some careful facilitation by the teacher, this isn't necessarily the case, and it does give learners a genuine sense of ownership of their learning, provided they are not investigating something that they find irrelevant, or a 'so what?' question (Johnstone, 1991). It has also been found to enhance learning by those with LD, possibly by ensuring that they have time to process experiences or data in their short-term memory, thereby increasing its retention by the long-term memory (Villanueva et al., 2012).

Experimental investigation is the most common form of enquiry-based learning used in science, although secondary data can be used too. Investigation is seen as an important way of giving pupils with SEND a feeling for the culture and processes of science and to experience at first-hand how scientific knowledge is generated (Villanueva et al., 2012). Practical investigation engenders meta-cognition, by encouraging discussion about ways of understanding the phenomenon under investigation. Pupils also develop recall and understanding of the vocabulary used to describe the processes of science when using the terms in a specific context. However, they may struggle to carry out a structured investigation, because the standard approach requires them to correctly identify variables in advance, and this may be difficult ahead of them having concrete experience of the phenomenon. An approach that is quite often observed is that a theoretical understanding is constructed retrospectively. The following observation below illustrates this alternative process,

> Today, as part of the 'Explosions' topic, the class made 'fizzy rockets', using effervescent Vitamin C tablets in the pots for blood sugar testing strips. I videoed them trying to get their pot to fly the furthest. I was interested to see that, even though they are the highest attaining group of students, they didn't plan their rockets, but set them off and then afterwards analysed the results to reach their conclusion. They discovered, by trial and error that there is a maximum number of tablets, after which the rocket won't fly any further.
>
> (Essex, 2020, p. 553)

As this example illustrates, due to the fact that investigations commonly consider multi-factorial phenomena, pupils with LD may find it hard to identify explicitly the individual variables that need to be controlled when conducting an investigation. Instead, they may simply want to make lots of changes at once, then see what happens! If this happens, it may be expedient simply to view these initial 'suck it and see' attempts as a pre-practical, or pilot, study and to employ a retrospective analysis of the results to inform which factor(s) to investigate in the next phase. Unfortunately, there is a deeply embedded commitment to deductive science, in which theory drives the design of experiments, on the part of curriculum writers, exam boards and textbook writers. This disregard for inductive approaches to science, in which observations shape knowledge, as in the example above, often precludes serious regard or assessment credit being given to other approaches to knowledge creation. In one instance that I recall, described below, two pupils came up with novel observations and were able, with help, to explain their findings but were still denied good marks for their assessed investigation because the mark bearing variables were temperature, concentration and surface area of reactant.

When I was a teacher, I had a group of low attaining pupils, most of whom had some diagnosed disability or special need. As part of their science course, they were required to plan and execute a scientific investigation for assessment purposes. I asked them to investigate the factors that affected the rate of reaction between magnesium metal and dilute acid. Having taught them the theory about what changes rates of chemical reaction, I expected them (with some support) to identify a factor they could investigate. Other pupils in the class opted to explore the effect of the temperature of the acid upon the rate of reaction, or the dilution of the acid. However, I was utterly taken aback when I asked two pupils what they were investigating and they said they were looking at the effect of the size of the beaker. I looked at their results and saw that they had tried dissolving the same amount of magnesium each time, in the same concentration of acid and always at room temperature. Their approach was in keeping with the expected approach to investigation, which is to control all the variables apart from the one that is under investigation. They then repeated the experiments in front of me and I observed what they had already noticed. When the experiment was run in a 150-ml beaker, then a 250-ml beaker and, finally a 400-ml beaker, the metal reacted more quickly each time. I was genuinely puzzled. We sat together and talked about what could be happening and their questions made me think that the diameter of the beaker might be affecting the way in which the product of the reaction was dispersed. Had they been studying science at pre-university level, we would have called it entropy. As it was, they called it 'stuff dissolving and moving away faster, so more new stuff could form'. I was really impressed and, even now, call this finding 'Emily's law' in their honour.

Another useful way of keeping pupils focused on altering just one thing a time is to assign different factors to different working groups and then to facilitate a plenary at which results can be shared and discussed. Pupils are liable to need very explicit support to understand and articulate the key stages in developing an evidence-supported answer to a research question but an approach to developing these skills, known as evidence-based enquiry, was found to be promising. In combination with scaffolding as pupils undertook the investigation, the shift in learning was seen to be large (Villanueva et al., 2012). A greater depth of understanding can be developed by promoting enquiry-based learning, commonly through experimental investigation. However, the time taken to carry this out may necessitate a corresponding reduction in the breadth of material covered (Harlen, 2010).

Reflective question:

What do you find are the most common difficulties with experimental work when you teach? Are these difficulties predominantly explained by the cognitive and psycho-social difficulties that were described previously or by the requirements of the experiments themselves?

Meeting different needs in shared learning opportunities

Differentiation, by which we mean providing different learning experiences to pupils but with a shared learning intention, is a mainstay of inclusion. It is the mechanism by which very different learners can be enabled to work alongside each other (Sola Özgüç & Cavkaytar, 2015). The importance of differentiating teaching and assessment is especially important in a subject like science that makes such steep demands of its learners. McGinnis (2013) notes the great value to pupils of introducing alternative mechanisms to secure equivalent learning in science. However, this is notoriously difficult for teachers to put into practice and is often beset by the fact that its implementation can convey low expectations to learners who have a history of low attainment. However, at its best, it offers an optimal learning experience for very diverse learners and is a key strategy through which inclusion can be achieved and through which attainment, including on tests, enhanced (Mastropieri et al., 2015; Westwood, 2001).

Three broad categories of differentiation are recognised; the following strategies for differentiation are considered according to these categories:

By outcome

Many learners who are considered to have special needs will have been noted previously to have performed less well than their peers, for the reasons that have been outlined in this section. As explored earlier in this section, this is problematic when the assessment requires a high level of recall or rests upon understanding abstract ideas. Criterion-referenced assessment may facilitate a better outcome, especially when these have been used formatively prior to being used for summative assessment purposes. Knowing that pupils with LD are especially sensitive to being deterred by failure (Park et al., 2019; Villanueva et al., 2012), it is important that assessments enable pupils to experience some level of success and this may require the assessment to be adjusted where possible.

By task

Be clear that this does not, however, mean that previously low attaining pupils should be given the least demanding and least interesting tasks, either to support learning or as assessment tools. Quite rightly, it is no longer considered acceptable to differentiate by having three learning intentions labelled 'must', 'should' and 'could', which is a license to avoid work for some pupils and leaves other feeling overwhelmed before they start the lesson. What is appropriate, however, is to have a range of equivalent tasks and assessment outputs that should be offered and pupil choice of task honoured, as the earlier discussion of multi-modal learning indicates (Boyle et al., 2020). This could be, for example, choosing which factor to investigate, or how to demonstrate learning criteria, for example explain how the flow of electric current can be altered, either in a presentation, a freeze frame animation, or a blog to help people revising. This is especially effective if the learning to be shown is given to pupils at the outset, so that they can formatively self-assess their work as it progresses.

Likewise, differentiation within an assessment task benefits from allowing choice. One example I have seen is that three different assessment tasks are offered and, as the challenge of the task completed successfully rises, so does the level of reward (such as merit points). A different example of how a differentiated task could yield unexpectedly positive outcomes was provided at the end of a science day on sustainability and how technology and human behaviour could influence this.

> I asked pupils to put something into a time capsule for pupils in 100 years' time. Their contribution was to show what their ideas about sustainability. Some pupils opted to write or draw postcards, other donated painted rocks. However, one dropped an empty chocolate wrapper into the tin. When I queried why he had done that he answered thoughtfully, 'I don't think anyone will be allowed to wrap food in plastic in 100 years and I think that they will be very shocked that we were.'
>
> (Field note, August 2021)

I thought his unprompted contribution demonstrated a strong grasp of how technologies and attitudes would change behaviours to promote sustainability but can't imagine how I could have ascertained this understanding with a standard assessment tool.

By support

Differentiated support link is a key way to enable pupils to achieve a common learning outcome (Sola Özgüç & Cavkaytar, 2015). Some teachers would say that assessing learning by measuring the amount of support that has been needed is a useful guide to learning. Strategic support also enables staff to ascertain the likely next developmental targets for a learner, based on Vygotsky's (1978, p. 86) notion of the Zone of Proximal Development. This phrase refers to what someone can almost but not quite do independently but is able to do with some support. Vygotsky considered that this showed what they would go on to be able to do independently. The support may take the form of structured questioning or formative feedback, giving prompts to aid recall or modelling what is wanted. It may also take the form of enabling further attempts at a task, ideally with further formative assessment, to ensure that it is fully learnt (Librea-Carden et al., 2021). This approach is the basis of 'mastery learning' which has become popular.

Mastery learning involves the use of formative assessment after a specified piece of content has been taught. Based on the outcome of the formative assessment, additional support is targeted at the identified areas of need for development needed for the pupil to 'master' the content. Once they have demonstrated mastery (as indicated by formative assessment) and this is verified by successful completion of summative assessment, the pupil is then ready to move on to the next section of content. Although this sounds time-consuming, it has been found to give a much more secure and enduring knowledge of the material taught. Another important aspect of mastery learning is that it takes the focus away from the inherent capacity of the pupil or some characteristic such as having a 'growth mindset'. Rather than seeking to account for any failure to learn in terms of pupil deficit, instead it focuses on the approach to teaching being deployed. This is a shift that can only be supportive for pupils whose label alone may depress expectations (Levine, 1985).

Group work may be another way of affording support through facilitating peer-to-peer support, especially when grappling with difficult concepts (Shayer & Adey, 2002). Contrary to common misconceptions, group work does not simply operate in a 'trickle down' fashion, whereby more highly achieving pupils re-teach pupils who are not attaining at the same level. The different insights and approaches that each learner brings can open up new avenues of enquiry to all parties (Librea-Carden et al., 2021). (This 'cross-fertilisation' of ideas can be very powerful, and I have seen academics have their ideas about teaching their subject transformed by interaction with neuro-diverse learners.)

One word of caution, however, about the form the support takes. Whilst support can be a powerful aid to learning, and 1:1 support especially so(Sola Özgüç & Cavkaytar, 2015), it is vital that it does not take the form of 'doing it for' pupils who are struggling. Blatchford et al. (2009) demonstrated that support inappropriately given suppresses attainment. Unfortunately, support workers often end up doing work, such as note taking for the pupil, to bridge the gap between teacher expectation and pupil capacity. What I would suggest is that tasks that result in this kind of support should be re-thought so that this sort of 'cover up' isn't needed. For example, if note taking is a problem for a pupil, could they have notes provided which they annotate, highlight or otherwise interact with?

Reflective question:

Differentiation is often seen to be a key way to reconcile diverse learning capacities in a classroom. How effectively can it do this, in your experience?

Unified responses to diverse needs

As shown in the preceding account, there are many barriers inherent to the curriculum and assessment tools. In response to these, there is a raft of strategies that school staff can deploy to counter these. Lest the reader feels that they are being asked to come up with a large number of individualised interventions, it may reassure them to see that, underpinning the myriad of practical steps at their disposal, there are some common strategies that will benefit all learners. Putting strategies in place that will benefit all learners, regardless of the fact that their primary target is SEND learners, is known as 'Universal Design for Learning' (UDL) (McGinnis, 2013). This is intended to improve educational equity, which is a way of describing the way in which opportunities are made equally available to all pupils. In the context of science lessons, it could also be viewed as a way of ensuring that all pupils have the chance to develop their science capita (Archer et al., 2012). It encompasses two key values, fairness and inclusion. Fairness is the principle that ensures that people are not denied academic success because of their characteristics, whilst inclusion is the notion that the same (or equivalent) standard of educational opportunity is available to all pupils. UDL is an approach that addresses both these requirements and, importantly, aims to make no prior distinction based on assumed needs associated with any individual given characteristic. The requirements of educational UDL are summarised below and illustrated further in Section 3.

Deconstruct the curriculum: Analyse the demands of the content, identifying those parts that are difficult because they deal with intangible phenomena, such as sub-microscopic particles, forces and energy. Look also at whether it requires learners to apply general patterns to predict what will happen in a specific situation (deductive reasoning). Finally, look at the different relationships between variables that the topic requires pupils to understand. Whilst direct proportionality (one thing gets bigger as another thing gets bigger) is an easier relationship to understand, the most challenging types of relationship are inverse proportionality (one thing gets bigger as another thing gets smaller) and multi-factorial variables (several factors contribute to an outcome).

Plan strategic omissions from the standard curriculum for different learners: Use your analysis of the demands of the curriculum and their centrality to assessment success to make strategic adjustments (Canning et al., 1997). Creating a differentiated curriculum, with pupils working on the same topic but in different ways, is essential if we are to stop a common curriculum spelling failure for some (McGinnis, 2013).

Set high expectations: Set challenging learning goals relative to attainment is advocated (Villanueva et al., 2012) and conveys high expectations which raise achievement (Rosenthal & Jacobson, 1968b). This does not necessarily require the use of challenging content, in terms of abstract thinking and complex mathematical approaches, but can focus on the elicitation of higher order thinking skills in Bloom's taxonomy. It is important that support commensurate with the challenge is available, including frequent monitoring and feedback which will provide reassurance to pupils who lack self-confidence in their ability to meet challenging expectations.

Plan for a gradualised development of demand: Construct your lesson sequence to ensure that the most demanding elements that you have identified are preceded by the less demanding elements. Plan for making explicit links between the different concepts, for example in the introduction to the new concepts and by using visual representations of how the concepts are related.

Build in graded support: As the conceptual demands of the topic increase, additional prompts are likely to be required by some pupils. Having identified the more challenging concepts, it pays to plan how to offer differentiated support for the potentially difficult aspects. Involve support staff in this stage, so that they are clear what adjustments you are proposing to implement and have the opportunity to share their thoughts on making the activities accessible.

Make it personalised: Get to know the pupils as individuals so that you can tailor challenge and support to suit their academic profile, and personal preferences. Knowing their interests will help you to make their science learning meaningful to them. It will also help you to know what rewards will be valued most highly by them. Knowing the pupils will enable teachers to provide the flexible and responsive pedagogic strategies that are at the heart of genuinely inclusive teaching (Villanueva et al., 2012).

Ensure plenty of experiential learning: Concrete or 'hands-on' learning, whether it is doing experiments or through physically engaging with the objects, enhances engagement and under-standing, as well as assisting with recall.

Create opportunities for repetition of key ideas and terms: Whilst this is not a call to return to 'rote learning', the value of re-visiting key ideas and key vocabulary throughout a lesson sequence is huge and of demonstrated benefit (Apanasionok et al., 2020). Although pressures to cover content may make teachers reluctant to re-visit material that has already been covered, failure to do so can mean that none of the material taught can be recalled or understood. Teaching mnemonics is an opportunity to repeat key content, whilst asking pupils to create and share their own mnemonics also requires active thinking about the subject matter and is even more effective. Similarly, the use of framework and similar visual organisers can support recall and help learners to generalise what they remember (Sola Özgüç & Cavkaytar, 2015).

Enhance active and explicit thinking: Deliberately encouraging the active processing of information enhances understanding of material, as does talking about one's own thinking which promotes meta-cognition. Asking pupils to use their prior learning to tackle a new problem can be used to introduce a topic or to consolidate learning or as a plenary activity at the end of a topic. It is important that pupils are not only asked to undertake activities that develop their understanding but are also encouraged to explain their ideas as they work through them. For instance, pupils might be sorting items into categories and they should also be asked to explain the basis of this classification.

Allow ample time for reflection: The most frequent piece of advice that experienced teach-ers of SEND learners offer, and the one they often say they wish they had known when they started, is to allow sufficient time for reflection and response. Pupils with limited or delayed processing capacity may need slightly longer to summon up their responses (McGinnis, 2013) but may have much of value to share if we afford them the additional time they need to retrieve it. Other pupils, if they are able to recall answers more quickly, can be asked to use to reflect on how they remember the answer.

Plan for frequent assessment and feedback: There are well-documented benefits of form-ative assessment, or assessment for learning (Hattie, 2012; Villanueva et al., 2012). In addition, pupils with SEND often know and understand far more than they can communicate and so practicing recall and application of learning is vital for their success. Frequent formative assess-ment not only helps pupils to learn (McGinnis, 2013; Therrien et al., 2017) but also helps staff to monitor learning, helps pupils to be clear about how well they have learnt thus far (something that they may not often be good to assessing accurately) and can give pupils agency in deter-mining their future learning targets. Formative assessments also provide valuable opportunities for active learning and meta-cognition.

Recognise diverse achievements in your feedback: Reward achievement other than aca-demic success. Without succumbing to stereotypes (such as the expectation that girls are tidy, or that people with Down's syndrome are always friendly) look for what attributes each pupil brings to the science classroom, whether it is personal characteristics, such as resilience, or skills, such as observing carefully, or asking challenging questions. These can often be benefi-cially linked to scientific processes to highlight their importance in the context of learning sci-ence (Villanueva et al., 2012).

Emphasise scientific processes: Although many formal assessments focus on recall of content, this is often difficult for pupils with SEND. Evaluation of process-based science, as opposed to content-based science, with SEND learners indicates that this approach enhances attainment. Process-based science still develops knowledge of content, but taking the pressure to remember large amounts of content reduces the pressure felt by pupils. Another opportunity that focusing on process opens up is that of 'embedded instruction' (Villanueva et al., 2012) or context-driven science. For example, a discussion about careers choices and possible jobs out-side the science classroom could incorporate a consideration of the sort of scientific skills that different jobs require, as well as simply what they would need to know.

Conclusion

This section has set out the multiple difficulties which face pupils with LD when they come to science lessons. Many of these are deeply entrenched in the culture and practice of science education and, as a result, it requires pro-active analysis of standard approaches to teaching and learning to anticipate the many obstacles that may deter pupils with LD from engaging and succeeding. Despite the major task that this may appear, it is important to be clear that making some adjustments, prioritising those that your knowledge of the pupils would suggest are most needed, is far better than simply ignoring their adjustment needs. Apart from any practical benefits these adjustments afford, making them signals your intention actively to include them and respond to their needs. Approaches that can mitigate these difficulties have been suggested and you will doubtless find discover more. The intention throughout is to reduce those aspects of standard lessons that prevent pupils with LD achieving their full potential for learning science, without singling them out as 'deficient' (sic) or meriting only a 'watered down' version of a standard curriculum.

References

Abrahams, I., Reiss, M. J., & Sharpe, R. M. (2013). The assessment of practical work in school science. *Studies in Science Education, 49*(2). https://doi.org/10.1080/03057267.2013.858496

Apanasionok, M. M., Neil, J., Watkins, R. C., Grindle, C. F., & Hastings, R. P. (2020). Teaching science to students with developmental disabilities using the early science curriculum. *Support for Learning, 35*(4). https://doi.org/10.1111/1467-9604.12329

Archer, A. L., & Hughes, C. A. (2011). *Explicit instruction: Effective and efficient teaching* (1st ed.). Guilford Press.

Archer, L., DeWitt, J., Osborne, J., Dillon, J., Willis, B., & Wong, B. (2012). Science aspirations, capital, and family habitus: How families shape children's engagement and identification with science. *American Educational Research Journal, 49*(5), 881–908. https://doi.org/10.3102/0002831211433290

Aydeniz, M., & Kotowski, E. L. (2012). What do middle and high school students know about the particulate nature of matter after instruction? Implications for practice. *School Science and Mathematics, 112*(2), 59–65. https://doi.org/10.1111/j.1949-8594.2011.00120.x

Bächtold, M. (2013). What do students "construct" according to constructivism in science education?. *Research in Science Education, 43*, 2477–2496. https://doi.org/10.1007/s11165-013-9369-7

Bakken, J. P., Mastropieri, M. A., & Scruggs, T. E. (1997). Reading comprehension of expository science material and students with learning disabilities: A comparison of strategies. *Journal of Special Education, 31*(3). https://doi.org/10.1177/002246699703100302

Beck, I. L., McKeown, M. G., & Kucan, L. (2013). *Bringing words to life: Robust vocabulary instruction* (2nd ed.). Guilford Press.

Belland, B. R., Glazewski, K. D., & Ertmer, P. A. (2009). Inclusion and problem-based learning: Roles of students in a mixed-ability group. *RMLE Online: Research in Middle Level Education, 32*(9), 1–19.

Biggs, J. B., & Collis, K. F. (1982). The psychological structure of creative writing. *Australian Journal of Education, 26*(1). https://doi.org/10.1177/000494418202600104

Blatchford, P., Bassett, P., Brown, P., & Webster, R. (2009). The effect of support staff on pupil engagement and individual attention. *British Educational Research Journal, 35*(5). https://doi.org/10.1080/01411920902878917

Bostian, L. R. (1983). How active, passive and nominal styles affect readability of science Reading. *Journalism and Mass Communication Quarterly, 60*(4). https://doi.org/10.1177/107769908306000408

Boxer, A. (2020). Practicals: Why you should take them slow. *Education in Chemistry*. https://edu.rsc.org/ideas/practicals-why-you-should-take-them-slow/4012186.article

Boyle, S., Rizzo, K. L., & Taylor, J. C. (2020). Reducing language barriers in science for students with special educational needs. *Asia-Pacific Science Education, 6*(2). https://doi.org/10.1163/23641177-bja10006

Breland, K., & Breland, M. K. (1944). Legibility of newspaper headlines printed in capitals and in lower case. *Journal of Applied Psychology, 28*(2). https://doi.org/10.1037/h0053815

Brigham, F. J., Scruggs, T. E., & Mastropieri, M. A. (2011). Science education and students with learning disabilities. *Learning Disabilities Research and Practice, 26*(4). https://doi.org/10.1111/j.1540-5826.2011.00343.x

Bronfenbrenner, U. (1979). *The ecology of human development: Experiments by nature and design*. Harvard University Press.

Bruner, J. S. (1960). *The process of education*. Harvard University Press.

Bybee, R. W. (1997). The Sputnik era: Why is this educational reform different from all other reforms? *Reflecting on Sputnik: Linking the Past, Present, and Future of Education Reform, October*.

Canning, C., Wilson, L., & Craig L. (1997). A model for teaching science to students with special needs. *Australian Science Teachers' Journal, 43*(4), 25–31.

Cawley, J., Hayden, S., Cade, E., & Baker-Kroczynski, S. (2002). Including students with disabilities into the general education science classroom. *Exceptional Children, 68*(4), 423–435. https://doi.org/10.1177/001440290206800401

Clawson, T. H., Leafman, J., Nehrenz, G. M., & Kimmer, S. (2012). Using pictograms for communication. *Military Medicine, 177*(3), 291.

Courtade, G. R., Spooner, F., & Browder, D. M. (2007). Review of studies with students with significant cognitive disabilities which link to science standards. Research and Practice for Persons with Severe Disabilities, 32(1). https://doi.org/10.2511/rpsd.32.1.43

DeWitt, S. (2007). The effects of note taking and mental rehearsal on memory. *Journal of Undergraduate Psychological Research, 2*, 46–49.

Department for Education. (2012). *Pupil behaviour in schools in England: Research Report DFE-RR218*. publishing.service.gov.uk

Department of Health. (2001). *Valuing People: A New Strategy for Learning Disability for the 21st Century*. publishing.service.gov.uk

Dexter, D. D., & Hughes, C. A. (2011). Graphic organizers and students with learning disabilities: A meta-analysis. Learning Disability Quarterly, 34(1). https://doi.org/10.1177/073194871103400104

DfEE (2004). Science accommodation in secondary schools, Building Bulletin 80. Department for Education and Skills. Retrieved July 2020 from http://science.cleapss.org.uk/Resource/Building-Bulletin-80.pdf

DFEE/QCA (1999). *The national curriculum: Handbook for secondary teachers*. HMSO.

Doherty-Sneddon, G., Riby, D. M., & Whittle, L. (2012). Gaze aversion as a cognitive load management strategy in autism spectrum disorder and Williams syndrome. *Journal of Child Psychology and Psychiatry and Allied Disciplines, 53*(4). https://doi.org/10.1111/j.1469-7610.2011.02481.x

Dougherty, J. M., & Moran, J. D. (1983). The relationship of Piagetian stages to mental retardation. *Education and Training of the Mentally Retarded, 18*(4).

Dunne, M., Humphreys, S., Sebba, J., & Dyson, A. (2007). Effective teaching and learning for pupils in low attaining groups (Research Report DCSF-RR011). *DCSF Publications*.

Elbaum, B., & Vaughn, S. (2003). For which students with learning disabilities are self-concept interventions effective? *Journal of Learning Disabilities, 36*(2). https://doi.org/10.1177/002221940303600203

Epistemic Insight website. Epistemic Insight | Bridging the boundaries between curriculum compartments

Essex, J. (2018). Why 'science for all' is only an aspiration: Staff views of science for learners with special educational needs and disabilities. *Support for Learning, 33*(1), 52–72.

Essex, J. (2020). Towards truly inclusive science education: A case study of successful curriculum innovation in a special school. *Support for Learning, 35*(4), 542–558.

Essex, J., Alexiadou, N., & Zwozdiak-Myers, P. (2019). Understanding inclusion in teacher education – A view from student teachers in England. International Journal for Inclusive Education, 25(12), 1425–1442.

European Agency for Development in Special Needs Education. (2012). *Teacher Education for Inclusion (TE41)*. https://www.unicef.org/albania/reports/teacher-education-inclusion-te41

Flesch, R. (1948). A new readability yardstick. *Journal of Applied Psychology, 32*(3). https://doi.org/10.1037/h0057532

Fry, E. (1968). A readability formula that saves time. *BMC Public Health, 5*(1) 849–870.

Gerstner, S., & Bogner, F. X. (2010). Cognitive achievement and motivation in hands-on and teacher-centred science classes: Does an additional hands-on consolidation phase (concept mapping) optimise cognitive learning at work stations? International Journal of Science Education, 32(7). https://doi.org/10.1080/09500690902803604

Gresham, F. M., McIntyre, L. L., Olson-Tinker, H., Dolstra, L., McLaughlin, V., & Van, M. (2004). Relevance of functional behavioral assessment research for school-based interventions and positive behavioral support. *Research in Developmental Disabilities, 25*(1), 19–37. https://doi.org/10.1016/J.RIDD.2003.04.003.

Grosslight, L., Unger, C., Jay, E., & Smith, C. L. (1991). Understanding models and their use in science: Conceptions of middle and high school students and experts. *Journal of Research in Science Teaching, 28*(9). https://doi.org/10.1002/tea.3660280907

Harlen, W. (2010). *Principles and Big Ideas of Science Education*. https://www.ase.org.uk/bigideas

Harrison, A. G., & Coll, R. K. (Eds) (2008). *Using analogies in middle and secondary science classrooms*. Corwin Press.

Hattie, J. (2012). *Visible learning for teachers: Maximizing impact in learning*. Routledge.

Hirsch, E. D. (2016). *Why Knowledge matters: Rescuing our children from failed educational theories.* Harvard Education Press.

Hitchcock, C., Meyer, A., & Rose, D., and Jackson, R. (2002). Providing new access to the general curriculum. *Teaching Exceptional Children, 35*(2). https://doi.org/10.1177/004005990203500201

Hodson, D. (2003). Time for action: Science education for an alternative future. *International Journal of Science Education, 25*(6). https://doi.org/10.1080/09500690305021

Inhelder, B., & Piaget, J. (2013). *The growth of logical thinking from childhood to adolescence: An essay on the construction of formal operational structures.* Routledge.

Johnstone, A. H. (1991). Why is science difficult to learn? Things are seldom what they seem. *Journal of Computer Assisted Learning, 7*(2). https://doi.org/10.1111/j.1365-2729.1991.tb00230.x

Kirschner, P. A. (2002). Cognitive load theory: Implications of cognitive load theory on the design of learning. *Learning and Instruction, 12*(1). https://doi.org/10.1016/S0959-4752(01)00014-7

Klein, N. K., & Safford, P. L. (1977). Application of Piaget's theory to the study of thinking of the mentally retarded: A review of research. The Journal of Special Education, 11(2), 201–216. https://doi.org/10.1177/002246697701100211

Krathwohl, D. R., Bloom, B. S., & Masia, B. B. (1965). *Taxonomy of educational objectives handbook II: Affective domain.* Longman.

Land, R. (2008). *Threshold concepts within the disciplines.* Sense Publishers.

Lenton, G., & Stevens, B. (1999). Numeracy in science. *School Science Review, 80*(293), 59–64.

Levine, D. (1985). *Improving student achievement through mastery learning.* Jossey-Bass.

Librea-Carden, M. R., Mulvey, B. K., Borgerding, L. A., Wiley, A. L., & Ferdous, T. (2021). 'Science is accessible for everyone': Preservice special education teachers' nature of science perceptions and instructional practices. *International Journal of Science Education, 43*(6), 949–968.

Lortie-Forgues, H., Tian, J., & Siegler, R. S. (2015). Why is learning fraction and decimal arithmetic so difficult? *Developmental Review, 38.* https://doi.org/10.1016/j.dr.2015.07.008

Lovitt, T. C., & Horton, S. V. (1994). Strategies for adapting science textbooks for youth with learning disabilities. *Remedial and Special Education, 15*(2). https://doi.org/10.1177/074193259401500206

Mastropieri, M. A., Scruggs, T. E., Irby Cerar, N., Guckert, M., Thompson, C., Bronaugh, D. A., Jakulski, J., Abdulalim, L., Mills, S., Evmenova, A., Regan, K., & Cuenca-Carlino, Y. (2015). Strategic persuasive writing instruction for students with emotional and behavioral disabilities. *Exceptionality, 23*(3). https://doi.org/10.1080/09362835.2014.986605

Mastropieri, M. A., Scruggs, T. E., Norland, J. J., Berkeley, S., McDuffie, K., Tornquist, E. H., & Connors, N. (2006). Differentiated curriculum enhancement in inclusive middle school science: Effects on classroom and high-stakes tests. *Journal of Special Education, 40*(3). https://doi.org/10.1177/00224669060400030101

McGill, C. (2022). *How to apply cognitive load theory to chemistry practicals.* https://edu.rsc.org/ideas/how-to-apply-cognitive-load-theory-to-chemistry-practicals/4015738.article

McGinnis, J. R. (2013). Teaching science to learners with special needs. *Theory into Practice, 52*(1). https://doi.org/10.1080/07351690.2013.743776

Meadan, H., & Monda-Amaya, L. (2008). Collaboration to promote social competence for students with mild disabilities in the general classroom: A structure for providing social support. *Intervention in School and Clinic, 43*(3). https://doi.org/10.1177/1053451207311617

Microsoft. (2022). *Get your document's readability and level statistics.* https://support.microsoft.com/en-us/office/get-your-document-s-readability-and-level-statistics-85b4969e-e80a-4777-8dd3-f7fc3c8b3fd2

Miri, B., David, B. C., & Uri, Z. (2007). Purposely teaching for the promotion of higher-order thinking skills: A case of critical thinking. *Research in Science Education, 37*(4). https://doi.org/10.1007/s11165-006-9029-2

Morin, L.L., Watson, S. M. R. , Hester, P. and Raver, S. (2017). The Use of a Bar Model Drawing to Teach Word Problem Solving to Students With Mathematics Difficulties. *Learning Disability Quarterly, 40*(2), 91–104.

Moseley, D. (2011). ACE Spelling Dictionary. LDA.

Moseley, D. (2012). Advanced ACE Spelling Dictionary. LDA.

Mulvey, B. K., Chiu, J. L., Ghosh, R., & Bell, R. L. (2016). Special education Teachers' nature of science instructional experiences. *Journal of Research in Science Teaching, 53*(4), 554–578.

Naylor, S. (2014). *Concept cartoons in science education: (The ConCISE project)* (3rd ed.). Millgate House.

NGSS Lead States. (2017). *Next generation science standards: For states, by states.* National Academies Press. https://www.nextgenscience.org/

OFQUAL. (2021). *GCSE subject-level conditions and requirements for single science (2022).* https://www.gov.uk/government/publications/gcse-subject-level-conditions-for-2022/gcse-subject-level-conditions-and-requirements-for-single-science-2022

Olson, J. L., Platt, J. C., & Dieker, L. A. (2007). *Teaching children and adolescents with special needs* (5th ed.). Prentice Hall.

Osborne, J., & Dillon, J. (2008). *Science education in Europe: Critical reflections*. The Nuffield Foundation.

Park, H., Kim, Y., & Jeong, S. (2019). The effect of a science festival for special education students on communicating science. *Asia-Pacific Science Education, 5*(1). https://doi.org/10.1186/S41029-018-0029-0

Parmar, R. S., Deluca, C. B., & Janczak, T. M. (1994). Investigations into the relationship between science and language abilities of students with mild disabilities. *Remedial and Special Education, 15*(2). https://doi.org/10.1177/074193259401500207

Paterson, D. (2018). *Improving practical work with integrated instructions*. https://edu.rsc.org/feature/improving-practical-work-with-integrated-instructions/3009798.article

Pellerin, M. (2014). Language tasks using touch screen and mobile technologies: Reconceptualizing task-based CALL for young language learners. *Canadian Journal of Learning and Technology/La revue Canadienne de l'apprentissage et de la technologie, 40*(1). https://eric.ed.gov/?id=EJ1030429

Piggott, S. (2002). Putting differentiation into practice in secondary science lessons. *School Science Review, 83*(305), 65–71.

Pisha, B., & Stahl, S. (2005). The promise of new learning environments for students with disabilities. *Intervention in School and Clinic, 41*(2). https://doi.org/10.1177/10534512050410020601

Poulton, E. C. (1967). Searching for newspaper headlines printed in capitals or lower-case letters. *Journal of Applied Psychology, 51*(5 PART 1). https://doi.org/10.1037/h0025098

Ramsden, S., Richardson, F. M., Josse, G., Thomas, M. S. C., Ellis, C., Shakeshaft, C., Seghier, M. L., & Price, C. J. (2011). Verbal and non-verbal intelligence changes in the teenage brain. *Nature, 479*(7371). https://doi.org/10.1038/nature10514

Reid, D. J., & Hodson, D. (1987). *Science for all: Teaching science in the secondary school*. Cassell.

Rickards, J. P., & August, G. J. (1975). Generative underlining strategies in prose recall. *Journal of Educational Psychology, 67*(6). https://doi.org/10.1037/0022-0663.67.6.860

Rosenthal, R., & Jacobson, L. (1968a). *Pygmalion in the classroom*. Holt Reinhart and Winston, Inc.

Rosenthal, R., & Jacobson, L. F. (1968b). Teacher expectations for the disadvantaged. *Scientific American, 218*(4). https://doi.org/10.1038/scientificamerican0468-19

Rudolph, J. (2002). *Scientists in the classroom: The cold war reconstruction of American science education*. Palgrave. https://books.google.com/books?hl=enandlr=andid=SLCADAAAQBAJandoi=fndandpg=PP1 anddq=rudolph+sputnik+curriculumandots=Mw5lp0iwOmandsig=6W4JPXQV0al99YDyycyGXXBOSk0

Scruggs, T. E., & Mastropieri, M. A. (2007). Science learning in special education: The case for constructed versus instructed learning. *Exceptionality: The Official Journal of the Division for Research of the Council for Exceptional Children, 15*(2), 57–74.

Sermier Dessemontet, R., Martinet, C., de Chambrier, A. F., & Martini-Willemin, B. M., and Audrin, C. (2019). A meta-analysis on the effectiveness of phonics instruction for teaching decoding skills to students with intellectual disability. *Educational Research Review, 26*. https://doi.org/10.1016/j.edurev.2019.01.001

Shayer, M. (2003). Not just Piaget; not just Vygotsky, and certainly not Vygotsky as alternative to Piaget. *Learning and Instruction, 13*(5). https://doi.org/10.1016/S0959-4752(03)00092-6

Shayer, M., & Adey, P. (1981). *Towards a science of science teaching: Cognitive development and curriculum demand*. Heinemann Educational Publishers.

Shayer, M., & Adey, P. (2002). *Learning intelligence: Cognitive acceleration across the curriculum from 5 to 15 years*. Open University Press.

Simon, S., & Richardson, K. (2009). Argumentation in school science: Breaking the tradition of authoritative exposition through a pedagogy that promotes discussion and reasoning. *Argumentation, 23*, 469. https://doi.org/10.1007/s10503-009-9164-9

Sola Özgüç, C., & Cavkaytar, A. (2015). Science education for students with intellectual disability: A case study. *Journal of Baltic Science Education, 14*(6). https://doi.org/10.33225/jbse/15.14.804

Southall, E. (2016). The formula triangle and other problems with procedural teaching in mathematics. *School Science Review, 97*(360), 49–53. https://dialnet.unirioja.es/servlet/articulo?codigo=5671733and-info=resumenandidioma=ENG

Stahl, S. (2005). Four problems with teaching word meanings (and what to do to make vocabulary an integral part of instruction). In E. H. Hiebert and M. L. Kamil (Eds.), *Teaching and learning vocabulary*. https://doi.org/10.4324/9781410612922-11

Steele, M. M. (2004). Making the case for early identification and intervention for young children at risk for learning disabilities. *Early Childhood Education Journal, 32*(2). https://doi.org/10.1007/s10643-004-1072-x

Steele, M. M. (2007). Science success for students with special needs science and children. *Education Database, 45*(2), 48.

Stroupe, D., Moon, J., & Michaels, S. (2019). Introduction to special issue: Epistemic tools in science education. *Science Education, 103*(4), 948–951. https://doi.org/10.1002/SCE.21512

Sullivan, A. (2018). *Phonics for pupils with special educational needs book 7: Multisyllable magic: Revising the main sounds and working on 2, 3 and 4 syllable words*. Routledge.

Sweller, J., Ayres, P., & Kalyuga, S. (2011). Intrinsic and extraneous cognitive load. In *Cognitive load theory* (pp. 57–69). Springer.

Taylor, J. C., Therrien, W. J., Kaldenberg, E. R., Watt, S., Chanlen, N., & and Hand, B. (2012). Using an inquiry-based teaching approach to improve science outcomes for students with disabilities: Snapshot and longitudinal data. *Journal of Science Education for Students with Disabilities*, *15*(1), 27–39.

Therrien, W. J., Benson, S. K., Hughes, C. A., & Morris, J. R. (2017). Explicit instruction and next generation science standards aligned classrooms: A fit or a split? *Learning Disabilities Research and Practice*, *32*(3). https://doi.org/10.1111/ldrp.12137

Therrien, W. J., Taylor, J. C., Hosp, J. L., Kaldenberg, E. R., & Gorsh, J. (2011). Science instruction for students with learning disabilities: A meta-analysis. *Learning Disabilities Research and Practice*, *26*(4). https://doi.org/10.1111/j.1540-5826.2011.00340.x

Tregidgo, D., & Ratcliffe, M. (2000). The use of modelling for improving Pupils' learning about cells. *School Science Review*, *81*(296), 53–59. https://eric.ed.gov/?id=EJ604061

van Driel, J. H., & Verloop, N. (1999). Teachers' knowledge of models and modelling in science. *International Journal of Science Education*, *21*(11). https://doi.org/10.1080/095006999290110

Villanueva, M. G., Taylor, J., Therrien, W., & Hand, B. (2012). Science education for students with special needs. *Studies in Science Education*, *48*(2), 187–215.

Vygotsky, L. S. (1978). *Mind in society: The development of higher psychological processes*. Harvard University Press.

Westwood, P. (2001). Differentiation' as a strategy for inclusive classroom practice: Some difficulties identified. *Australian Journal of Learning Difficulties*, *6*(1), 5–11.

White, J. (2005). *Howard Gardner: The myth of multiple intelligences*. Viewpoint, 16. London: Institute of Education, University of London.

3 Assessment for success

Introduction: The problems with assessment

Many who teach pupils with learning disabilities (LD) will recognise the comment made about the science curriculum and the associated assessment, which was noted decades earlier to represent a *'drive for fairness through uniformity, objectivity and anonymity'* (Reid & Hodson, 1987, p. 147). The same authors go on to note that low attainment should not be explained by lazy stereotypes and the following section considers the factors in school science education that contribute to low attainment.

Apanasionok et al. (2020), when investigating the impact of a highly structured teaching intervention for primary pupils with LD, described that the study's sampling protocol required pupils to be able to access both the learning and the format of the assessment. Unless both of these conditions are met, pupils do not have a realistic chance to demonstrate learning. In school, teachers cannot generally select which pupils are assessed, so it is inevitable that those with LD will be entered for assessments with which they will have difficulty on which they are liable to perform poorly. If the assessment is unsuitable, it is liable to result in pupils feeling powerless and that they failed. However, assessment at its best can be motivating and a valuable source of feedback for teachers as well as pupils (Reid & Hodson, 1987). Where the chance to differentiate the assessment that pupils take exists, this can be hugely helpful to capture a range of attainment. For example, Scotland's wide range of recognised qualifications ranging from National Level 1 through to Advanced Higher Level offers the ability to offer a wide range of possible outcomes. Regrettably, school management teams can exert pressure for pupils to be entered for 'benchmark' qualifications, despite the fact that these may not give all pupils the best experience of assessment or enable them to achieve at the highest level that they can.

In this section, I considered the combined effect of the multiple barriers that impede science learning by those with Learning Difficulties. It is self-evident that pupils who have learnt less, or understood less, are disadvantaged in assessments. They are also prone to achieving even less than they are capable of because they have a sense of science being something beyond their everyday lives. This feeling of 'otherness' also deters them from drawing on what they know from outside the science classroom. For this reason, relevance in assessment is as important as relevance in learning. Other common difficulties are those with memorising and recalling what they have memorised than their peers (see Section 2 for more on this). This is a major obstacle in assessments which are heavily knowledge-orientated, especially exams. Although the impact of reduced memory on assessment outcomes is not as clear-cut as might be expected, there is a general trend for reduced memory capacity to lower assessment outcomes (Kalmbach & Larsen, 2011). Exacerbating this is evidence that the stress occasioned by formal assessment reduces working memory capacity, which already tends to be lower than that of their neuro-typical peers anyway, so further impeding retrieval of what has been learnt (Sweller et al., 2011).

The cumulative effect of these factors is to prevent those with LD from demonstrating their learning effectively, most especially under test or exam conditions. Several considerations arise from this. Firstly, assessment should, as far as possible, promote learning as well as measure what has already been learnt. Integrating assessment into routine activities within lessons can enhance the value of the activities whilst decreasing the anxiety felt by pupils (Reid & Hodson, 1987). Questioning a staple of the classroom can have multiple purposes and can constitute both assessment and teaching. For example Chin (2007) notes that questions can help to develop new ways of thinking by developing a sequence of concepts or helping to elucidate the links between different bits of content. Questioning can also be used to engage a class and elicit interaction, to initiate further thinking or to help to construct a synopsis of prior learning as well as its more traditional uses in checking prior knowledge (Muijs & Reynolds, 2017).

They can also be used to structure learning, by sharing a 'big question' (one that does not have one simple answer) at the start of the lesson. Pupils can then be encouraged to reflect on

DOI: 10.4324/9781003167815-4

how their learning is helping them to formulate a response as the lesson proceeds, concluding with their responses during the plenary at the end (Wragg & Brown, 2001).

The second way in which assessment can enhance attainment is by promoting pupil response so that we get as accurate a picture as possible of what has been understood. To this end, strategies should be as varied as possible, so that evidence better reflecting learning can be gathered. Another aspect of enhancing response is to seek a visible reaction or answer. This could be by asking pupils to arrange cards or point to something or give a 'thumbs up' sign, as well as giving verbal or written answers. One of the most powerful, and easy to implement, devices to enhance pupil response is to give thinking time after asking a question. This is the top tip of numerous teachers widely recommended in academic sources, such as Chin (2007), Wiliam and Leahy (2015), Wragg and Brown (2001). The benefits of allowing thinking time, which can be enhanced by allowing pupils time to discuss the question, include increasing the number of responses, increasing the length of answers, increasing pupil confidence and increasing the number of pupils offering answers. For this to happen, it is essential that we create a climate where it is safe to make mistakes. Teachers promote this by responding sensitively to incorrect or partial answers. Although we may feel exasperated by a wrong answer, these are more valuable to us in knowing where we need to re-teach or change future teaching.

Thirdly, when testing, including external exams, is required, adjustments should be made as far as can be done. Additional time for assessments enables pupils to have further time to process the questions fully and to retrieve information they have learnt from their long-term memory. It also allows those with short concentration spans to take short breaks in attending to the assessment. The same adjustments that would be offered for reading or writing in a teaching situation should be considered for use during assessments. For example reading questions aloud allows frequently enhances performance, as it reduces the stress that many poor readers feel and enables them to focus their efforts on recalling recording answers. Text-to-voice options, combined with individual headsets, mean that this option can be made available selectively in a whole class setting. Likewise, text-to-voice functions facilitate the checking of written answers. Pupils with significant difficulties with handwriting will benefit from being allowed to word process answers or even to record spoken answers, which can later be converted to text. Whilst such adjustments require formal approval for external examinations, they should be routinely considered for internal assessments. As well as providing a truer picture of what has actually been learnt, success with internal assessments is liable to enhance motivation for future learning.

Reflective question:

Do you recognise the description of assessment as a major disincentive for pupils to study science? If you do, how do you rate the difficulties presented by different types of assessment that you are involved in?

Teaching to the test

Tests in science and written questions, more generally, are beset with many of the barriers that render the science curriculum and associated text sources so inaccessible. An analysis of exemplar questions intended for upper primary and lower school pupils published in teacher guides textbooks that are widely used in Scotland is set out below. Thirty-seven questions were analysed, and the findings are summarised below. (Of the three stated aims of the course associated with the books, the correspondence between questions and the three aims are shown in Figure 3.1.)

Course & assessment aim	Number of questions assessing the aim
Knowledge and understanding	34
Developing investigative skills	2
Developing informed attitudes	1

Figure 3.1 The number of questions addressing each of the three course aims in the assessments questions that were analysed.

Piagetian level	Number of questions
3B Late formal	3
3A Early formal	14
2B Late concrete	9
2A Early concrete & below	10
[Pre-operational]	1

Figure 3.2 The number of questions addressing each of the Piagetian levels.

The text of the questions intended for 9 to 12 years old and had an average Flesch Reading Ease score (for which 100 is the most readable) of 81.9, but the score ranged between 58.1 and 96.2. This means that some questions were accessible by neuro-typical 14 to 15 years old, significantly above that of the target audience.

The level of conceptual demand the questions made were mapped against Piagetian levels, as shown in Section 2, Figure 2.1. The distribution of conceptual dems is shown in Figure 3.2.

Given that multiple studies by Shayer and Adey suggested that around 88% of pupils would be able to operate at level 2A by the age of 16 and only around 32% would achieve level 3B, the demand would appear to be very challenging if not unattainable by the target learners. Those with developmental delay would fare still more badly and might well reach the conclusion that science really was not for them.

Finally, the extent to which the sample questions relied specifically on sub-microscopic or intangible phenomena was assessed. Fourteen of the 37 questions fell into this category, which, in most instances, raises the question to the level of formal reasoning and certainly precludes any chance of children drawing on everyday experiences to scaffold their understanding of science.

The result of these multiple exclusionary features is that written questions commonly compound the difficulties presented by the curriculum and provide an especially poor measure of true learning. Nevertheless, in anticipation of pupils being required to take 'pencil and paper' tests in science at some point in their school career, it is advisable to start preliminary preparation far in advance of the test itself. In approaching written exam-style assessments, familiarisation and rehearsal for the format provide gradualised support, through which pupils can be helped to develop the skills required for success in tests. This would typically involve pupils actively participating in assessment-style processes, including the analysis of typical assessment items. Involving pupils in writing test questions and corresponding answers is one way to do this. In response to this, pupils generally rely on factual recall questions, which are easier to compose and which reflect the knowledge-orientated disposition of many exams. This in itself can be a useful stimulus to consider what they could reasonably be expected to remember in a test and how they can know. Other devices I have used is asking pupils to rank order three specimen test questions to encourage discussion of what aspects of each question they think they would find hard about them. This, in turn, can point you to where skills development is most needed. Asking pupils to highlight process or instruction words in one colour, either with marker pens or digitally, highlights the range of terms they may encounter. Similarly, asking them to highlight essential information in the question in one and 'padding' in another helps them to see that not all the content does the same job. Although such approaches may seem quite mechanistic, it can empower pupils to see how assessment questions are structured. This can then help them to understand how to structure their response. This strategy can then be extended to get them to analyse some specimen answers to a question; where have they responded to the process terms? A colleague strongly recommends a 'bullet point per mark' approach to extended and heavily weighted, in terms of marks allocated, answers. An example of this is given below.

To a question scoring a possible six marks that asks '*Explain how why some fractions of crude oil are processed by chemical cracking. Refer to some of the products that are formed*', the teacher could give a set of marking criteria:

- Have I said how cracking is carried out (chemicals involved including any that speed up the process, that it is heated)? (2 marks)
- Have I said why crude oil is cracked? Have I talked about which chemicals are most common in oil and which chemicals people want to buy most of? (2 marks)
- Have I given the names of at least two chemicals produced by cracking? (2 marks)

This structured approach helps pupils to self-assess their answers formatively thus to know whether they have recalled all that is expected. Criterion-based assessment, if the criteria

The answer should show	Pupil ✓ or comment	Teacher comment (if needed)
How I arranged the circuit		
Say what happened when I added more lamps		
Say why I think the change happened		

Figure 3.3 A possible way to facilitate pupils' self-assessment of writing about an experiment.

are limited in number and comprehensible, as exemplified in Figure 3.3, permits the same approach to assessment, as does provide examples of what a good answer would constitute. Carefully structured questioning is another way to elicit a collective model answer, which can then serve as a benchmark for future responses. This can be thought of as an assessment-focused application of genre pedagogy. Genre pedagogy aims to ensure that all pupils are aware of the linguistic 'code' in a subject, including the codes used in assessment tasks (Hyland, 2007).

One of the most powerful tools that I have ever deployed is to ask pupils to mark specimen answers, using the mark scheme that would be applied to the questions. Far from objecting to doing my job for me, they took to it with great gusto and were far harsher than I might have been. The impact was very evident in their next assessment. The account below describes one such class.

A year 10 class full of disaffected, demotivated youngsters, all of whom had SEN or additional social issues to contend with. They had declined to engage seriously with two successive of assessed investigations I felt exasperated. I was keen for them to gain credit for something that I knew they could succeed in, as I was getting increasingly anxious about their likely results in the forthcoming exam. They liked practical work but wanted to approach it by trial and error, rather than planning, then doing, a structured investigation, of the sort that would earn marks. I decided to spend some time drafting three write ups of investigations from three fictitious pupils, each in a different handwritten script, each bearing suitably implausible names, including Bertha Jellybean. I started the lesson by saying that I had been very busy hadn't finished my marking was really worried about getting into trouble with the Head of Science. Would they, I asked tentatively, be able to help me with the marking? They said they would, perhaps detecting something unusual afoot. So, I distributed the same mark scheme that they had ignored completely during the previous two assessed investigations, plus copies of the 'scripts'. They set to, interrogating the meaning of the marking criteria debating the scripts with interest. I was amused to hear one of the most uninterested members of the group say loudly with some evident disgust, 'This Bertha Jellybean is just stupid. She hasn't even said what she is going to change in her experiment.' I duly collected the marked scripts in, thanked them very much for their help. The next lesson, I produced another investigation for the class to do, my last chance to get some assessable work from them. I was astonished when they started to talk about what they were going to change and why. Third time lucky, they duly delivered some model plans and write ups, exceeding all expectations. My delight was only tempered by the reaction of the Head of Science at the internal moderation meeting when he said, 'You can't give high marks like these to those kids. They're bottom set.' It was a great shame that the person in charge was so much less willing to learn than the pupils had been!

(Field note, May 2002)

In another instance, I observed a class of 12-to-13-year olds who were studying acids, alkalis and indicators. The observations of one class taking just one test raise serious questions about the suitability of paper–pencil style tests for those to whom they present such major difficulties. The difficulties that the internal end-of-topic test caused far exceeded the difficulties they had experienced during the lessons, despite the fact that numerous adjustments were made in the administration of the test by an experienced teacher of pupils with LD. The pupils were allowed to have their workbooks with them, to aid recall, and the number of questions had been reduced in comparison to the number answered by other pupils. In addition, classroom support assistants were available to help individuals and the teacher read the questions aloud one at a time. Despite these support measures, the pupils struggled during the test and exhibited unsettled behaviour. For example I noted that,

The teacher read a question in the end-of-unit test aloud, 'If I add 50 ml of water from one beaker to another beakers of 75 ml water, how much water would there be?' Ben scowls squirms. Teacher, 'You need to add it'. The classroom support assistant sitting next to Ben models the finger method of addition, 'If I had four fingers on this h no fingers on that one, how many would there be?' After four attempts, Ben. correctly calculates the total volume of water.

(Field note, March 2020)

The test also caused high levels of anxiety, reduced self-esteem and heightened self-doubt, to which pupils with LD are known to be prone (Elbaum & Vaughn, 2003). An interaction that captured the pall that the test cast over the pupils was overheard towards the end of the class test:

Teacher. How's Miss Lizzy doing?
Pupil, emphatically, 'Not well!' (Field note, March 2020)

The uncertainty over what success would look like in an assessment that was perceived as high stakes was expressed by another pupil as the test papers were gathered in. She said despondently, *'Not sure how well I did in the test questions.'* This sort of uncertainty points to the especial importance of formative assessment for pupils who may need more explicit guidance in how to gauge their success. It also testifies to the supremacy of norm-referenced assessment, which defines 'winners and losers' when self-referenced assessment, or assessing progress from an individual's starting point, may give a clear sense of attainment. This can be captured by asking pupils to work on an open-ended task, such as a concept map, at the start of a teaching sequence and then re-visiting it again, using a different coloured pen to show how their thinking has evolved.

What is being assessed?

In Section 1, a list of possible outcomes associated with learning science was given. All of these can be assessed in some way or other, though some, notably affective (emotions and values) outcomes are challenging to assess with any degree of certainty rest heavily on teacher judgement. In the interests of capturing the development of diverse learners, teachers may have to resist the '*drive for fairness through uniformity, objectivity and anonymity*' (Reid & Hodson, 1987, p. 147). Assessment, like the rest of teaching, is as much an art as a science; however, much educational managers wish it were not so. Just as planning lessons require a solid correspondence between stated learning intentions, assessment needs to be planned with a focus on the outcomes for which evidence is being sought. This is the quality of validity, which means that we are measuring what we want to measure, in this case learning. Pencil-and-paper style test may be considered a valid way of measuring a blend of literacy, recall and attention span which could be considered some aspects of what we call 'learning', they are not a valid indicator of attitude or practical skills. They clearly present distinct difficulties to pupils with LD, as the account of the test on acids shows.

Pupils who do not do well on such tests should not be assumed not to have learnt, but rather not to have learnt the skills required to bring about success in tests. Despite this, such tests are a staple of school assessments, partly because they are reliable, in that they give similar outcomes with equivalent pupils on repeated occasions. Their role in external assessment, by which schools are benchmarked, makes them politically strategic. For this reason, it is important that adjustments and accommodations are made to facilitate the optimal performance by pupils with LD. These may include the provision of printed resources in different sized fonts, an amanuensis to read questions aloud, the provision of a keyboard or voice recorder for recording answers and additional time to complete the assessment. However, more fundamentally, there is also a strong case for assessing in other ways.

Recall the example in Section 2 of the time capsule exercise, in which pupils with LD were asked to select and justify objects for a time capsule that will be opened at a summer school on climate change and sustainability in 100 years. This was used to probe the participants' understanding of the concept of climate change and sustainability.

One participant chose to contribute a plastic chocolate wrapper, justifying it thus, 'I don't think in a hundred years' time that people will be allowed to use plastic to wrap food in and I think that they will be shocked that we ever were.'

Another put in two shells and a stone that they had been carrying round most of the day and stroking, having gathered them from the beach that morning, 'Because they're beautiful and I think people may not have beautiful things then.'

Two young people contributed painted stones, one simply reading 'I love life' the other depicting a scene of the beach on one side a picture of pollution clouds skeletons on the other.

Still others wrote or drew on postcards, drawing mainly animals and plants. Habitat was alluded to twice, one drew a view of the polar ice cap and another described the beach, One described future change, contingent upon human behaviour 'There will be fewer people if we don't look after our planet.' Others had noted down things of more immediate concern, such as a comment on their hobbies or relationship matters.

(Field note, August, 2021)

Although the task required more inference than a multiple-choice test, it revealed far more about what the young people had understood of what they had been taught. My observations over the years have led me to conclude that, in order to probe learning in this way, requires the assessment task to be:

- Practicable, can be done in the time and with the resources available.
- Open-ended, also termed 'variable response, as opposed to fixed or limited response assessment, thus permitting wide differentiation and individualisation by outcome.
- Challenging because they not only had to contribute an object but were also asked to explain their reasoning.
- Low stakes, in that there were no adverse consequences to their choice of item. For example cards were anonymous and were not pulled out for a public critique of the spelling or drawing on them.
- Multi-modal, permitting objects, pictures, text and spoken word to be used to represent their ideas.

Not all learning can be assessed in such an open-ended way, but it is worth doing something of this sort when checking out learning about complex or emotive topics. I would suggest that the type of material, in conjunction with the learning intentions, can indicate the type of assessment that will be best suited to find out what learning has taken place.

The following account uses Reid and Hodson's (1987) framework of learning intentions to group the types of assessment tool that could be appropriately used. Revisiting the outcomes associated with learning science, discussed in Section 1, not all of them fall within the scope of standard assessment of learning, but all of them are important and can be both assessed reinforced through the mechanism used for assessment.

Skills

Whether they are transferable, such as data processing, communication, manipulative skills, analysis, evaluation and problem-solving, or specific skills, such as can be most meaningfully assessed in the context of tasks that are integral to science learning. It is helpful to be explicit about exactly what is being assessed what isn't. It is also very helpful to model success in the target skill looks like. For example if data processing is being assessed during an experiment, different outcomes can be set out or exemplified, such as:

a. Collects and records several measurements.
b. Organises measurements, for example in a list from smallest to biggest or in a table.
c. Recognises a pattern in the measurements, for example plots a graph or describes a trend such as the hotter the liquid, the faster the reaction.
d. Can suggest what might happen in experiments that they did not carry out, for example guess how long a reaction might take if the liquid was a temperature that they did not use.

Criterion-matched assessment, using statements like these, is a powerful mechanism for formative assessment of skills, since it helps learners to know what they have achieved and what their next target should be. It can also provide the material for some useful conversations that develop pupils' ability to self-assess, which is especially valuable for a group of learners who may struggle to know how they are performing.

Affective development

Including feelings and attitudes, can only be explored meaningfully through open-ended tasks, which permit a wide range of valid responses. Discussions are good for exploring attitudes and feelings, whilst 'washing line' assessments permit a quick assessment of feelings or attitude along a spectrum of values, for example: How important is it for us to stop climate change? Put your name card at the point along the line, from 'It has to happen now' to 'It isn't important'. As with many other questions, much deeper meaning can be derived from the responses if they are asked to explain **why** they chose the answer they did. Other favourites of mine are to ask students to nominate somebody or something related to what they have been learning about for an award, for example which of the rocks you have seen deserves the 'building material of the year' award? To get even more creative, get them to work in groups to design a web page, or a monument or a trophy to an inventor or discoverer or idea. This relies on the pupils' judgement there cannot be one right answer, but it is a great way to explore their understanding reasoning in a non-judgemental way.

Similarly, discussion and debate are excellent ways to explore the role of science in everyday life. The place of science as an aspect of culture is an important reason for science education being a universal entitlement but is one that is not commonly assessed, not least because this requires judgement in an area in which teachers may not feel confident or even comfortable. However, it would be inappropriate and insensitive to laud some contributions belittle others, or to dismiss some views above others, may cause much controversy. I think, for instance about some of the heated arguments about whether portraying creationist views alongside the 'Big Bang' theory are 'unscientific' (Reiss, 2008). Nevertheless, we can assess whether pupils are prepared to consider different views, possibly with support, to understand which views are well supported by scientific evidence and which are not.

Acquisition of factual knowledge

This is the type of learning that is traditionally assessed by recall questions. Although knowledge is the lowest form of cognitive process according to Bloom's taxonomy (Krathwohl, 2002), it is not necessarily easy for pupils to demonstrate. Demonstrating knowledge is commonly not motivating, in an information-rich age, and simply does not seem an especially worthwhile activity on which to spend time. Allied with the difficulties that such learners commonly have with memorising and recalling factual information, pupils frequently under-perform in tasks requiring the recall of factual knowledge. Asking pupils to use factual knowledge in some way, rather than simply remembering it, may help, for example choosing a false statement out of a list of three or four correct statements may enable you to get an idea about what they are familiar with, whether or not they can recall it when asked. Other sorting activities with given pieces of factual information might include organising facts (which could be written in text boxes on a digital device) under given headings, such as facts about electric currents, facts about static electricity, facts about measuring electric current, both assess familiarity with, and reinforces, factual knowledge, whilst enabling pupils to ask for further guidance if they need it. Another popular activity is to give pupils bits of information then ask them to devise a question to which it could be a correct answer, for example the answer is 6 volts, what might the question be?

> How commonly do you hear about or observe teachers assessing factual knowledge? Why do you think that it is by far the commonest aspect of learning to be assessed?

Matching assessment to learning intention

Concepts and terminology

Learning intentions assessing the understanding of concepts place greater assessment demands on teachers than knowledge alone does. Although learning terminology may appear to require recall of the words, it also requires an understanding of their meaning and hence is included along with concepts. Assessment of understanding can make for a more interesting assessment for the pupils, if we choose it to be. Pupils' grasp of terminology is often assessed using DARTS (directed activities related to text (Pamelasari & Khusniati, 2013), of which the most common is the Cloze exercise ('fill in the blanks'). These have the advantage of being highly structured and straightforward to assess. They can also give some senses of whether pupils recognise the linguistic function of the vocabulary, such as whether it is a noun, an adjective or a verb. However, they can be dull to complete so should be used judiciously.

Testing understanding more generally is typically done by asking for an explanation, but this may be hard for pupils with literacy or oracy difficulties. Approaches that I have used successfully include those which involve the use of images or artefacts to represent what they have understood, of the sort used to assess their understanding of sustainability that was described earlier. Asking pupils to draw symbols to represent ideas or words, or to match images or symbols to given concepts is a useful way to check understanding. (Signs can also be a helpful representation; see Section 6 for where to find out the British Sign Language signs for scientific terms.) Bear in mind that understanding does not have to be assessed separately from factual knowledge; for example pupils can be asked to pair up pieces of information with the correct (brief) explanation or to choose the best explanation from a list of two or three possible options.

Reflective question:

One of the arguments for teaching technical vocabulary and assessing whether pupils have understood it is that it embodies deep meaning in a word or phrase. Based on your teaching, do you think that argument is as true for pupils with LD as for others?

Classification

Classification is not only a learning intention but can also be an excellent way of probing the depth and generalisability of pupils' understanding. This is the reason for the use of examples and non-examples is a recognised strategy used in the technique of explicit instruction, described in more detail in Section 2. So, for instance pupils are frequently asked to group energy sources into renewable and non-renewable sources; this becomes a much more revealing activity if they are asked to justify their choices. Try adding some lesser known sources of power to the types classified and listen to the discussion about them. For example how would they classify a dance floor that generates electricity when people are dancing on it, or collecting the excess heat from underground railways and pumping it into people's homes to keep them warm? How, and why, they categorise these unusual examples can reveal a lot about their understanding.

Trends and sequences

To understand the notion of trends (successive incremental changes) requires pupils to identify that the changes are all in the same direction, such as getting faster each time. It also requires pupils to evaluate the nature of the changes to evaluate the pattern, so relies on higher order skills. Talking through the changes qualitatively is a good starting point, for example helping pupils to identify that as a beaker of water stays longer over the Bunsen flame, the hotter it gets. It may be helpful to have pupils identify the two related sets of data into rank order and then get them to notice that they get bigger or smaller at the same time. For instance

Here are three voltages that are applied to a circuit:

Experiment 1: 2 volts
Experiment 2: 4 volts
Experiment 3: 6 volts

(Or three drawings of an analogue voltmeter showing the needle at successively higher readings)

Ask the pupils what the scientist has done to the voltage in each experiment (turned it up or made it bigger each time)?

Here are the three currents that flowed through the circuit:

Experiment 1: 1 amp
Experiment 2: 2 amps
Experiment 3: 3 amps

Ask the pupils what has happened to the flow of electricity when the voltage was turned up (gone up or got bigger each time).

The next conceptual step is to relate the two trends, so that the pupils recognise that as the voltage gets bigger, the current gets bigger.

This understanding of the correlation between the two features (voltage and current) paves the way for pupils recognising that one thing is changed by the experimenter (the 'input variable') and the other changes because of that (the 'output variable'). It also paves the way for graph plotting, in which the two variables are shown together and which provides a representation of the trend. Other ways of interacting with a simple data set could be to 'fill in the gaps.' For example what current do you think there would be if we applied 8 volts? Or to work out what voltage gives a current of 5 amps.

Experimental techniques

Although experimental techniques are quite often examined indirectly, by asking pupils to write about an experiment, there are various reasons to advocate assessment as they do an experiment, or at least have an experiment accessible to them. It is an aspect of science in which pupils can demonstrate far more success than in written work and is often very popular with them, so frequently benefit from their full engagement. It can also help to build up their confidence which will pay dividends in other aspects of their learning. Much has been written about the assessment of practical experimental work (Abrahams et al., 2013) it is a well-documented undertaking for the general school population. The adjustments required for those with LD are mainly practical, for instance bearing in mind that the teacher may be needed to give more support and so can undertake less assessment than might be done in other groups of the same size. The urban myth about pupils with LD being inherently more unsafe in the lab is not borne out by evidence (Cawley et al., 2002) so is not a reason to avoid assessment activities in the lab. Whilst compulsory assessment of practicals for external assessment can be very burdensome for teachers, the potential benefits of being assessed in an area of success should not be underestimated. This need only be for internal use involving assessing one skill using a simple list of assessment criteria in order to be achievable. The payback for this effort is that pupils can rapidly get positive feedback on the assessment, which is hugely motivating.

Knowledge creation (epistemology)

Accepting that science is often presented as an absolute truth (which it isn't, just the best understanding we can achieve with the evidence that we have), it is important that learners have experience of creating knowledge and understanding the uncertainty inherent in the process. One useful approach is to ask them how certain they are about their interpretation of phenomena (Bonello & Scaife, 2009). For instance in the circuit activity described above, if they predict that the next current will be 4 amps, how sure are they? How can they test their idea? Once pupils are confident in their ability to predict results, it can be good to deliberately introduce activities that don't work as pupils expect. There are various examples that facilitate this more exploratory discussion, such as:

- What happens when you hang a weight from a wire loop around a block of ice let the weight hang? Why doesn't the block get cut in two?
- Burning a candle in water in an inverted jar and seeing how much the water goes up inside the jar. Why isn't it the 21% or one fifth that we would predict?
- Adding coloured ice cubes to a mixture of oil and water. Where do they sit and what happens as they melt (Griffiths, 1999)?
- The behaviour of cornflour as you add increasing volumes of water to it presents a challenge because the changes in viscosity that are observed do not show a steady shift.
- The behaviour of different food items when dropped in a fizzy liquid, such as lemonade, is not easy to predict, relying on several characteristics of the food and their relative impact on the nett motion.

This approach enables pupils to develop a two-part explanation, the first one upon they base their erroneous prediction, and a refined one once they have had a surprise result.

Another approach that can help you to assess how well they understand how scientific knowledge is constructed is to give them an accepted piece of information ask them how they think the scientists worked it out. Even better is if they can design an investigation that lets them test their idea about how scientists might know this.

Reflective question:

How comfortable do you feel teaching and then assessing open-ended tasks, to which you may not know all the possible answers? What support would you like with this aspect of teaching, which many people find especially anxiety-inducing?

Societal and ethical issues

Discussing complex issues may seem like a very challenging task for pupils who have additional difficulty with thinking and learning, but these aspects of science have two distinct advantages. Firstly, their relevance is very evident. Secondly, there is rarely a clear-cut right answer and so they do not carry the fear of failure that science content may instil. Weighing up different factors and deciding where the balance lies is a challenging task, relying as it does on synthesising multiple ideas. This is not a reason not to engage with complex ideas but rather to scaffold understanding by breaking the relevant information into smaller pieces, for example pupils were asked to consider whether they think it is a good idea to have a newly released Covid immunisation, they could be given single 'for and against' points. They could then sort these bits of information (ideally supported with suitable pictorial symbols) on cards into positive, negative or unsure piles. For each pile, they can then sort them into groups of very important, fairly important and minor considerations. They can then decide where the balance lies, based on their judgement of the significance of possible outcomes. A group might decide to group arguments about the immunisation as shown in Figure 3.4.

Importance	Plus	Negative	Unsure
Very important	Covid kills people and makes them very ill, especially old people and ill people.	It's a new injection and we don't really know how safe it is yet.	We don't know enough about how long the jab keeps us safe for, so we might need more in the future
	If you get Covid and you have had the jab, you will probably be a lot less ill	Viruses can change so the jab might not work for new Covid viruses	The jab has been tested on a few people but I might not react in the same way as those people
	Having the jab means that your body can fight the virus so you don't pass it on to other people as easily		
	The jab has been through a lot of tests so we know it's not dangerous		
Quite important	If people get Covid when they didn't need to, the health service can't look after other ill people as well	There are tablets that some people can take if they get Covid, so we don't need a jab.	Young people are probably not going to die of it but could give it to other people who might get very ill or die.
Not important	It's free to have the jab	Jabs hurt	
		You have to wait in a queue so it wastes your time	

Figure 3.4 Consequence of having a new immunisation arranged on a 3 × 3 table.

Reflective question:

How effectively do you think you assess the full range of possible learning outcomes associated with science lessons? Which of the outcomes would you like to assess more frequently and which less frequently, if the choice was yours?

How to respond to assessment outcomes

As illustrated above, the developmental assessment can be embedded in the learning. This is beneficial for all learners (Black & Harrison, 2000) and especially important for those who find learning extra difficult and for whom formal assessment can be especially intimidating. In these circumstances, whilst the notion of formative assessment, in which the assessment shapes future learning, is understood to be important I would suggest that for learners with LD, assessment needs to be even more two way than for other learners. This can mean that it appears to be simply a conversation with an individual as the teacher circulates, rather than a 'proper' formal assessment. My observation is that assessment for such learners frequently resembles a coaching interaction, with multiple small pieces of feedback and guidance which inform next steps. The benefits of this approach to a group that commonly has processing difficulties and may also lack self-confidence are easy to understand. As is often the case, the issues that pupils with LD highlight wider issues in teaching.

Whilst choosing the right way of carrying out assessment is important, so is the way that we feedback. The difficulties that beset our best intentions are indicated in a study that showed that feedback often makes attainment worse (Kluger & DeNisi, 1996). Given the effort that goes into assessment, this is a depressing finding. There are several problems with typical feedback, on top of the learning difficulties that we are considering in this book.

1. Feedback is too generic. This is commonly how teachers deal with the expectations of extensive feedback, they have a statement bank, either digitally or in their head, which makes the task manageable. However, this requires the recipient to relate the feedback to their own work; many pupils struggle to apply general feedback to their specific answer. (This is deductive reasoning, which is an abstract process, see Section 2.) It is far better to show exactly what aspects of the answer merit the feedback. So instead of saying that a piece of work shows a poor understanding of life processes, link it to what was said. 'It's not quite right to say that plants 'eat' starch, because they don't take it in from outside and break it down. Instead, we say that they break up starch stores in the leaf when they need food.' If possible, relate the feedback directly to the specific part of the work, in the margin or on a sticky note on the part being commented on.

2. Feedback isn't focused enough and talks about too a wide range of issues. For pupils with limited processing capacity, they feel overwhelmed rather than informed about how they have done. I would recommend that feedback focuses on the learning intention associated with the task (probably those for the lesson during which the work was given) one or two other points, such as literacy (most usefully on key technical terms or very commonly used (Tier 1) words). This clear focus makes assessment purposeful and bounded for teachers too, so is of mutual benefit.

3. Feedback is often about what hasn't been done, rather than on what has been done. Teachers can be quick to point out what is inaccurate or incorrect this can be very demoralising for learners who have to put in extra effort to get things correct. A balance of affirmative comments and pointers to things to change is much more powerful as a way of driving further positive change than a litany of problems.

4. Feedback should model what is wanted as well as identifying what isn't correct. When you assess, consider offering an alternative that demonstrates a preferable answer (see the example in point 2 above).

5. Be aware of thinking normatively about attainment that is holding all pupils to a common standard. This may be necessary in preparation for formal assessments but may take attention away from relative progress on an individual basis.

6. Be prepared to use assessment data to inform a decision re-teach previously covered material, to a group or to the whole class. Bear in mind that the very sequential nature of

science means that meaning missed at this point is likely to be a barrier to the next stage of learning. However, re-teaching doesn't mean teaching it a second time in the same way but re-covering the same concepts again but taught in a different way. Repetition should not be viewed as failure but rather the basis of secure learning and has its roots in Benjamin Bloom's (of Bloom's taxonomy) ideas about learning. He maintained that many more pupils can learn if given sufficient time, along with material broken down into small, manageable sections (Bloom, 1968).

7. Use assessment to find out what the underlying issues might be, this could be failure to recognise vocabulary or misunderstanding comm words or misconceptions about the topic.

Conclusion

Assessment takes a great deal of teachers' time and effort and can be especially fraught for those who work with pupils with LD. Assessment undoubtedly causes staff a great deal of stress because they feel judged by their pupils' 'performance'. Despite this, its role as a stimulus for review and as a powerful aid to learning means that well-chosen assessment is at the heart of optimal development by teachers and pupils. It, therefore, merits at least as much planning and resourcing as any direct teaching.

References

Abrahams, I., Reiss, M. J., & Sharpe, R. M. (2013). The assessment of practical work in school science. *Studies in Science Education*, *49*(2). https://doi.org/10.1080/03057267.2013.858496

Apanasionok, M. M., Neil, J., Watkins, R. C., Grindle, C. F., & Hastings, R. P. (2020). Teaching science to students with developmental disabilities using the early science curriculum. *Support for Learning*, *35*(4). https://doi.org/10.1111/1467-9604.12329

Black, P., & Harrison, C. (2000). Formative assessment. In J. Osborne & J. Dillon (Eds.), *Good Practice in Science Teaching: What Research Has to Say* (pp. 183–210). Oxford University Press.

Bloom, B. (1968). Learning for mastery. Instruction curriculum. Regional education laboratory for the Carolinas Virginia, topical papers reprints, number 1. *Evaluation Comment*, *1*(2), 1–11.

Bonello, C., & Scaife, J. (2009). PEOR-engaging students in demonstrations. *Journal of Science Mathematics Education in Southeast Asia*, *32*(1), 62–84.

Cawley, J., Hayden, S., Cade, E., & Baker-Kroczynski, S. (2002). Including students with disabilities into the general education science classroom. *Exceptional Children*, *68*(4), 423–435. https://doi.org/10.1177/001440290206800401

Chin, C. (2007). Teacher questioning in science classrooms: Approaches that stimulate productive thinking. *Journal of Research in Science Teaching*, *44*(6). https://doi.org/10.1002/tea.20171

Elbaum, B., & Vaughn, S. (2003). For which students with learning disabilities are self-concept interventions effective? *Journal of Learning Disabilities*, *36*(2). https://doi.org/10.1177/002221940303600203

Griffiths, T. (1999). Good – It's gone wrong; secondary; science and technology. Times Educational Supplement, 31 December.

Hyland, K. (2007). Genre pedagogy: Language, literacy L2 writing instruction. *Journal of Second Language Writing*, *16*, 148–164.

Kalmbach, R. D., & Larsen, J. M. (2011). *The impact of visual memory deficits on academic achievement in children adolescents*. ProQuest, Umi Dissertation Publishing.

Kluger, A. N., & DeNisi, A. (1996). The effects of feedback interventions on performance: A historical review, a meta-analysis, a preliminary feedback intervention theory. *Psychological Bulletin*, *119*(2). https://doi.org/10.1037/0033-2909.119.2.254

Krathwohl, D. A. (2002). A revision of Bloom's taxonomy: An overview. *Theory into Practice*, *41*, 212–218.

Muijs, D., & Reynolds, D. (2017). *Effective teaching: Evidence practice* (4th ed.). Safe.

Pamelasari, S. D., & Khusniati, M. (2013). The Effectiveness of directed activities related to texts (DARTs) to improve reading comprehension for science students. *The Foreign Language Learning Teaching International Conference (FLLT Conference)*.

Reid, D. J., & Hodson, D. (1987). *Science for all: Teaching science in the secondary school*. Cassell.

Reiss, M. J. (2008). Should science educators deal with the science/religion issue? *Studies in Science Education, 44*(2). https://doi.org/10.1080/03057260802264214

Sweller, J., Ayres, P., & Kalyuga, S. (Eds.) (2011). Intrinsic extraneous cognitive load. In *Cognitive load theory* (pp. 57–69). Springer.

Wiliam, D., & Leahy, S. (2015). *Embedding formative assessment: Practical techniques for k-12 classrooms*. Learning Sciences International.

Wragg, E. C., & Brown, G. A. (2001). *Questioning in the secondary school*. Routledge.

4 Approaches to teaching exemplar science topics

Introduction

The following section considers how the preceding sections, on practical approaches to making science inclusive and accessible, might be enacted within specific subject areas, specifically during the first 3 years of secondary school. The suggestions take particular account of the barriers that are often integrated into commonly used approaches but which are not necessarily integral to the key concepts being taught. Everyone reading this book will teach in a different context, including different lesson lengths and technical resources. You may find that, in your context, you need to spread the contents of a suggested lesson out over two of your lessons or to abridge the lessons. In addition, all pupils, whether identified as having one or more of the characteristics of diversity or not, will vary. Finally, schools differ in how pupils are grouped so some readers will have pupils of similar levels of prior attainment together, others will be teaching groups showing a wide range of prior attainment levels. If the latter is the case, you will need to have available 'stretch and challenge' elements for each activity, for instance looking at how a sub-microscopic model can explain what has been observed, using more technical vocabulary or handling quantitative aspects of the activity in a more formal and less supported way. Those pupils who are able to take on these additional challenges will benefit from gaining a secure conceptual grounding provided at the outset.

The implementation of the ideas offered in this section relies on the judgement of the individual teacher to make the concepts and content accessible in their teaching situation. I have taken account of the fact that many teachers may not have access to a lab for some, or all, of their lessons and so consider ways of using everyday materials that can be used out of a lab wherever possible. Note that wherever practical activities are suggested, the expectation is that individual teachers will carry out the risk assessment in line with the expectations of their school. If a pupil's support needs make risk assessment difficult to judge, you are encouraged to seek further guidance from SSERC if you are in Scotland or CLEAPSS for the rest of the UK. (See Section 6 on further sources of support.)

These examples illustrate the small, sequential conceptual steps that can enable pupils with learning disabilities (LD) to make meaningful progress in science, especially at the early stages of learning key ideas. They are founded in many years of experience that suggest for atypical learners, experiential learning is even more important to developing understanding than it doubtless is for their peers (Driver & Fensham, 1988). None of these approaches are intended to set any limit on learning and all can be used as the basis for developing more formal approaches to the concepts, by differentiation on a lesson-by-lesson basis. They focus on topics that might typically be taught to lower secondary aged pupils but can be used outside that age range if that is appropriate.

The approaches to developing understanding exemplified here can be incorporated into far more activities and topics than just the ones below. You are encouraged to find activities that you think are suitable for your pupils and which are feasible in your situation. Teachers are endlessly resourceful in devising new activities and resources, they are also very generous with their materials. For this reason, you are encouraged to engage with the professional bodies and other sources of teaching material listed in Section 6 and to adapt ideas you find there to suit your teaching situation.

Matter

This module is used to teach about why 'stuff' is like it is. It offers ample opportunities for hands-on and experiential learning, using familiar materials. There is also plenty of scope for

DOI: 10.4324/9781003167815-5

simple lab activities and many schools use it early on as a way of introducing pupils to the lab. The key concepts that this module seeks to impart are:

- Scientists can explain why material/stuff has the properties it does
- It is useful to scientists to classify/group things that are similar
- Scientists use ideas (called models) to describe what happens, to explain what happens and to predict what is going to happen
- There is an idea/model that explains why solids, liquids and gases behave differently to each other
- The model of matter says that it is made of very tiny pieces that we can't see
- Scientists can explain why solids, liquids and gases are different by describing how the very tiny pieces are arranged and how they move

Although this topic is commonly taught with an early focus on particle theory, this instantly presents major conceptual difficulties to those with LD. It is preferable to start by looking at examples of solids and liquids, encouraging pupils to focus on what physical characteristics the two groups of material display. Gases should be considered last as they are trickier to make tangible without being associated with a solid or liquid in which they can be contained. The two concepts in this topic that require a shift from concrete thinking (Piagetian level 2, or Johnstone's (1991) macroscopic representation) are deliberately at the end of the list so that this is not encountered early in each lesson or made a focus of the beginning of the topic.

Lesson 1: Comparing examples of solids, liquids and gases

These can be everyday substances and objects, such as a piece of wood, a cup, tap water, cold tea, air in a balloon and helium in a balloon. For learners who have very limited capacity for processing information, it would be wise to start with solids and liquids, which are more tangible, and establishing the difference in their properties. Solids and gases can then be compared in a similar way and the distinctive properties of gases noted. Finally, liquids and gases can be compared, which should consolidate awareness of both these states.

The next phase of the lesson could then be differentiated with some pupils identifying the state of a further set of materials, to consolidate their ability to classify material into the three groups, whilst other could consider why the different states have their different properties. The use of so-called runny solids, such as sand, sugar or red lentils, can be used with both groups, as it can develop their understanding that fluidity is seen when pieces (whether they are visible or too small to see) of the material are able to move over each other.

Pupils can then extend their understanding of the relationship between state, properties and uses by considering which of a set of materials could be used for given purposes. For example, pupils could be asked to match samples of the materials to cards giving their state and some key properties and to their use. Some examples are shown in Figure 4.1.

Material	State at room temperature	Use
Carbon dioxide	Gas	Bubbles in fizzy pop, push the air away from fires to put them out.
Water	Liquid	To drink, to cool things down, to dissolve things
Iron	Solid	To make objects that are strong and have the right shape e.g. nails, tools
Glass	Solid	To let light through but keep liquids where they should be
Vegetable oil	Liquid	To mix into food, to fry food, to stop objects rubbing against each other
Stone	Solid	To make objects that are strong and heat proof e.g. walls, fireplaces
Petrol	Liquid	To flow into fuel tanks to be stored, to be turned into a gas so it burns easily in engines
Hand gel	Liquid	To spread over skin to stop any disease causing 'bugs'
Oxygen	Gas	To get into animals' lungs and to react with fuels to make them burn
Mercury	Liquid	Used in thermometers to show what temperature something is
Sugar	Solid	Can be sprinkled on food to make it crispy or dissolved in drinks and food

Figure 4.1 Some materials, their state at room temperature and their uses.

Lesson 2: Classifying more mixtures

Looking at mixtures and seeing whether they behave in the way that would be expected from the constituent parts is a useful way to reinforce the properties of the three states. Suitable mixtures might include examples of:

- Foams (liquid and air), for example detergent solution and air, hair mousse or bathroom cleaning foam
- Emulsions (two or more different liquids), for example mayonnaise
- Suspensions (small pieces of solid in a liquid), for example cornflour and water, jelly, hair gel

These mixtures offer the opportunity for pupils to do some simple chemical engineering activities, trying different proportions of each component and seeing how the properties change. Adding increasing amounts of water to cornflour makes the mixture less thick and easier to stir, for instance, but less water gives a fluid that stiffens when you apply pressure to it and which has been called 'liquid armour'. An activity that enables pupils to see this effect is shown in Figure 4.2.

Similarly, they could look at the 'pourability' of different prepared jelly samples which contain different amounts of edible jelly.

Lesson 3: Changes of state

Having securely established the three states of matter and associated properties, the focus can move on to changing matter form one state to another. Note that it is still not essential for pupils to have fully grasped the notion of atoms or molecules as this is notoriously difficult concept to grasp fully, and it can be considered very small pieces and this concept can still be considered at the level of 'stuff'. If it is essential for the assessment that pupils will undergo, or you feel that some have a secure grasp of the different states, this may be a point to introduce formal particle theory, either as a physical model (often done using pupils as model particles) or using digital

Figure 4.2 Investigating 'liquid armour'.

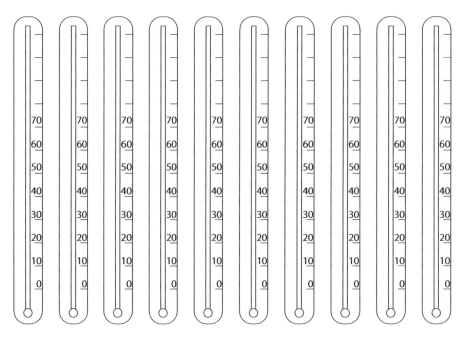

Figure 4.3 A chart for recording changes in temperature.

animations. These can be used to visualise what is happening during the changes of state. They can understand that solid material can turn to liquid material without grasping the particle model that is used to explain this. Equally, this is a common point to introduce this for those who are able to understand it, even if only partially, as it helps to explain at a deeper level the association between energy transfer and changing state.

A common approach to melting and boiling is to heat up ice. Ice is readily available and low risk, though bear in mind the risk of steam burns. The classic approach is to heat up ice in a beaker over a Bunsen burner and take its temperature. If so, I would not recommend that this is the pupils' first use of the Bunsen burner, as the demands of using the burner and executing the experiment are liable to exceed what many learners can process. A trial attempt, simply heating up some water as a prelude to the ice-melting experiment, is advisable. The other problem that may be encountered is the gathering of data about the rising temperature whilst heating. Rather than having pupils timing the readings of their thermometer (this may be difficult for some) and recording them, I would use a set of thermometers such as that shown in Figure 4.3, on which they could colour the height of the blue fill or red fill in the thermometer. This could still be done every minute but I might undertake to call out each time a reading needed (or use a digital timer that went off every minute), which reduces the number of things the pupils need to focus on. They would still get a representation of the temperature changes over time and have a record of how it plateaus at the start, then rises rapidly once the ice has melted, before changing more slowly as boiling point is approached then plateauing once more at boiling point. (Note that this is not 100°C if the water is not pure or the atmospheric pressure is not 1 atm. For this reason, tap water in hard areas commonly boils at 103°C in my experience.)

One of the great benefits of using water as a typical substance (though it is not typical in lots of ways, chemically speaking!) is that pupils can also see the vapour coming off the hot water and so have tangible evidence of water existing in all three states.

'An alternative approach to melting a solid, which may present fewer risks and does not rely in Bunsen burners, is to use stearic acid. This is widely sold in the form of waxy granules and is used for candle making; it is inexpensive. The granules can be put in a test tube standing in a beaker. Then near-boiling water form a kettle can be poured into the beaker and the temperature of the thermometer read each minute, as described previously.

The concept cartoon discussion about how to stop a snowman form melting (Naylor & Keogh, 2000) can be a useful activity as it both considers what is needed to make a solid melt and also links to the real-life issue of the rapid melting of the polar ice caps.

Lesson 4: Applications of state of matter

It can be useful, if time and your access to lab glassware permits to build upon the previous lesson by reinforcing the reversibility of the changes in state. This underlines that the chemical has not been turned into a new chemical but just its state. A follow up to the boiling of water experiment could be to generate steam and passing it through a water-cooled (Liebig) condenser, then the condensed water frozen back to ice, showing the complete state of water cycle. (It is expedient to have some pre-frozen ice ready to show rather than waiting for the same sample to be frozen!) If you have heated stearic acid previously, you could show how their test tubes from the last lesson have now re-solidified as they cooled.

You might usefully consolidate learning up to this point by consider the uses of solids, liquids and gases, and their interconversion. This could take the form of a 'circus' of mini-experiments with questions relating to different scenarios, for example:

- Why do we use liquid chocolate to coat chocolate biscuits?
- What changes of state take place when a candle burns?
- Why do manufacturers make ceiling paint solid, not liquid, when it is in the pot?
- When we dry things by heating them up, for example putting wet clothes in a tumble drier or heating salt water to make salt crystals, what happens to the liquid water?
- How do the bubbles in a fizzy drink make it nice to drink?
- Why do we use things that turn easily into a gas when we want a nice smell, for example perfume or room freshener?
- Fires happen when gases react together, do fire extinguishers use gases to put the fire out? (Your local fire service may well be happy to help you to talk about fire safety and supply educational resources for this. It is also possible to make a small-scale fire extinguisher to demonstrate. Instructions are on the RSC Teach Chemistry website.)

Whichever scenario(s) are chosen should be relevant to the pupils' everyday experiences and, where relevant, to local industries and industrial heritage.

Lesson 5: Comparing anti-freezes

It is common to conclude a topic with an investigation. This both reinforces prior learning and provides an ideal opportunity for individualised support or additional challenge, whilst developing investigative skills and promoting scientific literacy. For those pupils who have understood the idea of particles or small pieces, anti-freeze can be described as a substance that gets in between the water particles and stops them getting close together and sticking. For those who are still working at the macroscopic level, it is sufficient to say that the anti-freeze makes it harder for ice to form and easier to melt ice.

In this investigation, you could investigate the de-frosting power of different substances upon ice cubes. The activity can be related to the application of anti-freeze to icy car windows on cold days. Although regular anti-freeze liquid for cars can be used, you may prefer to use other low-toxicity substances. These include table salt (sodium chloride), glycerol (a naturally occurring oily liquid that is added to icing to stop it being very brittle) sugar or urea crystals. Although it is tempting to be highly directive about how pupils do the investigation, emphasising the need for a fair test or controlling variables, there is often more learning gain in letting them try it out themselves, including making their own mistakes. They could choose to compare the different substances or look at the effect of different concentrations of one, or try out the effect of mixtures of anti-freeze compounds.

If time permits, they can suggest a follow up investigation arising from their findings and different solutions, of their choice or yours, can be put in ice cube compartments and put in the freezer. They can then see which mixtures froze and which ones did not. Using food colouring to distinguish the different experiments is recommended. A possible approach is set out in the 'Life in the freezer' materials available online through the STEM learning website. The approach creates a higher level of logistical demand on you and your technicians, however, and is also lengthier which is why the de-frosting investigation may be more practicable.

Materials

The coverage of materials as a collective term for substances that are useful may be spread out between different modules, depending on your school's practice. Those working outside mainstream settings may, however, find this a useful banner under which to teach a set of ideas in a format that they can support with hands on activities. Accepting that many with learning difficulties will struggle with the formal concept of atoms and molecules, it is a useful opportunity to develop their understanding of the relationship between the properties of materials and what they are made of.

The following lessons are intended collectively to give pupils the chance to meet the following learning intentions:

- To know how materials are different from each other
- To understand that these differences make materials useful for different uses
- To explain what makes materials different from each other
- To know how materials can be changed from one sort into another sort
- To recognise that humans change many materials to make them more useful

Lesson 1: Mixtures and single substances

Teaching about mixtures is an excellent place to start because it lets pupils see the connection between real-world things and how scientists think about them. I have deliberately called the constituent components of a mixture a single substance, rather than a simple one, lest there be any confusion between a chemically pure substance, one that is uniform in its composition and properties, and a 'simple substance', which is also used to describe an element.

There are lots of mixtures that can be separated without specialist lab equipment, such as flour and whole grains, sand and gravel, which are relevant to their preparation. (Whole grains that get through the milling process can be separated and returned to the mill for further grinding when flour, whilst sand and gravel are quarried together and can then be separated for different purposes.) My own favourite is the separation of rock salt (road grit) because it can be linked to later work on rocks and Earth materials and is a material that is seen everywhere, so is universally recognised by pupils. You can buy a bag from hardware shops if you can't get any from school. I usually start by asking pupils to think about how we could separate the two 'ingredients' and a few minutes trying to sieve it can really prepare them for the need for a method that doesn't rely on the size of the pieces. If pupils need further scaffolding, ask them what happens to the rock salt when it goes on the road and what is left once the ice melts, which may help them to recognise that the salt dissolves but the sand and rock do not.

In a lab, the mixture can be warmed over a Bunsen but water formed in the kettle is quite enough. A filter funnel and filter paper are used to filter the rock and sand off (apart from the very small grains of sand). Out of the lab, wooden coffee stirrer can be used to stir the mixture and it can be filtered through several layers of paper towel or kitchen roll spread out in a kitchen sieve.

The activity can be done at two levels, qualitative and quantitative. In the space of a lesson, there will not be time to do both but, if you can do this over two lessons, pupils can try out the separation method in the first lesson and focus on weighing the rock salt in the next lesson. Allowing for the time it takes for salt to evaporate and the sand to dry, it is advised that you ask all the pupils to separate a pre-weighed sample (25 g is plenty, using 100 cm^3 water keeps the evaporation time manageable). You can then weigh the dry sand and salt in the second lesson and work out the proportion of each. I would recommend the bar method (see Section 2, Figure 2.9) as a way to help pupils to understand the relationship between the weights of the rock salt and the rock/sand plus the salt.

Lesson 2: Mixtures and single substances

Chromatography (colour writing) is a staple of school chemistry and, in more sophisticated forms, is used widely in research and industry. This separation technique can be carried out with ink, such as in water soluble felt tip pens, or food colourings. These are usually linked to a forensics style context, such as 'who wrote the ransom note when a theft took place?' It is possible to do this out of the lab using strong white paper towels if you cannot obtain filter paper. To obtain suitably small spots, I strongly recommend the use of cocktail sticks which are inexpensive and can be disposed of, in preference to glass capillary tubing which often snaps.

Although this is a safe and low-cost experiment, which can be repeated if errors are made, the method has multiple stages and so presents genuine challenges for pupils with processing or recall difficulties. One of the most helpful ways to reduce the cognitive load is to get the paper marked (in pencil, in case biro ink runs) before any spots of colour go on to it. If the level that the water should reach is shown to be below the level at which the ink is spotted, you can minimise the risk of washing the ink sample off by mistake at the start. Similarly, marking the level to which the water should rise before you take the paper out helps pupils to know when to remove it. I have also found it helpful to hang the paper from a wooden splint using blue tack, rather than trying to secure it with paper clips or hang it over the edge of the beaker or jam jar. These modifications are shown in the instruction sheet in Figure 2.6. Note that laminating it will let pupils tick off each stage as it is complete, which helps them to recall what they have already done and what needs doing next.

Pupils do not generally seem to find the analysis of the results difficult as, by looking at the paper, they can directly compare the colour(s) that emerge from the reference colour, say the ink from the ransom note, with the colours from the other ink samples. Pupils with colour vision impairment may use a colour identifier app (which will give the name of the colour that it is pointed at and may speak its name) but can usually manage well by comparing the distances that the different colours move to identify which inks contain the same colour.

Lesson 3: Solutions and dissolving

Having seen that some colours move faster in water than others in the chromatography activity, looking at dissolving is a logical next step. This lesson uses household items and, whilst it takes some planning to get the different materials assembled, can be done outside a lab.

My favourite introduction is to gather the pupils round and to tell them the story of the Parsis (Persians) coming to the city of Mumbai (former Bombay) in India. I have learnt that story telling is a great 'hook' into science learning and recalls Reid and Hodson's (1987) observation that narrative is the most accessible form of communication. It is a nice activity to prompt discussions about citizenship, why people travel, how we should respond to strangers. As props, I use a watch glass (a saucer would work as well), a beaker or jug of water, some table salt and a nice head scarf. I put the watch glass or saucer on the scarf, the scarf representing a priceless rug on the floor of a beautiful palace. You can enhance the atmosphere by displaying an Indian palace at the same time. I tell them that

The Parsis came hundreds of years ago from a country called Persia, where they were being punished because they did not follow the same religion as the rulers of Persia. The Parsis fled their homeland and travelled until they reached Mumbai. Their leader went to speak to the local prince who ruled the area, to ask for permission to settle. The prince said that they could not because the city of Mumbai was very full, there was not room for any more people in it. The Parsi leader then asked for a bowl of milk to drink and some salt, because he was very thirsty after his long journey. The prince did not want these refugees to stay but did not want to be rude, so he called a servant to bring a jug of milk, a bowl to drink from and some salt. The Parsi leader put the bowl on the floor in front of where he was sitting and poured milk into it until it could not hold another drop. (At this point, put the watch glass or saucer on the scarf and fill it until the water is bulging from the top but not overs=flowing.) *The Parsi leader then picked up the salt and said to the prince, 'My people will be to your city, what this salt is to this milk'. He took a pinch of the salt and held it over the water.* Pause at this point and ask the pupils whether the milk will spill when the salt is added? The bowl is already completely full and if the visitor gets milk on the beautiful carpet the prince will be very angry and throw them all into prison or cut off their heads. Ask pupils whether he should risk adding the salt or not? Why do they think that? Finally sprinkle a generous pinch of salt into the water; it does not overflow. *The Parsi leader told the prince that they would 'flavour' the city make it more interesting and better, but not push out the people who were there already. The prince gave in and agreed that they could stay. There are still Parsis on Mumbai and they are famous for three contributions to the city's life; being successful merchants who buy and sell goods, being good doctors and being very funny comedians. In this way they have added character to the city without overwhelming it.*

Pupils can start by exploring the question of 'what dissolves?' by testing out everyday materials in a beaker (or any other container, preferably with colourless sides) of cold water. Suitable examples include sugar, instant coffee, coffee grounds, tea leaves, flour, dried milk, salt, rock salt, a piece of fizzy vitamin C tablet, piece of grated candle wax. It is interesting to ask them to predict which will dissolve, as this encourages them to draw on everyday experiences. They can then record whether the substance dissolves, using a simple results chart of the kind shown at: https://edu.rsc.org/download?ac=14845. Pupils should be encouraged to note that dissolving substances produce a transparent liquid, if the liquid is cloudy, it means that there are still pieces of the stuff big enough for us to see. They should also have their attention drawn to the fact that we have not melted the stuff because we have not heated the water. The candle wax is useful to illustrate this point.

Once they have added small amounts of the different substances to water, you will be left with some solutions and quite a lot of suspensions. Ask pupils to tip the contents of the experiment into a nylon kitchen sieve over a bucker or large beaker so that you catch the solid particles rather than them blocking the drains. They may notice that the solutions go through the sieve (very noticeable with instant coffee or tea infusion) but that other mixtures leave bits behind, such as coffee grounds or tea leaves. Milk powder and flour create a cloudy liquid that passes through the sieve, showing that the pieces are bigger than in the solutions but not as big as some of the solids that are trapped by the sieve. They are suspensions, rather than mixtures.

The next thing to look at is how dissolving changes when we heat the liquid up. This can be done successfully out of a lab if you can have kettles in the room. Pupils can be asked to see how many teaspoons of sugar they can get to dissolve in a fixed volume of water at different temperatures. (The potential difficulties of measuring volume can be overcome by marking the level on the receptacle using a water-resistant marker pen or even placing a rubber band at the desired height on the container.) Pupils can be provided with a prepared results chart showing the temperature of the water and the number of spoonsful of sugar that dissolved. (They do not need to measure temperature accurately, they can simply describe it as cold, warm, very warm, hot boiling.) A clear trend should be visible, which is the hotter the water, the more sugar dissolves. If the hottest solution is put aside to cool until the next lesson, they will see sugar crystals forming because the cool water cannot dissolve as much sugar as the hot water did. In other words, the sugar can 'undissolve' again. This demonstrates that the sugar has not disappeared but broken into such tiny particles that we cannot see them.

A further investigation could be conducted into how different sized pieces of stuff dissolve. This could look at how quickly the same amount, for example a teaspoonful of different types of sugar (icing sugar, caster sugar, granulated sugar and coffee sugar crystals), dissolve. The beakers can be set up in a row and the sugar put in in quick succession, then dissolving time compared. The different sugars put into a rank order. Pupils will see that bigger pieces dissolve more slowly. The results can be explained in terms of dissolving involves the breaking up of the sugar into tiny pieces; icing sugar is already in much smaller pieces, so does not take as much breaking up to dissolve.

Returning to the legend of the Parsis makes a good plenary activity. Can they now explain what happened? What advice would they give to the Parsi if he ever wanted to do this again and be even more sure that it would work? (Pupils may suggest fine ground salt, warm milk) What should the Prince of Mumbai do to stop any unwanted visitors tricking him again with the milk and salt request? (Give the visitor large salt crystals, make sure the milk is really cold, smear detergent in the bowl to stop the 'bulge of the water forming so it spills more easily.)

Lesson 4: Elements around us

It is important to understand that the notion of an element conveys two distinct ideas. One is the idea of the simplest substance, one that cannot be broken down any further into anything purer or simpler, and the other is of an atomic 'building block' from which new substances can be built up. The first definition stems from the days before we had the idea of an atom and so maybe especially useful for pupils who will find the notion of intangible particles inaccessible. Bear in mind that it served some very influential chemists perfectly well and is certainly sufficient for pupils at lower secondary level.

Conveying the notion of not being possible to break it down any more is much simpler if you have a lab available to show some attempts to break things down. As pupils carry out or watch each experiment, underline the point that the parent chemical is very different from the elements that it is made from. Below are two sets of experiments that could be carried out to support this idea; if you do both, you can probably expect this to be a two-lesson slot.

First, microscale approaches make it possible to do electrolysis on a very small scale so that pupils can break down compounds, including those that release chlorine gas, in a well-ventilated room (Worley & Paterson, 2021). Microscale chemistry can be used to show the breaking down of copper chloride to form copper metal and chlorine gas. Sodium chloride (table salt) solution can also be broken down to release chlorine, although sodium is not formed because it is too reactive to exist as an element in water.

The same microscale apparatus can also be used to split acidified water into hydrogen and oxygen (just add drops of dilute bench acid until indicator paper shows it is just acidic). The splitting up of the water into two gases is very visible and, although the amounts do not permit you to test them with a glowing or lit splint, the faster rate of hydrogen production (at the negative electrode) is very visible. Whilst this approach does not show the relative quantities of the two gases, it is certainly sufficient to establish that water is not an element but can be broken down into elements.

Second, as a demonstration of breaking down a compound, copper carbonate undergoes very visible changes. Combining two standard practical activities, heating copper carbonate and reacting copper (II) oxide with sulphuric acid, you can break down the parent compound into one of its constituent elements. Methods for each of these are widely available, see for instance the RSC Education website and the Practical Chemistry website, respectively. [See https://edu .rsc.org/experiments/thermal-decomposition-of-metal-carbonates/450.article https://edu.rsc.org/ experiments/reacting-copperii-oxide-with-sulfuric-acid/1917.article]

Although both these experiments are done by upper secondary pupils, I would suggest that there is a lot of 'noise' in each of the activities (Johnstone, 1991) and a demonstration enables you to focus on the 'signal', the message that substances are made of elements (simplest substances) and we can break substances down into their elements. Although it is not possible directly to separate out the carbon and oxygen, the loss in weight can be very clearly shown as the carbon dioxide is evolved. Done as a demonstration, this can be an opportunity to show the use of a balance and to set out the calculation of the loss in weight of the pre-heated tube of green powder by subtracting the weight of the black copper oxide powder that is formed. If you think that this is liable to cause delay and distraction, a simple balance can be constructed from a suspended ruler. If you have two pre-weighed heatproof test tubes whose weight balance prior to heating, you can remove one and heat it. You can show that a gas is being produced by having a delivery tube attached to the tube you are heating and collecting the gas over water, remembering to remove it before removing the Bunsen burner. (This can be tested with lime water but I don't think this adds to the narrative of breaking down the copper carbonate and simply adds unnecessarily to the cognitive load pupils have to bear.) Once cool enough to handle safely, re-suspend it to show that the heated powder is now lighter, because it has broken down to release a gas. Note that neither the powder nor the gas is an element but they are simpler than copper carbonate, in the sense that it contains only two elements.

(If you wish to show the carbon that is in the gas, a 'hack' to do this is to show the pupils a piece of glassware or ceramic that has previously been held in a yellow Bunsen flame. The soot is made of carbon particles that form when full oxidation of methane is prevented by reduced air flow and so shows the carbon precursor of carbon dioxide, rather than a breakdown product of carbon dioxide. However, this demonstration works perfectly well for the intended purpose!)

The resultant copper oxide can be dissolved in warm 0.5 M sulphuric acid to form copper sulphate. Electrolysis of the copper sulphate solution will then yield copper metal, one of the three elements that made the original copper carbonate.

If you are working outside a lab, you could still do microscale electrolysis. Another possible approach is to use videos to show some of the experiments described above. If you do this, I would limit it to no more than two video clips and would choose the two stages of breaking down copper carbonate into copper as the subjects.

An alternative experiment to show that breaking a compound down yields the elements that it is made of is to break down a metal oxide (copper (II) oxide or silver (I) oxide) with carbon. This can be done by putting a spatula of both the metal oxide and carbon powder on a square of ceramic paper and holding it in a roaring blue flame. Once the mixture has glowed bright orange, the paper should be put into a beaker of cold water. (This can also be carried out in a small ceramic crucible or in a porcelain combustion boat, but this approach demands far greater dexterity. The mixture should be covered with a thing sprinkling of carbon powder to stop the metal formed from re-oxidising instantly.) Pupils are left with a small amount of orange or silver metal which, when cool, can be glued or taped into the pupils' books.

It is tempting to combine the focus on breaking things down to their elements with the counter notion, that of building elements up to make new substances. I would counsel against this because approaching the two ideas in the same lesson, or even using the same experimental approach, is liable to lead to confusion.

Lesson 5: The Periodic Table

The Periodic Table (PT) is so iconic that it is easy to go off on a tangent, or several! I like to present it as a 'chemical dictionary' that lists all the elements that we know about. Pupils may be interested to learn that it was written to help chemistry students remember all the elements,

1 Hydrogen	2 Helium	3 Lithium	4 Beryllium	5 Boron
A very light, colourless gas that burns very easily	A light, colourless gas that does not burn.	A soft, silvery metal that is very light and quite reactive	A soft, silvery-white metal that is light. It is fairly reactive.	A dull black powder. It is very reactive and used to start the fire in fireworks.
6 Carbon	7 Nitrogen	8 Oxygen	9 Fluorine	10 Neon
Usually a dull black solid but also occurs as diamonds. It conducts electricity and can join to lots of different elements.	A colourless gas that does not burn.	A colourless gas that reacts with fuels and makes them burn. Living things need it to get energy from their food.	A very reactive and dangerous gas. It is yellow-green in colour.	A colourless gas that does not burn. If it is put in a lighting tube, it gives out bright red light.
11 Sodium	12 Magnesium	13 Aluminium	14 Silicon	15 Phosphorous. Two sorts:
A soft, grey metal that floats on water. It reacts instantly with air or water.	A silvery-white metal that burns easily and give out a very bright white light.	A light silvery-white, lightweight metal. It is soft and easy to shape.	A non-metal that has very shiny blue-grey crystals. It conducts electricity.	1. A harmless red powder 2. Like white wax but very poisonous. It glows in the dark and catches fire if left in the air.
16 Sulphur	17 Chlorine	18 Argon	19 Potassium	20 Calcium
Is a yellow powder or crystals. It reacts with air to give smelly gases.	A reactive and dangerous gas. It is green in colour.	A colourless gas that does not burn. If it is put in a lighting tube, it gives out very bright white light.	A soft, silvery metal that floats on water. It reacts very quickly with air or water.	A soft, silvery-white metal. It reacts quickly with air or water.

Figure 4.4 The first 20 elements of the Periodic Table.

which they had to learn off by heart as well as what they were like. Those who struggle to memorise large amounts of information are often appreciative of Mendeleev's efforts! Although it can be linked to the atomic structure of each element, this is not needed at this level and is likely simply to bemuse pupils who face additional barriers to learning. Instead, it can be described as listing elements in order of how heavy they are, similar to the way that most dictionaries list words alphabetically. However, that order on its own would simply give us a very long list of almost 120 elements. It is the next bit of the organisation that makes the PT so useful (By 'the' PT we mean the standard medium-form Periodic Table). The list is then 'cut' so that elements that are most like each other are placed in a column above and below each other. In other words, we group by property, even if it means them not quite being in the correct order of their weight. (If additional principals are used to group the elements, we get other types of PT of which there are reckoned to be around 130 different forms in total.)

One way to help pupils see how the PT has been constructed is to give them a long strip of paper, listing the first 20 elements with their number in the order. I would recommend making a document like the one shown in Figure 4.4 and printing it on A3 paper, then cutting it into horizontal strips. (This could also be done by having the elements in separate draggable squares displayed in the same format on an interactive whiteboard.) Get them to check that they are in the right order from the lightest (number 1) to heaviest (number 20). Then ask them to see which of the labelled elements belong in families using samples of the elements, if possible, or using the RSC's interactive PT [https://www.rsc.org/periodic-table] *or elements cards if you have them. Suitable elements for examination are:*

- Oxygen (a test tube of air with a stopper in)
- Nitrogen (a second test tube of air with a stopper in)
- Lump sulphur

- Carbon in the form of a piece of graphite or soft pencil lead with the wooden shaft whittled back to show an appreciable length of graphite
- Aluminium foil (kitchen foil)
- Magnesium ribbon
- Helium in a balloon
- Chlorine gas (which can be made outside the lab by adding an acid, such as vinegar to a small quantity of chlorine-containing bleach) in a small test tube with the bung securely tapes on and placed into a second container, such as screw top jar, to prevent leakage
- Argon, in an old-style (incandescent) light bulb
- Neon, in a car indicator bulb
- Silicon can be bought on-line in small pieces. Note that products, such as baking sheets, labelled as silicon are actually silicone, a polymer-containing silicon and oxygen, rather than the element.
- A piece of lead metal
- Securely sealed mercury, for example a mercury thermometer in a taped clear outer casing

As there is a lot to look at in this list, you will probably find it works better if you give them fewer elements, rather than all the one above, perhaps half to each of two groups. Ask pupils to look at the elements, their appearance and uses, and to put them into chemical 'families'. It may help them to colour in the element's squares withal the similar elements colour coded the same colour or shown with a distinct symbol (star, triangle). If time permits, get different groups to work together to see that the 'tricky to place' elements may have become easier to group as more elements were discovered. Based on the similarities, where would they cut the strip so that the most similar elements lie in a column? Although this is a challenging task, it encourages careful observation and underlines the importance of judgement when grouping the elements.

If you have access to a lab, this is a great excuse to go on to look at the Group 1 metals and calcium, if available. This usually helps to clinch the way that the strip should be cut. It doesn't matter that their cut strips give a table that is not like the standard one; that only happens if you make the cuts at the second, tenth and eighteenth elements points. What you can say is that scientists grew a lot more confident about what elements went into which families as they discovered more and more about each of the elements.

Lesson 6: Insulators and conductors

This is a lesson that can be placed into the topic on electricity, in which case the materials tested do not need to be elements, and also comes well after a look at the PT. In the latter case, pupils can look at different elements and relate their behaviour as conductors and insulator to where on the PT they are shown. The approach suggested does not consider what happens when an electric current flows, or the nature of the charge, it is simply treated as a mass flow of electricity and with it the energy to light up the bulb. By viewing it this way, conductors (meaning 'guide through') allow electricity to pass through whilst insulators (meaning 'island') stop the electricity from moving.

The elements listed under lesson 4 (apart from chlorine gas) can now be augmented with additional metals from the d-block (central block) of the PT, including copper and iron. They can infer that the argon and neon don't conduct because of the way they behave in the light bulbs. They are often very surprised that graphite (carbon) conducts, providing it is not snapped. If you have a lump of graphite, rather than a pencil, it only conducts along the layers, not across the layers. Pupils will often ask to test silver and gold jewellery but be aware that these are rarely pure and alloys (mixtures of metals) conduct much less well than the pure metal element.

The lesson takes the form of using a simple circuit with a low voltage power source, leads, a light bulb and a pair of crocodile clips at the end of two adjacent leads. Pupils should check that the circuit works by touching the crocodile clips and seeing that the bulb lights up. They can then test a range of materials by placing it between the crocodile clips and seeing whether the bulb lights up. They can record their results in a simple results table or by sorting the materials into two groups, 'lets the bulb light' and 'doesn't let the bulb light'. Once they have done this, see what patterns they can deduce. They usually see the correlation between being a metal and letting the bulb light up quite quickly. Conversely, the non-metals sulphur, oxygen and nitrogen do not carry electricity and, correspondingly, the bulb does not light up. They may well be slightly puzzled by the carbon and, if available, the silicon which they do not expect to carry electricity.

At this point, ask them to look at a PT and find where the electricity carrying elements are (colouring in the squares in one colour, or marking with a symbol, is a good idea). Then do the same for the electricity blockers (insulators), using a different colour or symbol. Encourage them to reflect on where the carriers and blocker sit on the PT. Finally, do the same with any 'surprising' element(s) and they will notice that they sit in between. They can be thought of an 'in between elements', part electricity carriers (if the electricity goes along the layers) and part electricity blockers (across the layers).

The lesson can be used to reinforce ideas about the PT as a dictionary of elements, where they occur on it tells us more about them, and to recognise how to test whether a substance carries or blocks electricity or can do both. If it is made to do both, the reinforcement of previous learning provides the type of rehearsal that learners with LD find especially beneficial and other pupils will not have their learning impeded by it.

Lesson 7: Different types of rocks and the rock cycle

Although Earth materials as a discrete curriculum requirement has fluctuated in significance, with it frequently being explicitly required only in passing, there is much to commend this as a context for exploring key concepts taught in topics that are more dominant in the curriculum. A session on the three main groups of rocks reinforces ideas about natural cycles and the interconversion of materials by both natural processes and human activity. It also consolidates concepts about how the composition of a material affects its properties and, on account of that, its uses. The other feature of rocks and other Earth materials is that they are ubiquitous and it is easy to find examples to look at, plus local field work to do. They thus offer extensive opportunities for concrete learning, which is especially beneficial for those with LD.

The teaching of this topic is often much impeded by teachers' keenness to impart all the names of the rocks on pupils who can easily develop cognitive overload. I would advise focusing on the three main groups of rocks: sedimentary (made of small solids that settle out of water), metamorphic (meaning 'changing shape' because they are modified sedimentary rocks) and igneous (fiery, formed by hot lava from below the Earth's surface) rocks. My approach is to use very concrete models and to avoid using technical terms until the main features of the three groups of rock are firmly established.

Igneous rocks can be modelled by making sugar glass. This emphasises the role of extreme heat in making them; at this stage, I refer to them as 'boiled rocks' to make the point. Pupils could do this in the lab with close supervision. If you do not have a lab, this can be made at home. The important thing is not to allow the sugar glass itself the focus but to consider how it resembles material made from molten rock.. To make it, you need to boil 100 g sucrose (table sugar) with 25 g glucose powder (which can be bought over the counter in a pharmacy) and 40 cm³ tap water. Boil it until it reaches between 145°C and 155°C, at which point it looks very impressive as it boils away; however, it should not be turning brown. Then pour it into a non-stick baking tray (or previously greased baking tray, or one lined with baking parchment). It will form a 'puddle' and then set over the next half hour or so, which may make it advisable to prepare one in advance even if you are going to make it in class. It can then be lifted off the non-stick surface.

The complete piece of sugar glass can be passed round for the pupils to feel. They can be asked what it is like and they will probably offer descriptions such as smooth, shiny and 'like glass'. These descriptors can be noted down and later used to identify igneous rocks. It is also a good idea to encourage pupils to take photos of their three rock models as they make them.

The next stage is the breaking up of the 'rock'. Although in real life this happens over thousands of years through the action of wind and freeze-thaw, this can be modelled by hammering the sugar glass (wear safety specs) or applying a rolling pin to the sugar glass and pressing down hard on it. This will be less messy of the sugar glass is put in a strong plastic bag before breaking it up. The fragments of 'rock' form sedimentary rocks.

Sedimentary rocks are made from small pieces of rock that are carried by rivers until the water slows, usually when it enters an ocean and the particles drop out. They are then cemented together by minerals in the water. In our model, 'bitty rock' is made from the pieces of sugar glass held together by play dough (play dough made at home from flour, oil and salt is ideal, bought play dough works but plasticene is too stiff to work). The pupils can work the sugar glass fragments gently into the play dough to make the 'bitty' rock. If they have used homemade play dough, they can put a small lump of play dough into a plastic box and pour water on to it to model the weathering of the rock. They will observe that the cement washes away leaving the small pieces of the model igneous rock. This illustrates how sedimentary rocks are easily weathered due to the cement breaking up and wear away more quickly than the other two groups of rock.

Keeping half the bitty rock for comparison, they use the rest of their model sedimentary rock, they can make a model of metamorphic rock, which I introduce as 'squashed rock'. In real life, the pressure comes from new layers of rock forming on top of them and the heat from the centre of the Earth makes them slightly softer and easier to squash. (Eventually they are pushed so far down that they melt and the material that they are made from becomes liquid rock. When the liquid rock is pushed out to the surface of the Earth, the cycle begins once more.) To do this, they need to flatten the play dough and sugar glass mixture and then fold the outside third of their pancake over the middle third. They should do this several times, noticing that the play dough warmed by their hands become more stretchy. They should then see that the sugar pieces are now no longer orientated randomly but are generally lying pointing along the long surface of their pancake, at right angles to the direction of pressure. This shows why metamorphic or squashed rocks have flat layers.

The different stages and the conversion of one type to the other can then be summarised on a suitable diagram of the rock chart. It may be helpful to have this superimposed on a diagram of the structure of the Earth, so that the processes can be recorded at the corresponding point on the diagram (igneous rocks around volcanoes, sedimentary rocks where rivers discharge into oceans, metamorphic rocks buried beneath surface layers of rock).

Lesson 8: Using rocks

If it is not possible for pupils to see rocks being used, it is also possible to gather rock samples, either by asking a monumental stone mason for samples, or collecting them when you are travelling around, or buying a commercial set of rock samples. However, the best learning is likely to come from seeing rocks in use and connecting their properties and their uses. Graveyards, especially older graveyards, are an ideal place to observe them, providing a risk assessment indicates no undue hazards at the site. Towns with buildings made form stone are another potential source of observational data. I would recommend not attempting to identify the individual rocks used but to focus on which of the three groups ('boiled', 'bitty' or 'squashed') they are in. (If pupils are insistent, there are apps for rock identification but there is the risk that you lose the key ideas in a surfeit of detail.) As pupils observe the rocks get them firstly to assign them to one of the three groups. As an alternative to photos, they can create rock rubbings with wax crayon and pieces of paper to show the surface of the rock. Then encourage them to notice what they are being used for, if their use is not ornamental, and how much they have weathered. One of the benefits of looking at gravestones is that they have dates, so pupils can compare stones of very similar ages when they assess how easily they are worn away. At the end of the visit, the plenary should collate their observations. A typical set of findings would be:

- Boiled/igneous rocks are very hard and shiny. They weather very little because they are very hard. (Although this cannot be directly observed, they are also very dense, so costly to transport.) Their extreme hardness makes them difficult to carve. This makes them the costliest stone to use.
- Bitty/sedimentary rocks are soft and weather the most. It is possible to see the small grains in them and these can be felt if pupils rub them with their fingers. It may be discernible that some layers wear away more quickly than others making the weathering uneven. They are easy to carve, so often used for very ornate stones.
- Squashed/metamorphic rocks are smooth because they are cut in the direction of the layers. They are hard, though not quite as hard as igneous rocks, and so weather very slowly.

Acids and alkalis

This is yet another chemistry topic that rests on the notion of grouping chemicals by their properties. It is also a topic that is especially feasible outside the laboratory, as it can be taught using everyday household materials. My advice on teaching about the two groups of substances is not to attempt cover the two major groups in one introductory lesson, but to consider acids in one lesson and make sure pupils have grasped what the distinctive features of acids are before moving on to alkalis in a separate lesson. Otherwise, you risk ending up with a problem I call 'same but different' where the details are not sufficiently different, so merge and become muddled, requiring further work to unscramble the confusion. When doing practical work, it may be helpful to use a quick-to-decipher code on the bottles to distinguish between acid and alkalis, for example a red triangle for acids and blue circle for alkalis. This helps to aid identification by pupils who are struggling to read the words on the label and those who have a colour vision impairment.

The combined learning intentions of this set of lessons are:

- To know how to recognise an acid
- To know how to recognise an alkali
- To understand how scientists use indicators to show whether a substance is an acid or an alkali
- To understand how acids and alkalis change each other when they react together
- To recognise some common reactions that involve acids and alkalis reacting

A lesson sequence might look like this:

Lesson 1: What are acids?

In this lesson, pupils can consider the properties of acids, as illustrated by everyday examples.

- They taste sour if edible, for example as the acid in lemon juice or vinegar. If they are working outside the lab, they can experience this directly. For any tasting activity, I recommend wooden coffee stirrers be dipped in tap water (if it is a powder, no need if it is a solution) and then into the substance, pupils can then taste the substance and throw the wooden stirrer away.
- Change the colour of indicators ('acid testers'). The topic of indicators is considered in more detail in another lesson and I would simply use universal indicator at this point.
- React with metals and metal 'tarnish'/rust. Although commonly not a requirement at this level, I include this characteristic because it enables pupils to carry out a simple investigation into which acid makes the best cleaner for tarnished copper (old 1 and 2 pence pieces are perfect). They can compare various acids, for instance those in lemon juice, vinegar, cola and a cut piece of rhubarb stalk. This helps them to remember that these all belong in the same group, acids, whilst giving them valuable experience of designing a simple and safe investigation.

As a plenary, pupils can be asked to use what they have learnt to design a logo for acids, which consolidates their learning and be used later as an *aide memoire*.

Lesson 2: What are alkalis?

Having spent the previous lesson focusing on the properties of acids, the second lesson can now shift the focus on to alkalis (an Arab word meaning 'the salt' because they are commonly white powders until they are dissolved).There is some debate about how to define alkalis in an accessible but accurate way, the opposite of acids is not strictly true; if it were, they would taste sweet rather than sour and put the tarnish back on the 2 pence coins! The term 'antacid' which I quite often use, or the expression that they 'cure the acid', is seen by some to imply that they destroy acids when they do not, although they do reduce the acidity and lessen or remove the acidic properties. However, the acid can re-form so has not been destroyed. The most accurate way to describe them is that they react with acids.

It is helpful to show the properties of alkalis in a chart that considers the same variables as the three headings under which the properties of acids were considered, taste, effect on an indicator and reactions.

Alkalis that are edible taste bitter. Pupils can test a small amount of baking soda (sodium hydrogen carbonate) to verify this.

Alkalis change the colour of indicators but in a different way to acids. This can be shown with universal indicator paper or solution.

Alkalis do not react with metals or metal 'tarnish' in the way acids do; this can be shown by putting a tarnished coin into a solution of an alkali, such as baking soda. They react with acids and stop them being acidic. (This can be demonstrated by getting an alkali to react with the weak acids in the grease that occurs on your skin. If they dip a finger in baking soda solution then rub it on the back of their hand, it will feel soapy.)

This may be a suitable point to discuss a good term for alkalis of the options given above, based on what they have found out. Design of a second logo, this time for alkalis, could be set as a plenary task and they could discuss the differences between their two logos with a partner.

If time permits a practical investigation, pupils could be asked to consider how similar alkalis are to each other by testing the effect of different alkalis and different concentrations of the same alkali on universal indicator. This can help to add a further level of understanding to what we mean by a chemical group, which contains chemicals that are broadly similar in several ways – such as tasting bitter or feeling soapy to touch – but not identical.

Lesson 3: Making and using different indicators

This is a standard lesson and one that is well liked by pupils and teachers. The classic source of indicator is red cabbage, because it contains three different colour molecules that change colour at different pH values, meaning that it has several detectable colour changes. Other possible sources of indicators, which are single colour change indicators, include red Poinsettia petals (good for pre-Christmas lessons!), turmeric, breakfast tea, cochineal food colouring and butterfly pea tea. I would suggest that you limit the number of indicators, preferably no more than four being tested or confusion may reign. The chosen indicator sources do not need boiling over a Bunsen burner, they can be made as infusions by adding boiling water from the kettle and, if filter funnels and paper are not to hand, the infusion can be strained through a kitchen sieve or tea strainer.

The recording of results can be made very easy by preparing a sheet for the experiment to be done on (once the sheet is laminated) and a corresponding sheet such as that shown in Figure 4.5. Notice that the sheet introduces the concept of neutral, which is represented here as being between acids and alkalis. It also skirts round the issue of pH numbers, which can present a major difficulty because there is an inverse relationship between pH number and the concentration of acid, in that a small pH number denotes a higher concentration of acid. As

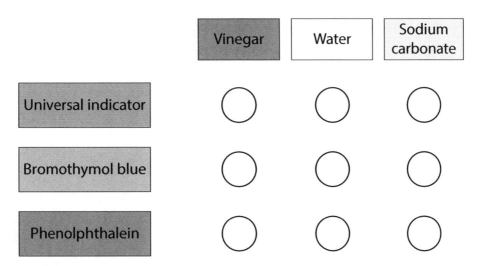

Figure 4.5 A microscale chemistry results sheet for indicators with an acid and an alkali, which also shows which liquids to mix.

indicated in the discussion of Piagetian levels in Section 2, this type of correlation requires a higher level of cognitive reasoning and will be unattainable by the vast majority of pupils with LD of a lower secondary school age. Pupils can then use to record the colour changes they see. This approach requires only one drop of the indicator and one drop of the acid or alkali solution so it only requires very small volumes, making it inexpensive and reducing the risk of the experiment, and is also very easy to clear up. A wipe of the laminate with a paper towel is all that is required.

Once pupils have tested the indicators, they will need orientating with respect to the meaning of their observations. It may help to ask them to talk to a partner about how they would answer the following questions:

- Which indicator gave the most obvious colour change?
- Which indicator gives more than two colours, meaning that it can show different degrees of acidity or alkalinity?
- Which indicator do you think is the cheapest to make?
- If you could only one indicator to do an experiment with acids and alkalis, which one would it be and why?

The plenary of the activity should recap that indicators are acid or alkali detectors. A few indicators can test for both acids and alkalis. The most useful indicators are usually the ones that are 'multi-purpose' and can detect different levels of acidity and alkalinity. That is the reason that universal indicator is so useful. A follow up homework can be to ask pupils to take away a few strips of universal indicator and test liquids around their home, such a juice, tea, coffee, shower gel, toothpaste, cleaning agents, and to see whether each of them is an acid or an alkali. This is a very well-liked activity and the follow up plenary enables the teacher to recap the properties of acids and alkalis. For example, foods are usually acidic, because acids give a sharp taste rather than a bitter one. Cleaning agents are often alkaline because that helps to dissolve grease, as they experienced back in lesson 2.

Lesson 4: Neutralisation 1

There are lots of examples of everyday neutralisation reactions that pupils can carry out in school. I think it is important that the first one that they observe lets them see clearly that when the acid and alkali react together, the acid becomes less acidic and the alkali becomes less neutral. For this reason, I would prefer to start with two liquids to which they can add a familiar indicator (universal) and establish that one solution is acidic, the other alkaline. Pupils can then try mixing the two liquids and see the two liquids being neutralised.

Because I am keen that they see the relevance of the science to their daily lives, I like to contextualise activities where ever possible. The use of indigestion cures to neutralise stomach acid is a plausible context and the pupils can be given 1.0 M hydrochloric acid, labelled 'stomach acid' to test different remedies. (If you are do not have lab facilities, white vinegar can be used.) Pupils should add universal indicator solution to establish that it is indeed an acid. Pupils can be told how much acid to use each time, I would suggest 20 cm^3 looks substantial enough but does not present a management challenge. They can then test the alkali substances that could be used as stomach ache cures. These could be over-the-counter remedies, such as Milk of Magnesia or solutions of alkalis labelled with fictitious names such as 'Gut-eze'. I like to include at least one carbonate solution and give it the name 'Burpo'. When they see the fizz as it goes into the acid, they can well imagine that it would make the drinker burp! They should add universal indicator to each of the remedies in turn and observe that they are all alkaline. They can then put a remedy into a measuring cylinder or draw it up into a large plastic syringe and add the alkali slowly, stopping when the indicator in the acid changes colour to show that the acidity has gone and the solution is more or less neutral. This process enables them to see that both the acidity has gone and so has the alkalinity. They then need to work out how much alkali solution has been used to neutralise the acid. (It may be helpful to mark the start and finish levels with a marker pen or small rubber band around the measuring device so that pupils have a record of the 'before' and 'after' measurements from which to calculate how much alkali was used.) They can then repeat the experiment using a different remedy and evaluate which one has the best acid neutralising powers, that is the one of which the least volume is needed to neutralise the acid. Note that asserting that the best remedy uses the smallest volume presents an inverse relationship and this may well delay understanding. Be prepared to say that is simply the strongest and leave it (for now) at that.

Lesson 5: Neutralisation 2

Bath bombs rely on the reaction between citric acid (which can be purchased over the counter from a pharmacy if you do not have access to laboratory resources) and sodium hydrogen carbonate (sodium bicarbonate/baking soda). This can be done outside the lab, and the most basic of 'recipes' uses twice the weight of the carbonate as the citric acid, for example 30 g of the carbonate and 15 g of citric acid. (Commercial bath bombs contain additional ingredients but they are not needed here.) If you not in a lab, the dry ingredients can be measured out in a 2:1 ratio using scoops that are used to measure volumes of flour or sugar in the kitchen. The two powders should be put in a small container (a disposable coffee cup is fine) lined with cling film. The powders should be mixed together and then oil (cooking oil is fine) is added a few drops at a time, to bind the powder together. The cling film is then lifted out and wrapped around the bath bomb mixture. The mixture is then pressed firmly between your hands to form a solid ball. This can then be dropped into some water and the bomb will explode with bubbles of carbon dioxide made when the acid and carbonate alkali react. If the water has universal indicator in it, they will see that the reaction between the acid and the alkali leaves a neutral solution.

   The activity can be extended by asking pupils to find out what difference the amounts of acid and alkali have on the bath bomb. They can try out different proportions of powders, for example 3:2 or 3:1. Another activity that consolidates their understanding is to ask them to design a wrapper for their bath bomb that explains the science behind it and explaining why the user does not need to worry about their bath being too acidic or alkaline.

Living and non-living things

This module provides multiple opportunities to understand how scientists classify things and the basis upon which they do so. It combines the reassurance of looking at familiar objects with some more open-ended or philosophical questions. It serves as an important platform for other biology topics, such as ecology and genetics. One of the most important aspects of this module is the opportunity for pupils to start to articulate their intuitive knowledge. By modelling ways of thinking about and, very importantly, talking about the basis for judgements, pupils are encouraged to build links between intuitive knowledge and scientific knowledge.

   The key concepts that this module seeks to impart are:

- Living things can be recognised because they are all able to do certain jobs ('functions').
- The ways on which living things carry out these functions can be very different.
- Many non-living things can carry out some of the functions but not all of them and they can't do them without help.
- Living things are made up of cells, which are the smallest things that can carry out all the processes of life.
- Scientists look at the features of living things and can use these to put living things into groups.
- The features of living things make them able to survive in certain places and not others.
- Some features are only helpful in certain situations, for example thick fur is only helpful in very cold places.

Lesson 1: Identifying living and non-living things

A useful approach is to give pupils examples or cards of living and non-living things and asking them to say why they classify each example as living or non-living. Suitable examples include common animals and objects that show some features of living things, for example a battery operated vehicle, a solar operated calculator, a thermometer. For additional challenge, they can also be asked to place things into a third category of 'has been living' and to include examples such as coal, wood, a seashell and leather. This third category, if used, reinforces the concept that living things possess a distinctive set of characteristics and these are lost when an organism dies.

Pupils' ideas about what distinguishes living and non-living things can be used to create a checklist, to which features can be added at the suggestion of the teacher to make up the standard MRS GREN checklist:

Movement
Respiration (obtaining energy from food)
Sensitivity (can tell what is going on around it and respond to changes)
Growth
Reproduction (making new living things)
Elimination (getting rid of waste)
Nutrition (taking in, or making, food)

They can then use the complete list to re-assess any of the items they were uncertain about. Alternatively, they can discuss an example that you provide (reading aloud if helpful), such as,

Many cars need fuel putting in them. They can then move, giving out waste gases as they burn the fuel. They detect how fast they are going and some can tell when it's dark and turn the lights on when needed. Can we say that a car is alive because it takes in fuel that it needs for energy, gives out waste gases, it moves and is sensitive to its speed and to daylight?

Or, more challengingly, *Viruses cause illnesses such as colds, cold sores and COVID. They are small packets of information covered in an outer coat. They don't need air or food to survive away from living cells and only a few can move themselves. They can only make new viruses by getting into the living cells of another plants or animal. When they get on to a living cell, their code goes into the cell. Inside the cell the virus' information joins on to the cell's own information. The cell then makes new strands of the virus code as well as following its own instructions. The new pieces of virus code make the cell burst and, when it does, lots of new viruses are released.*

For pupils who may find learning unfamiliar terms along with their meanings difficult, it may be helpful for them to scaffold them with a set of icons to reinforce the meaning, or to get pupils to devise a set of physical signs for the functions or make a collective set of pictograms that illustrate what each of the words mean.

Lesson 2: How do scientists make decisions about living things?

In order to ensure that pupils get repeated opportunities to engage with the seven processes of living things, teachers could introduce the idea of branching keys (which are often taught as a mechanism for identification of species) as a 'choice machine'. Each of the functions can be presented as a choice point, and only things that show evidence of each of the seven functions of living things emerge as living (Figure 4.6).

Further reinforcement of how a branching key is constructed can be given by asking pupils to identify between four and eight (depending on time available) of the examples used in lesson 1. (It is important that the features considered are integral to the object rather than something that can be changed by the environment.) Building intentional repetition of ideas and materials is a good way to help pupils gain a confident grasp of what has been covered.

Lesson 3: Seeing cells, the 'building blocks of life'

Cells are a useful way to show how the macroscopic functions of living things can be linked to the smallest unit of life, namely cells. The introduction to the idea of the smallest unit is best done through microscopy. However, it is important that pupils succeed in seeing cells, rather than air bubbles or stray hairs! In teaching microscopy, there is a significant risk of losing what Johnstone (1991) describes as the 'signal', which we want pupils to see, and 'noise', the distracting incidentals like air bubbles on microscope slides. Digital microscopy enables the pupils to see a projection of what we want them to see before they look for themselves. The observations that we want pupils to make are that living things are made of lots of small units, which we call cells (so called because plant cells reminded the early microscopists of rows of monks' cells in a monastery). Digital microscopy does not bring a fragile lens close to the specimen and so works well without the additional steps, and additional processing demand, associated with a standard light microscope. If your circumstances require you to use these, I would suggest giving pupils prepared or purchased slides to begin with and then introducing the method for making a slide

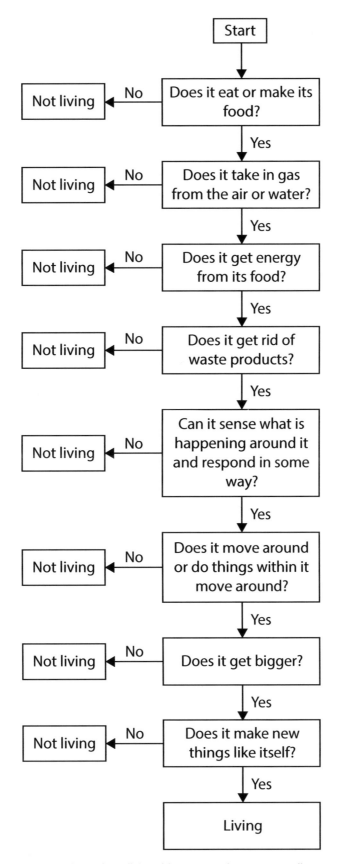

Figure 4.6 A branching key that shows how living things must demonstrate all seven functions.

using a drop of liquid and a cover slip. It is helpful if students do not have to make drawings of what they see under the microscope, capturing a photo is faster and induces far less performance anxiety about the accuracy of their drawing. The two 'classics' of microscopy in school are onion cells and cheek cells. Other fresh specimens of animal cells are messier and liable to upset the squeamish but insect specimens, including bees and cochineal beetles, can be bought on-line and observed directly.

Once pupils are able to use the microscope confidently, they can be set to look at a wider range of plant tissues plus prepared animal tissue slides, if time permits. It is beneficial to look at what have been living and non-living materials for comparison. Pencil shavings and paper are readily available and show plenty of structure but no cells.

The plenary should highlight that living things contain cells but not all cells are the same. They may have noticed that plant cells have more regular shapes ('are more like bricks') and thick walls whilst animal cells are irregular in shape and have only a very thin 'skin' or membrane. If a physical difference between plant and animal cells is established, it helps to pave the way for learning about the ways in which plants function differently to animal cells.

Lesson 4: Cells, where living processes happen

[If time permits for a nine lesson sequence, there are advantages in including a consideration of cells in a unit on living and non-living things. If this is to be covered elsewhere, lessons 4 and 5 can be omitted.]

This lesson links the preceding one on cells to the previous work on the functions of living things. Rather than making this a list of incomprehensible names, the focus can be put on to identifying the parts of the cell that carry out the different functions that they have encountered previously. Notice that this is a mini-spiral curriculum in that they are re-visiting previous concepts but extending their understanding of them.

Light microscope images should enable them to have seen the following features:

- The **nucleus (**'control centre') of the cell. It stores information and sends out chemical instructions to the cell. This information includes making new cells so it is essential for **growth** and **reproduction** (making new living things).
- The **membrane** (cell's barrier) controls what chemicals get into the cell and out of the cell. In this way, it controls **elimination** (getting rid of waste) and **nutrition** (taking in, or making, food). It also detects what is going on around the cell and so is responsible for sensitivity.
- The **cell wall** (the thick outer covering of plant cells) stops the plants cell from swelling too much and bursting.
- The **cytoplasm** (liquid inside the cell) lets chemicals **move** round inside the cell. Some cells, such as muscle cells and sperm cells, have special structures inside them that are able to move round the whole cell.

A more powerful microscope (electron microscope) also shows the 'power stations' of the cell (mitochondria, singular mitochondrion, meaning a thread with granules), where food reacts to release energy. This release of energy is called **respiration.**

To reinforce the fact that all these parts are needed, an activity requiring the pupils to gather up cards representing these cell parts and associated functions can be organised. This could take the form of a quiz for teams of pupils or asking team members to take it in turn to win one of the cell part cards, for example by finding a piece of information on a poster or successfully classifying an object as living or non-living. Alternatively, pupils can have information on one organelle and they have to draw how they think they will fit together in a whole cell.

A plenary could take the form of a group discussion of the question above regarding whether a virus is living or non-living, with a reason (there are several possible explanations but in this context the major one is that it only possesses the information to reproduce and cannot carry out the other six functions. Instead, it relies on the cell it infects for these functions).

Lesson 5: Meeting the needs of different living things

The next lesson should build a secure understanding of how the features of all living things is associated with what they need from their environment. One way to do this is to ask pupils to consider sending a plant and an animal on a space rocket to the moon. What would they have to put in the rocket of the organism is to survive? They can be asked to draw a plan or to build and label a capsule using modelling and craft materials that are available. The advantage of this approach is that it makes pupils conscious that they will have to think of everything that must be put in the space rocket, they can take nothing that is available on Earth for granted. This can raise interesting questions about what we mean by 'need', and many pupils will talk about psychological needs, such as company and things to occupy the animal travellers. It also enables pupils to draw on their personal knowledge, of keeping a pet or helping with plants at home, and so can build useful bridges between their out-of-school life and their learning in school.

Their plans can be self- or peer-assessed by considering how well each plan caters for the seven functions of living things. For example, have they thought about waste material? Will there be air or oxygen to allow the food to react and release energy?

The topic can be extended by looking at how different types of living thing can interact constructively, so people can eat plants whilst plants take in the waste gases from the humans. This may suggest that a combined crew of plants and animals would be the best, which prefaces considerations of communities of organisms sharing habitats on Earth.

[Stimulus material can be found at: https://www.nasa.gov/feature/can-space-gardening help-astronauts-cope-with-isolationandhttps://www.nasa.gov/feature/the-menu-for-mars-designing-a-deep-space-food-system]

Lesson 6: Focusing on feeding

This lesson picks up on one element of the planned spaceflight task, by focusing in on the function of feeding. It may be useful to start by asking pupils what food they had included in the space capsule for their animal. Although all animals need to feed, they do not eat the same food. It is interesting to ask pupils why they think animals eat different food, they often see it as an adaptive response to environment. 'They eat what's there' (rather than understanding that they are living where there is food that they can eat). When it comes to humans, the story is complicated by culture and economics and this difference between human animals and others is worth highlighting.

The introduction could be to think about the space travel activity in the previous lesson and to discuss which animals from a list could share an enclosure in order to save space on the journey.

Although in this unit the focus is on providing what is needed to sustain life functions, rather than on the physiology of digestion, the difference in the mouths of animals that eat meat, plants or both gives a useful illustration of how animals have adapted to get the most food out of what they eat. If you do not have them in the school, see if you can borrow some skulls or teeth samples. Neighbouring schools or university departments, local museums or local collectors may be able to help. Sheep skulls from which the flesh has completely rotted away are quite commonly found in upland areas and provide an excellent example of the mouth and teeth of a plant eater. (They should be scrubbed with a bleach and water solution before pupils handle it.) Alternatively, good photographs are easy to obtain on-line.

Pupils can then be asked to be mouth detectives and look at the skulls to see if they can find the following features:

Meat eaters (carnivores) have:

Small, sharp cutting teeth at the front of their mouth

Sharp pointed teeth at the side for grasping meat and tearing it

Few back teeth are needed for grinding because the meat is torn up by the front teeth

Herbivores (Plant eaters):

Front teeth tear the plants up and do not need to be sharp

Side teeth are usually rounded, rather than pointed

Lots of grinding teeth at the back. These are wide and often have ridges on to help grind the plants into pieces.

Omnivores ('eats all') can eat meat and plants:

Pretty sharp cutting teeth at the front

Quite pointed side teeth

Ridged grinding teeth at the back

To reinforce the activity, they can be asked to discuss in groups what sort of teeth the animal that they thought about sending into space would be expected to have and why.

The session can be concluded with a plenary that reinforces that the different groups of animals are able to eat certain foods because they have teeth that can break the food up effectively. You can also point out that the fact that different animals eat different foods helps to reduce competition for one particular type of food.

Lesson 7: Diversity and adaptation

This lesson focuses on the observation that plants and animals are usually found in places where they have everything they need to thrive. One has to be careful that this does not lead to teleological thinking, the notion that organisms change in direct response to their environment, for example giraffes grow long necks to enable them to reach the leaves high up on trees. Although the genetic basis of adaptation, and how it arises through evolution associated with environmental pressures, is not expected at this stage of the curriculum. It is appropriate, however, to point out the 'fit' between animals and plants and the places they thrive in.

A common approach to this is to consider animals (I consider plants as a separate topic) which survive in hostile environments, such as deserts and polar regions. There is also merit in including more familiar animals, such as foxes and seagulls which have shown exceptional behavioural adaptations to urban environments. You may also choose to include animals of local significance, for example marine animals and seabirds in coastal areas that rely on tourism. This is popular but it is easy for it to lose focus, as pupils just gather lots of facts about an animal that interests them. One way to reduce this risk is to structure their thinking and independent research around the seven functions of living things and to show how the animals have adapted to be able to carry out these functions in extreme environments. The use of this framework is illustrated below as a series of prompt questions:

How does the way it **moves** help it to survive?

What changes in the environment does it **sense**, and how does responding help it to survive?

How does it get food to give it **nutrition**? Is it a carnivore, herbivore or omnivore? (to reinforce the previous lesson's learning)

How does the animal get enough food and air to obtain energy from food (**respiration**)?

Can the animal get enough food to **grow** where it is?

What does the animal do to make sure its **young** survive in its environment?

How does the animal get rid of any **waste** from its body in its environment? (*This question is most relevant in hot arid environments where limited water makes urine production challenging. Losing heat is also a problem for warm-blooded animals*).

If pupils do independent research on an animal, individually or in pairs, they can then pair up with another research team and compare how their respective animals are able to survive animals. (Ensuring that each team has looked at a different animal to enhance peer teaching.) The key learning outcome will be that survival requires the animal to have ways of carrying out all the seven functions of live, wherever they live.

Lesson 8: Living things in their place

This lesson moves the focus on from individual animals to communities in a given habitat. You may wish to look at the habitats that were used when considering survival in extreme conditions or you may want to introduce other habitats. There are plenty of resources on resource sharing site and there are also two attractively illustrated documents about 'Our forests and jungles' and 'Our grasslands' available through the World Wildlife Fund website's Education area: https://wwf.panda.org/projects/our_planet_netflix_wwf_nature_documentary/education/. Although the text is likely to prove inaccessible, these resources provide illustrations of some of the key animal species that can be found in each of these habitats.

Pupils can be asked to consider how the habitat (place where they live) gives one of these animals everything it needs to survive. Ideally each pupil will consider a different animal in whichever habitats you are focusing on. You will notice that this is effectively a reversal of the previous analysis, which focused on the adaptations of the individual animal. They can then conduct a plenary with other pupils, according to the habitat, to see how one habitat can meet multiple needs.

An appropriate closing activity is to ask pupils to consider what would happen if the habitat was destroyed. Could their animal survive somewhere else? This should not only reinforce the fit between animals and their environment but also highlight the importance of saving habitats if we wish to limit animal extinction.

Lesson 9: Balancing every organism's needs

This previous lessons may well leave areas that need to be re-visited or completed. If time permits, a useful consolidating activity is to look at one habitat, either one that has been considered previously or one that is relevant locally, and to assign tasks to different groups that revise what has already been covered. A personal favourite of mine is to bring in compost from the bottom of a well-rotted compost heap and to allow pupils to observe the invertebrates that live in it. (The compost must be away from anywhere where pets could foul it and have been left for at least 3 years to be well rotted. It is advisable for pupils to wear disposable gloves for this activity to protect them from any pathogens. They should also wash their hands afterwards.) A couple of serving spoons full of the compost can be put into a disposable bowl and turned over for invertebrates by pairs of pupils. Using tweezers to pick out any inhabitants and put them into a petri dish, and then putting the lid over it to prevent accidental escape, they can photograph their finds and count how many of each there are. Most of the animals they find will be herbivores, and they will clearly see the plant material that is being eaten in the compost, but if they find spiders they have an example of a carnivore.

Keys to aid the identification of Earthworms, terrestrial invertebrates, Woodlice and Centipedes can be purchased from the Natural History Book Service [https://www.nhbs.com/1/series/field-studies-council-aidgap-guides].

In terms of classroom organisation, it would probably work best if pupils focused on just one group of animal and one corresponding key. The key will help pupils to identify what they have found and also let them see how a branching key is used to aid identification.

Plants

This is a topic that is often dismissed as 'boring'. However, it offers numerous opportunities for practical work that it offers, with no concern about the ethicality or issues of squeamishness to contend with. It is also an essential precursor to understanding ecology. The topic is liable to bring about processing overload because it considers multiple factors affecting plants' photosynthesis. The suggested approach introduces key concepts gradually and explicitly re-visits key concepts several times to ensure that learning is consolidated.

The learning intentions of a module on plants could be expected to be as follows:

- Plants make a wide range of materials that are important for animals.
- Plants use waste products from animals and use them to make new substances.
- Green plants make their own food (starch) when sunlight falls on them.
- When plants make their food, they also make oxygen which is essential for animals.

Lesson 1: The importance of plants

Concrete preparation, that is the linking of what is being learnt to everyday tangible experiences, is essential to learning and this is a stage that is all too often omitted. Teachers say that they do not have the time or that 'it isn't on the test'. However, time spent on orientation and eliciting interest is absolutely not wasted time. It is what more academically able students are more frequently able to manage without, instead drawing on the remembrance of past experiences. Pupils with LD cannot rely on the retrieval of relevant memories in the same way, so teachers need to provide the necessary concrete experiences.

My preferred way to do this is to bring in a selection of plant foods, preferably with the leaves where relevant, as in the case of carrots, and ask them to discuss which parts of the plant humans eat. They should be able to see that people eat all the parts of plants (though not all the parts of every plant, for instance rhubarb leaves are toxic but rhubarb stalks are edible):

- Leaves such as cabbage, lettuce or herbs like parsley or mint
- Flowers: Edible flowers include pansies and nasturtiums which are used decoratively, and crystallised rose petal are available for cake decoration
- Seeds

- Fruits (the part around the seeds): There are numerous examples of edible fruit, such as apples, tomatoes, oranges, grapes. This is an excellent opportunity to introduce some less familiar fruits if available, such as star fruit, and to extend pupils' awareness of the very varied ways in which people around the world meet their food needs. The fruit should be cut into pieces so that pupils can see the seeds inside
- Stalks such as celery, rhubarb and Pak choi stems
- Roots/bulbs such as ginger root, potatoes, carrots, garlic bulbs

Although testing leaves for starch comes later on in the topic, this may be a good place to introduce the idea that humans eat plants because they contain sugar and starch and to introduce or revise the use of iodine as a test for starch. Pupils can then test pieces of food such as potatoes, carrots, lentils, oats and rice for starch. This is excellent preparation of the testing of leaves for starch that comes later in the topic. If time permits, this can be extended by testing food derived from animal sources, such as milk, tuna flakes or meat, to show that they, by contrast, do not contain starch.

If no practical work is possible, it is still possible to look at dried and tinned food items, including spices and herbs (preferably the actual items rather than pictures), and sort them into those that come from plants and those that come from animals. They should see that the majority of the human diet, and for some people all their diet, is supplied by plants.

Extension activities could involve asking pupils to decide how many non-food items in their classroom (or at home, if given as homework) come from plants. They can be asked to audit the location for the following materials:

Wood/timber
Rubber (from rubber trees)
Paper or cardboard
Cotton, linen or bamboo textiles
Rope or string
Scented oils in candles and diffusers
House plants
Indigo dye (used to dye denim blue)
Herbal remedies such as turmeric capsules, ginseng products
Vapour rub for colds, which contains strong-smelling plant oils
Henna hair dye
Plant extracts in shampoos, conditioners and other cosmetics
Wood pulp in disposable nappies

The plenary should emphasise the importance of plants to humans and how humans can choose to protect, use or exploit plants to their advantage.

Lesson 2: Imagining a world without plants

The focus of this lesson is to present the idea that plants and animals depend on each other. The first lesson focused on commodities that come from plants, this lesson focuses on the inter-dependence of animals and plants in terms of the production of or use of carbon dioxide and oxygen. A simple example of an experiment to demonstrate this is Priestley's experiment in which he placed a mouse and a mint plant into a sealed jar and left in the light. If only the mouse or a mint plant were put into the sealed jar, they died. However, when both were put in the jar, they both lived. Pupils can be asked what they think was happening. They may well offer the idea that they 'need each other' and, if they do, they are correct in inferring that the plant is making something that the mouse needs to live, whilst the mouse makes something that the plant needs. They can be asked how they could find out what it might be and how they could test their idea. Their discussion can lead into testing the gases in the different jars.

If you are working in the lab, you can give the pupils tubes of gas to test:

1. One labelled, 'Carbon dioxide', containing carbon dioxide
2. One labelled, 'Mouse breath', containing carbon dioxide
3. One labelled, 'Oxygen', containing oxygen
4. One labelled, 'Air from a green plant', containing oxygen
5. One labelled 'Air from green plant **and** mouse', containing air.

Pupils can test each of the tubes with a glowing splint (made by blowing out a burning splint and using it whilst the edges are still glowing orange). Oxygen will relight the splint. They can then test those that don't relight the splint by pouring the gas (carbon dioxide is denser than air) into some lime water in a second test tube (or drawing it up into a dropper pipette and then bubbling it into the limewater).

This should enable them to see that the mouse and plant help each other to carry out the functions of living things if they have studied these. The mouse breathes out (excretes) carbon dioxide, whilst green plants give out (excrete) oxygen. This means that plants make the air suitable for animals, which need oxygen to release energy from their food (respiration). By contrast, the plant needs the carbon dioxide to build up its food.

To consolidate their learning, pupils could be asked to apply what they have learnt to a new situation. For example, they could be asked to think about what they think would happen if someone put a goldfish into a jar of water and carried it a long way. What do they think would happen and why? Would the outcome be different if the fish had some pondweed in the jar? [Alternatively, they could look at what happens in a sealed terrarium, some of which have lasted for decades, but in this case, the oxygen is used by micro-organisms that cause dead plant material to rot.]

Lesson 3: Plants as starch factories

Having established the role of the two different gases, carbon dioxide and oxygen, pupils can be asked to look at what plants need to make food. This can also extend the pupils' understanding of how scientific investigations are set up and how they can generate information. Water is a difficult factor to investigate because plants only wilt and die quite slowly, and dead is quite a remove from not making food. Most pupils who have any experience of plants intuitively recognise that they need water. As a backup, it may be worth bringing in some dried leaves (such as herbs) in sufficiently large pieces to be identifiable from leaves. Pupils may be happy to accept that these are no longer living. However, as a means of reinforcing the work of the previous lesson, these dried leaves can be put in a test tube in advance and then the test tube stoppered. Testing for oxygen, as they did in the preceding lesson, will show that no oxygen has been made, so the leaf is not alive or making food. Note that this is the type of repetition that is very helpful in developing long-term memories that can be retrieved; the material is re-encountered but in a new context rather than being a re-run of what has already been done.

Although there is a temptation to deal with the environmental factors needed for starch production and test leaves for starch in the same series of experiments, this places a high cognitive load upon pupils. For this reason, my preference would be for exploring the environmental factors that green plants require and then to consider the food that is made separately. Note that this is not only an experiment or investigation but rather a verification activity and a way to develop pupils' scientific literacy by showing them how scientists use evidence to generate knowledge. One of the disadvantages of plants is that the experiments can be quite slow and for this reason it is very helpful to have the plants prepared several days in advance, and to explain retrospectively what has been done. (If you are teaching outside the lab, it is still possible to use pre-treated plants and for pupils to examine them. 'Geranium' (pelargonium) house plants are commonly used but other plants with soft leaves can be used.) The usual experiments that are set up are:

1. A 'control' plant which is left in the air and in light, for example on a window sill
2. A plant that has been deprived of carbon dioxide gas by keeping it in a sealed colourless plastic bag along with a beaker of soda lime, which removes carbon dioxide from the air. It can be introduced as a 'carbon dioxide snatcher'.
3. Optionally, an additional plant can be set up with a carbon dioxide 'supplement' by keeping it in a sealed colourless plastic bag along with a beaker of sodium hydrogen carbonate solution. The solution breaks down to give off carbon dioxide gas which is then available to the gas. Pupils do not need to know this but simply to know that the liquid is 'carbon dioxide maker'.

The plants can then be compared by appearance, for example how green they are, whether they are wilted. At that point, the standard test for starch can be introduced as a way of checking whether the plant has made food. (If you do not have access to a lab for this lesson, a kettle can provide hot water which you can put in a heat-proof container such as a jam jar or mug to 'cook' the leaf. The 'cooked' leaf can then be put into a test tube with a little ethanol and the test tube can stand in the hot water to bring the ethanol to the boil.) Because this is a multi-stage process, and pupils can lose track of the steps, I recommend doing this as a demonstration (which can be projected via a web cam for better visibility) and giving pupils a check list of the steps for them to check that you are doing the experiment in the correct order. [See https://practicalbiology. org/standard-techniques/testing-leaves-for-starch-the-technique] It is quicker if you carry out one stage for each of the 3 (or 4) leaves but keep careful note of which leaf comes from which plant! The four pieces of leaf can be passed round for examination on a white tile with each one placed on a labelled white tile (or labelled areas on a single white tile for easy comparison). Pupils should be encouraged to identify which leaves have turned the iodine blue-black because they had made starch.

Their thinking about the purpose of each of these steps can be extended, once they have seen the practical being done, by asking them to match the step with the reason for doing it:

Steps

- Boiling the leaf
- Putting leaf in alcohol
- Putting the leaf in water
- Putting iodine on the 'cooked' leaf

Reason

- To break the leaf down and let the starch out
- To remove the green colouring, so you can see any colour change clearly
- To wash the alcohol off the leaf
- To see whether the leaf has starch in it

The pupils should see the correlation between increasing levels of carbon dioxide and the amount of starch with plant 3 (if set up) having the most starch, plant 1 the next most and plant 2 showing little or no starch. This points to the role of carbon dioxide in making starch. Plants also need water, so at this point, pupils can see that there is evidence to support the fact that:

$$\text{Carbon dioxide + water} \rightarrow \text{starch}$$

They can be reminded that the experiment with the mouse and the mint plant shows that the plant makes oxygen, so the final equation is:

$$\text{Carbon dioxide + water} \rightarrow \text{starch + oxygen}$$

This formalises their earlier understanding that animals need what plants make (starch for food and oxygen to release energy from food).

Lesson 4: How light affects plants 1

This lesson builds upon the previous one by using the same experimental techniques but this time the factor being looked at is the presence or absence of light. The two equivalent plants, which need to be prepared several days in advance, should be:

1. A plant that has been open to the air and kept in the light (the control)
2. A plant that has been open to the air but deprived of light by keeping it in the dark (in an unsealed black bag is ideal)

Pupils can then carry out the experiment that saw demonstrated, using the same checklist as last tie but this time checking off the experiment as they do it. This is yet another example of adopting a spiral curriculum approach to learning, albeit in a very small way, by creating opportunities for re-visiting material and also by developing the concepts or skills in some way that is new.

Because the ethanol is flammable, I would use hot water from a kettle so that no Bunsen burners need to be lit whilst ethanol is out. If you are working outside of a lab, iodine solution presents no great risk though stains hands and surfaces. Very small plastic dropper bottles, containing a maximum of 5 cm^3, are a good idea to minimise the risk of spillage.

Having established that the leaves do not make starch of deprived of light, even when they have carbon dioxide and water, the word equation for photosynthesis that has been successively built up now needs one final modification, the presence of light, as shown below.

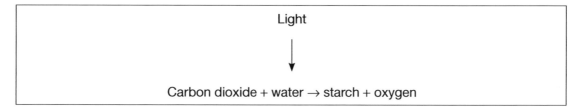

Light

↓

Carbon dioxide + water → starch + oxygen

The complete equation provides a good device for developing and modelling scientific literacy, and for reviewing the material covered in the two lessons, by asking pupils what evidence they have for each part of the equation. This is also a suitable point to reflect on the word that scientists use to describe the process by which plants make starch and oxygen, photosynthesis. Using a morphographic approach (see Section 2), the word has three root parts, 'photo' meaning light, 'syn' meaning 'with' and 'thesis' meaning 'joining together'. Pupils should now see that this is a suitable word to use for when the plant makes starch and oxygen when there is light.

Lesson 5: How light affects plants 2

The use of Elodea (Canadian pond weed) to investigate the effect of light on the rate of photosynthesis is a standard practical. The pupils need to be clear that they are using the number of oxygen bubbles made as a way of knowing how quickly the pond weed is making starch. The standard experiment (see, for example, https://www.saps.org.uk/teaching-resources/resources/190/demonstrating-oxygen-evolution-during-photosynthesis-using-pondweed/) involves counting the number of bubbles in a minute with a lamp at different distances. The introduction of this much quantification in one go may cause difficulties to pupils with LD, due to their difficulties with numeracy and their difficulties with processing multiple pieces of information simultaneously. One way to scaffold their learning is to ask them to observe the bubbles when the lamp is turned off, when it is a long distance away and then what happens as they move the lamp nearer. Once they have established that the closer the lamp is to the pond weed, the more bubbles are made, they can be asked to measure the distance from the pond weed and to count the number of bubbles. Measuring distance can be done quite simply by securing a metre stick or ruler (with blue tack or Sellotape) and ensuring that the 0 cm point is next to the beaker. They can then place the front of the lamp base at three, four or five points along the metre rule. If pupils are going to struggle to time a minute and count bubbles, it is acceptable for them to sketch the presence of bubbles at the different distances. They can then stick their sketches on to a second piece of paper on which the distances along the metre rule are shown. This then provides a simple graphic summary of their results; if pupils have managed to count the bubbles in a minute, they can use their measurements to plot a bar chart showing the correlation (Figure 4.7).

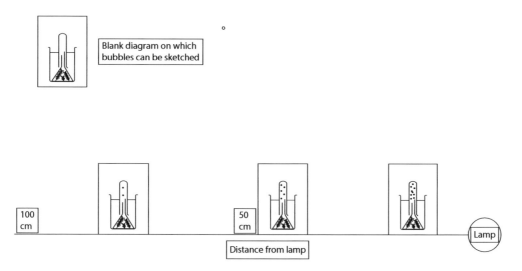

Blank diagram on which bubbles can be sketched

100 cm

50 cm

Distance from lamp

Lamp

Figure 4.7 A suggested way to record the bubbles released from pond weed at different distances from the light.

Whether pupils have measured the release of oxygen or sketched the incidence of bubbles, they should see that the closer the lamp source is to the weed, the more oxygen is given off. This means that the plant is making more starch when it is closer to the light. They can be asked to explain why this happens, and answers may include that the plant needs light to make food or that the light is stronger closer to the lamp. Without getting into an explanation of the fall in intensity as distance increases, this should pave the way for the explanation that the light gives the plant the energy it needs to make starch and oxygen. The more light the plant gets, the more starch and oxygen it makes. Likewise, the less light the plant gets, the less starch and oxygen it makes. They may notice that the fall or rise in number of bubbles is not linear, for example doubling the distance between the lamp and the plant does not give half the bubbles and this need only be explained in terms of the light spreading out as it leaves the lamp so it gets a lot less strong over a short distance.

Lesson 6: Travelling plants

Because the topic has introduced a multi-factorial variable (something, like photosynthesis, that depends on more than one factor), it is especially important to recap and consolidate the learning. One possible synoptic activity would be to design a plant carrier that would keep green plants alive over a period of months. This could be the form of re-visiting the question about sending an animal into space that was presented in the Living Things module but now focusing on sending plants into space, either alongside the animals or on their own. Considering sending them together provides a good opportunity to re-visit the concept of the inter-dependence of animals and plants.

An alternative problem, which can be used to introduce some technology into the lesson, is to design a case that could be used to keep plants alive for the months it took eighteenth and nineteenth century plant collectors to travel back from around the world to the UK. Plants that were carried in these cases included tea plants, cinchona trees whose bark gives us cinnamon, ferns, mosses and grasses. The plants and the plant collectors travelled by boat and the plants had to be protected from sea water spray and cold during the journey. However, they could not be totally sealed in, because they needed carbon dioxide gas and fresh water. Two plant collectors devised similar cases, Allan Maconachie and Nathaniel Bagshaw Ward. The cases came to be known as Wardian cases and you can find illustrations of them on-line. Pupils can build their plant carrier as a 'junk modelling' exercise and could even be asked to carry a plant home in it afterwards. In order to keep the focus on this as a revision and re-cap exercise, it might be helpful to ask pupils to present their designs having self-evaluated or peer-assessed their designs and state how they have met the plant's requirements of carbon dioxide, water and light during the journey. They could also be asked to think about how to stop the plant from freezing and how to keep splashes of sea water off it.

Electricity

Electricity is often viewed as difficult topic to teach, partly because it tends to be taught as a numerical topic at a point when pupils may still be struggling to grasp more fundamental concepts and partly because circuit board work can be frustratingly unreliable. The number of concepts implicit in the teaching of the topic helps to explain the conceptual challenge of the topic. This challenge is further compounded by their being brought about by sub-microscopic changes, the transfer of electrons which are, by virtue of their intangibility, abstract concepts. The learning intentions are to know:

- Charge is of two opposite types, negative and positive.
- A thing with a positive charge and a thing with a negative charge are attracted towards each other.
- Two things that have a positive charge or two things with a negative charge will push each other away.
- An object can be made charged by gaining or losing negative charge.
- Electricity is caused by charges moving.
- Charge must have energy to move, and when charge moves (electric current), it carries energy.
- When charge with energy is applied to a conductor, the charge passes along the conductor.

Lesson 1: Static electricity

Static (or 'staying in one place') electricity is often treated as a separate and less interesting aspect of electricity, of use only for children's party games or to explain thunderstorms. Its use-fulness appears to be limited, confined to making laser prints and photocopies, spray painting and attracting dust that would otherwise come out of chimneys into the environment. It is prob-ably more easily recognised as a problem, damaging items with a microchip in, making clothes in a tumble drier stick together and causing unwanted fires. However, it provides an accessible way to explore some of the key concepts associated with electricity. It can be done quite easily outside a lab. These include the nature of opposite charges, the way that electricity generation requires energy and that the electricity can then be used to transfer energy. It provides further practice at classifying materials according to how they behave. This lesson also reinforces the inherent nature of the properties of materials, in that the same materials consistently loose or gain negative charge.

A typical lesson involves pupils rubbing solids, such as polythene rods, pieces of acetate strip and other materials with a piece of cloth and then seeing whether they are charged by using them to pick up small pieces of expanded polystyrene or paper. Similarly, a charged rod brought near to a stream of water (but not touching it) will cause the water to deflect towards the rod. Rubbing an inflated balloon on a jumper will make the balloon stick to the wall. It is easy for mis-conceptions to creep in if the teacher does not have a secure and accurate grasp of the scientific concepts needed to explain what is observed. The first misconception is that it is the rubbing that makes the charge move, by pulling the charge off the material or pushing charge on to it. The reason that repeated rubbing repeatedly promotes the transfer of charge increases the amount of contact between the cloth and the rod. The second one is that the pieces of polystyrene or paper are that rubbing causes the charge to be unevenly distributed on the material. They are then attracted to the oppositely charged rod or piece of material.

Although it is simpler to assign the material that you are charging into two categories, as is shown in Figure 4.8, you need to be aware that it is the *difference* in their ability to attract or lose charge that matters. This means that things that are both in the polythene group (tend to become negative) could become like glass or nylon if they were rubbed with something that became negatively more easily than them. To support learners who are working hard to cope with lots of new concepts, the two-category approach simplifies things, however. I have intentionally not included metal rods, although metal can be electrostatically charged (see lesson 2), because pupils are liable to confuse metals' behaviour as a conductor with how it behaves when the charge cannot flow away and spread out, usually by 'going to earth'.

The next stage is to establish that the charge developed on the plastic rods is of two differ-ent types that attract each other. This should be done with between four and six rods, depend-ing on what is available to you. A rubber balloon can be suspended directly by tying string to the knotted neck. This can be demonstrated by getting pupils to suspend the charged (rubbed) rods or pieces of fabric in paper 'slings', suspended on thread. These can be suspended from a pair of retort stands if you are in a lab. Alternatively, pupils can each hold up one of two charged rods on a 30 cm rule and slowly bring them towards each other. Observe the way that they swing in their 'hammock'. Do they move towards each other or away from each other? I would show how to do the first pair of rods, modelling the interpretation of observations. For example, 'This a rod A (polythene) attracts this rod C (glass rod). This means that have oppo-site charges'.

They should then note which rods attract each other (have opposite charges) or repel (have the same charges). As the names of the polymers can present substantial problems, it might be helpful to stick or write a letter on them that can be used to identify them.

Part of the circuit	Which part of the model shows this?
Battery	Hands pulling
Light bulb	Hand squeezing the rope
Wires	Rope
Electricity	Moving rope
Buzzer	Hand squeezing the rope

Figure 4.8 How some common different materials become charged.

A simple results table might take the form of filling in the letters on a pro-forma such as the one shown in Figure 4.10

The interpretation of this will require significant scaffolding. Starting with one rod, for instance polythene which was labelled A, pupils might have recorded that

'Rod A attracts C and D. Rod A pushes B and E away'.

where B is a rubber balloon, C is a piece of silicon baking sheet, D a piece of silk fabric and E a piece of nylon.

The interpretation depends on the identity of rod A as either negative or positive, so it is important that you know what the rod is and how it becomes charged when rubbed with the cloth. Polythene develops a negative charge, so material C must have a positive charge. The positive and negative charge attract each other, and the rods move together. However, for material B and E, their charge pushes against the negative charge of rod A. This means that B and E both had the same negative charge as A.

Pupils should then be asked to group the rods into two groups, positive (has a similar effect to the charged polythene) and negative (has the opposite effect to charged polythene).

As a consolidation activity, pupils can be asked to explain one of the following events, using their experiments to explain the scenario.

When you put clothes in a tumble drier, they all brush together, again and again. When you take the clothes out, they often all stick together. They sometimes make a spark when you pull them apart.

When you photocopy a picture, charged ink powder sticks to a moving drum. The places the powder sticks to depends on the picture you are photocopying. Then the drum runs over a piece of paper and the ink sticks to the paper.

When a lorry's tyres turn on the road, they become charged. The charge can build up and causes a spark. If the lorry is carrying petrol, it has a metal chain that drags along touching the road. The charge can go down the metal chain and on to the road. This stops the spark forming and prevents the petrol catching fire.

Lesson 2: Charge moves

If it is at all possible, a demonstration with a van der Graaff generator is a highly popular and memorable illustration of static electricity in action. If that is not possible, it may be possible to borrow a plasma ball which illustrates similar behaviour but transfers charge by ionising gas in the sphere. If you touch the glass, the small amount of charge flows across you to the ground. There are also some good videos of the apparatus in action that can serve as a provocation for discussion if hands-on experimentation is not possible. Another useful piece of kit is the 'Fun Fly Stick' which has a very small van der Graff generator inside to generate static electricity safely.

You must take up-to-date safety advice from a suitable body, such as CLEAPSS or SSERC as the voltages involved are very high. The Institute of Physics also offers guidance on how to use it as a teaching tool. (If operated correctly, it is safe because the charge involved is very small.) You must also be trained to use your school's specific apparatus, including the safety aspects of using it in a class situation. You should only allow children to be models who are genuine volunteers and after warning them that anyone using any type of 'active implants' such as a cochlear implant, pacemaker or insulin pump should stand at least 6 m away from the machine before it is turned on.

The apparatus gives pupils an introduction to the notion of the two features of electricity that they will go on to measure, one is the amount of electricity (the charge that moves in this instance is only a very small amount) and the other is the energy that the electricity carries (which is large in the case of the van der Graaff generator).

The usual approach would be to show that the moving belt charges a plastic rod inside the metal dome at the top in the same way that the plastic rods were charged by the moving cloth. The plastic rod in turn charges the metal dome. The charge on the dome can be demonstrated by placing a bundle of fibres close to it, and then into direct contact with it. The way that the fibres repel each other should be linked back to their observation of the rods which repelled each other when they were both positive or both negative.

If a pupil is willing, they can stand on an insulator (an upturned Gratnell tray is ideal) and touch the dome to show that their hair becomes charged and adjacent hairs repel each other. (It may be good class management to delay repeating this activity, which is hard to surpass in terms of tension and drama, until the end of the lesson.) The charged dome can also be demonstrated to charge materials by placing pieces of paper or polystyrene on top. As they become negatively charged, they will start flying away from the negative dome. Another impressive demonstration is to add a small pile of foil cases (from mince pies and the like) and then switch on the van der Graff generator. The cases fly off one by one.

The next stage is to show that when charge moves it carries energy. The moving charge can be used to light up a low voltage fluorescent bulb that is brought close to or touched on the dome. If pupils are willing, they can then be used to show that charge can be transferred across several insulators. To do this, pupils need to hold hands in a line and the two pupils at either end of the line of pupils touch the van der Graaff dome with their free hand. It is recommended that no more than three are standing on trays and that the circle is not allowed to be large, because the build-up of charge can be too great for safety. (Check local guidelines on how many pupils could safely transfer charge with the generator you are using.) The generator is turned on and allowed to run for a minute or so. Some pupils may experience their hair starting to stand on end, especially those with long, clean hair. However, when the generator is stopped and pupils stop holding hands, they will hear (and may see, if the lights are down) sparks flying as the charge moves between the pupils.

This lesson is fun and shows a number of science 'tricks' so it is important that the plenary focuses on the scientific concepts that have been illustrated by the activities. One way to do this might be to reflect on the activities, possibly listed an illustrated, and to decide which of them provides evidence for the following statements:

- An object can be made charged by gaining or losing negative charge.
- Two things that have a positive charge or two things with a negative charge will push each other away.
- When charge moves, it carries energy.

Lesson 3: Charge flows, models of electricity

There are arguments for letting pupils try out simple circuit board equipment before trying to explain it or represent it. One helpful approach to introducing the circuit board equipment for those with LD is to focus on what it does, rather than what the different parts are called and what symbol is used to represent them. For example, pupils can be asked how many ways they can find to send a message using light bulbs to the circuit board components. This is open-ended, encourages pupils to explore without fear of getting it wrong, provided they have no more than two batteries (to prevent overheating). They should be warned to stop immediately if anything in the circuit is getting very hot.

Once you reach a point of seeking to explain how the moving charge is behaving, models provide a useful and very concrete way of talking about current electricity. There are numerous models of electricity, though none of them provides an especially accurate picture of how current flows through a circuit. Despite their imperfections, they help pupils to gain a concrete grasp for how current works. Models, such as energy, represented by sweets or counters, in cups and passed between a circle of pupils, illustrate the movement of imperceptibly small particles. A marble run model or a circular model railway does a similar job. Such models can also show how parallel circuits work, by introducing junctions where flow can go in more than one direction. Marble runs can also be used to illustrate that different types of work can be done by electricity, for example turning a paddle wheel, going noisily down a spiral tube or jumping a gap can be likened to making a light bulb light up, running a motor or turning on a buzzer. What these models do not show is how each charge creates a field around it that causes nearby charges to move, in the way that that charged materials interacted during the static electricity activities. (It might be worth re-visiting this experience by showing a set of three rods made of identical material charged, two of them suspended in paper slings and then bringing a third similarly charged rod up to the one at the end.) A related limitation is that the models described imply that there may be a large gap between the charges, in the way that there is a substantial gap between the cups or marbles. For this reason, the circle of rope model is especially helpful as it shows the continuity in the current. As pupils move the loop of rope around from hand to hand, they can also see how the electricity transfers energy by gripping the rope more tightly and seeing how their hand gets heated up as he rope moves through it. At the same time, the other pupils have to pull harder to keep the rope moving.

In order to consolidate learning, pupils should be asked to apply the model that you have chosen to use to the circuit that they made at the start of the lesson. For example, if you have used the rope model, pupils can be asked to complete a table like the one in Figure 4.9.

Rod A attracts …*C*…*and* ….*D*…………………………………………………..

Rod A pushes *the rubber balloon and plastic E*……. away

Like A	Not like rod A
B	C
E	D

Figure 4.9 A comparison between the components of a circuit and their representation in a rope loop model.

Lesson 4: Electricity divides

Having used a simple (series) circuit, pupils can then look at circuits in which the charge can take more than one possible route, a parallel circuit. (The treatment of parallel circuits is considered qualitatively only here.) This lesson involves pupils setting up a series of circuits for investigation and comparison and it can be most easily managed by running it as a step-by-step 'staged practical', as described in Section 2. If you set a simple one battery (which needs to be fresh to light two bulbs) two bulbs in parallel circuit on a circuit board, this can either be displayed using a web cam and projector, or by being clamped in an upright position to display it to all pupils. You may also find it helpful to draw the course of the circuits in washable pen on the circuit board, with the battery and bulbs shown using standard symbols, to show the line of the wires once the components are removed; this can be a precursor to circuit diagrams. Pupils' attention should be drawn to the fact that there are two loops, side-by-side, both driven by the same battery. Pupils can then be tasked with setting up their own parallel (side-by-side) circuit. They should then be encouraged to try removing the bulbs one at a time to see what happens.

It is useful then to contrast this with a series circuit with the same number of bulbs, where the removal of one bulb causes them all to go out, because the charge can no longer move through the circuit. This can be a good point at which to conduct a mini-plenary, possibly in the form of an evaluation. Which circuit was easier to set up? Which one needs more wires? Which one lets one bulb go out without all of them going out? Which arrangement do they think is the best one over all? If you take a note of their thoughts at this point, they can further review these at the end of the lesson.

Their understanding can be reinforced by returning to the model of electricity that you are using. If you are using the rope loop model, the parallel circuits can be represented by two or three loops of rope or string, all of which are pulled together by pupils and which then separate out into three separate, parallel strands. If you are using the marble run model, the parallel circuit is represented by the marbles passing through a junction at which some marbles follow one route and other marbles follow an alternative route. A pupil of mine memorably remarked that, '*Parallel circuits are when the electricity has a choice point*'. The models used to illustrate the idea of branching prepare them for the next investigation.

Once they have understood the notion of multiple alternative routes for the charge to move along, they can start to explore the way in which the two different arrangements use the energy provided by the battery. One way to achieve this is to ask them how many bulbs can be made to light up using just one battery using different circuits. Their findings that the parallel circuit lets one bulb light up multiple bulbs, whereas the series circuit will not let the battery light up more than two bulbs lighted up discernibly. This gives them insight into the way that parallel circuits can use a common power source to provide energy to multiple devices which function independently of each other. They may even be able to see that this is how the ring mains in their home operates, with each appliance operating independently of the others.

A suitable plenary might be to re-consider the list of features of the parallel circuit and to add any other points that they have thought of. Alternatively, they can be asked to match each of the earlier evaluative statements to the type of circuit, series or parallel, to which it applies. Either approach provides a useful re-visiting of the key features of the two types of circuit.

Lesson 5: Measuring electricity 1

Attempting to quantify electricity is only of any value once pupils have gained a secure grasp of what is happening in a circuit. At this point in the development of their understanding, the model of electricity that has been selected will provide crucial 'anchoring', ensuring that pupils are clear exactly *what* is being measured. It may be helpful to separate the measurement of voltage and current over two lessons, focusing each lesson on one variable, so that you can avoid unintended conflation of the two. One of the practical problems that all pupils encounter when measuring voltage and current is that they commonly use multi-meters to measure current and voltage. As a result, the same device is set up differently and connected into the circuit differently, which causes confusion. It is for this reason that teachers working with pupils with LD often prefer to use old-style analogue ammeters and voltmeters. These enable pupils to see current or voltage increasing or decreasing easily, even if they find reading them challenging. They can also put sticky spots to show where the needle was and read them later.

If you start with voltage, you can get pupils to look at different batteries, the settings on a power pack, the voltage marked on a mains plug and the voltage of the van der Graaff generator. It may be helpful to get them to arrange these items (or photographs of them) along a voltage line marked on a bench up to 100,000 V to show the relative scale of the varying voltages. This gives them a sense of the scale of voltages that we commonly encounter.

This is a suitable point for pupils to see what the effect of different voltages is. This can be done quite simply with standard circuit board equipment by putting three 1.5 V bulbs in a circuit and showing the pupils the effect of one 1.5 V on the bulbs, then adding in a second battery to give a voltage of 3 V and, finally, a third battery to give 4.5 V. This is a good point at which to model how to measure voltage (which has to be read in parallel with the item, or 'across the thing'), using whichever meters are available. If you have a choice, digital readouts are usually easier, although decimal points may present problems. If this is the case, the pupils concerned may prefer to use an analogue meter and read it to the nearest whole division on the meter scale. This experiment demonstrates that increasing the voltage provides more energy. Pupils can then set up a simple circuit with a single battery and see what voltage it takes to drive the electricity through a single bulb by measuring the voltage across the bulb. They can then try two bulbs, or a buzzer, or a motor. This shows them that different devices require different amounts of 'push' (voltage) to give them enough energy to work. For example, circuit board bulbs are commonly rated as 1.5 V, a small buzzer is also rated 1.5 V but a small motor is often rated higher, at anything between 1.5 and 3 V.

Having established that the values of the voltages vary substantially, and that changing the voltage increases the energy carried round the circuit, they now need to consolidate their understanding of how an increased voltage affects the amount of energy available. At this point, your chosen model can be re-introduced to show how the voltage affects what happens in the circuit. If you have opted for the rope model, this can be represented by having more pairs of hands pulling the rope so it can move through hands that are gripping more tightly; if you are using the marble run model, the same point can be made by increasing the height of the run so that the marbles run faster at the bottom.

A useful plenary is to ask pupils to explain in their own words what they understand by the voltage and to conclude with a definition that you provide. This might say that 'Voltage is the way we measure the energy that is given to equal amounts of charge', or other words of your choosing, to that effect. They could also prepare a pictogram of the word voltage. (See Section 2, a pictogram is a way of displaying a specified word in such a way as to give a pictorial representation of the meaning of the word.)

Lesson 6: Measuring electricity 2

If you are able to spend two lessons on the quantification of electricity, it enables you to spend longer on both voltage and current, and this is likely to give greater consolidation of both concepts. Assuming that you are in a position to do this, the second lesson can then focus on current. The understanding that you are looking to develop is that current is the way we measure how much charge flows in the same time. Although it is technically the amount of charge each second, this definition introduces an inverse relationship (between current and time) and, as shown in the consideration of Piagetian levels of cognitive development in Section 2, this is likely to make it hard or impossible for most pupils with LD to access.

What changes in the current mean in practice could be illustrated by firstly showing how to measure the amount of current with an ammeter. Measure the current that flows when you have one 1.5 V battery and one 1.5 V bulb. If you then add a variable resistor, which you can describe as a 'blockage' to the moving charge, you can show how increasing the 'blockage' reduces the current. Pupils could then measure how much current flows in a circuit with one battery and one bulb, or two bulbs, or a buzzer or a motor. Having established that different devices draw different currents, this observation can be linked to your model of electricity. If you are using the rope loop model, this can be shown by loops of the same length but different thicknesses of rope/string. If the resistance of the devices in the circuit is modelled by gripping increasingly tightly on the rope, they should observe that thinner rope/string gets stopped by the tightened grip but the thicker loop pulls through. The ammeter measures the amount of charge in the same way that we could measure the thickness of the rope. If you are using a marble run model, the current can be described as the number of marbles that run down the run in a certain time. If more marbles run down, it is equivalent to more charge moving in the same time.

If time permits and you feel that the pupils have a secure understanding of what current means, you could extend their exploration of it by getting the pupils to measure the current at different points around a series circuit to see that the current is the same all the way round and help them to recognise that this is because the charge moves steadily through the wires, rather than forming 'bottle necks'. (They may see variations in the range of hundredths of amps but these can be blamed on the meter if anyone notices them.)

As with the lesson on voltage, it is important to gather pupil's understanding of the term current, both for the purpose of consolidating it and also to spot any misconceptions or inaccuracies that they may have formed. They could be asked to propose one model to show what we mean by current and explain why they have chosen this model. Alternatively, they could be asked to write an acrostic poem about current. An acrostic poem is one where each new line starts with a letter of the target word, for example:

Circuits carry charge
Under the watchful display of the ammeter
Riding round the wires, the energy travels to light bulbs
Riding round the wires, the energy travels to buzzers too
Electricity flows, sometimes tiny amounts and other times a flood
Never stopping our current until the circuit is broken
Timed and travelling, our charges move onwards to work your world

As another alternative, pupils could be asked to devise an icon that could be used to represent the idea of 'current'.

Lesson 7: Electricity doing work

A lesson on electricity and work would commonly look at the relationship between current, voltage and time, to show that the work done by an electrical device is directly proportional to each of these. You may choose any of the activities below to demonstrate the relationship associated with it, according to your equipment and room. I would recommend not over-focusing on the numerical aspects of this but rather to show pupils that the work a device does gets bigger when the voltage is bugger, the current is bigger and the time is longer. Because work is a multi-factorial variable, requiring Piagetian level 3a to make sense of it, it is especially important to start with a very familiar concrete example. For that reason, my top choice is the model of an electric toaster.

a.   How does a toaster work? Showing the effect of varying the current
Pupils can be reminded of the way on electric toaster works, preferably with a demonstration. They can see, if the toaster is turned on its side or a web cam pointed down on it, that there are heating elements that toast the bread. You can then show them the effect of changing the setting to give more heat, for browner toast, or less heat, for lighter toast. They can see that the heating elements glow more brightly on the dark toast setting and less brightly on the pale toast setting.
You can then use a circuit board model to show them how the toaster works. This comprises a series circuit containing a power source, for example of two or three 1.5 V cells, a 1.5 V bulb to represent the heating element and a 10 Ω variable resistor. First of all, join up the circuit without the variable resistor to show the brightness of the bulb. Then add the variable resistor set at minimum resistance to show that, when the resistor is not stopping current going through, the bulb is as bright as ever. However, as the variable resistor is turned up, less charge flows and the current is less. They can see that the light bulb gets gradually dimmer, which is the same as moving the toast setting being changed from dark to light. The

charge passing through the circuit is less because the resistor makes it harder for the voltage to push the charge through. As a result, the toaster does less work when it toasts the bread.

b. Running an electric motor: showing the effect of changing the time.

c. Pupils can first lift a mass (500 g is ideal) to see that it takes work to lift it. There is then a demonstration activity to show that more work is done by the electricity over a longer period. The mass can then be attached by a string that is fixed to a spindle that is turned by an electric motor. The mass should be on the floor, whilst the motor needs to be standing on a base that is clamped securely to the table. Once the motor is turned on, the spindle starts to wind the string on itself and the weight will start to rise from the floor. Run this once, so that pupils see what happens and from that you can get an idea of how long the motor and eight combinations have taken time. Pupils should then measure different time intervals, possibly at 5 s intervals, possibly using the stopwatch on their phone. You should turn off the motor at each of the different times and measure how far the mass has been pulled up. A quick way to do this is to tear a strip of paper, such as ticker tape paper, to the height of the mass and mark it with the time. As they probably anticipate, the mass is lifted higher the longer the motor is moved by the electricity. The more general point is that the longer the charge flows, the more work is done.

d. Turning a kettle on for different times: showing the effect of changing the time 2

This is a simple activity that could be done outside a lab because it only requires an electric kettle and a thermometer per group. Pupils either place a thermometer down the spout or take the kettle lid off, if possible, turn on the kettle and measure the temperature of the water every minute. (Because of the risk of steam burns, they should not heat it above 50°C.) They can note down the temperature very easily on a chart, such as the one shown in Figure 4.3. The results clearly show that the longer the charge flows, the hotter the water gets.

e. Electromagnetism: showing the effect of changing the voltage 1

Making temporary electromagnets using an insulated wire in a spiral around an iron nail is a standard experiment. [See https://spark.iop.org/simple-electromagnet.] The strength of the temporary (or 'turned on') magnet is assessed by finding out how many paper clips the magnetised nail will pick up. In this instance, it is being used to show that a larger voltage, or electrical push, transfers more energy to the nail and turns it into a stronger magnet. It is recommended that the voltage used does not exceed 1.0 V so, in practice, only low (1.0 V) and very low (0.5 V) values can be tested.

f. Electrolysis of copper sulphate: showing the effect of changing the voltage 2 or the effect of changing time 3 [See https://edu.rsc.org/experiments/electrolysis-of-copperii-sulfate-solution/476.article].

Electrolysis is one of the topics for which the notion of moving charge is especially useful since it does not differentiate between electrons in a metal wire and the mobile ions in a beaker of electrolyte. This activity can reinforce the idea of elements as pure substances whilst developing ideas about moving charge in circuits. The purpose of the experiment I would suggest is presenting a demonstration because it involves a number of steps which pupils may find very difficult to get correct or do in the right order and even if they do so they are likely to lose the sight of the purpose of the experiment. However, it will help to increase pupils' involvement if they are assigned roles and are not simply passive spectators of your experiment. The point of it is either to show that the greater the voltage, or the longer the charge flows, the more copper metal is deposited. To start, rub two pieces of copper foil with emery paper to remove any copper oxide. Mark them with a + and a – sign with a marker pen, and weigh each one, noting down the weight of each. Use these as your electrodes and connect these with crocodile clips, two leads connected to the positive and negative terminals of a low voltage power supply. Place the electrodes into a beaker of 0.5 M copper sulphate solution, ensuring that they do not touch. If you are demonstrating the effect of varying voltages, set up a series of three successive experiments with the voltage set at 2, 4 and then 6 V, respectively. For each run, record the weight of the negative electrode before and after. For ease of comparison, the pieces of copper foil with further metal formed on it should be kept in order for pupils to compare them all at the end, pre-labelled petri-dishes are ideal for this purpose.

You will see that the weight of copper metal formed is greater each time. (If, however, you increase the voltage any higher than 6 V, you will still get more copper formed but it will no longer be shiny orange metal but will be brown, dull sludge. This is because when the voltage rises, hydrogen gas starts to form and this stirs the solution and causes very tiny copper crystals to form. It is called 'burnt copper' and sells for a lot lower price than the shiny metal. So depositing copper more slowly ends up being more profitable.) The learning point is that when the charge is given more 'push', more charge will pass to the blue copper in solution and turn it to solid copper metal.

If you are showing the effect of time, run a series of experiments with the positive electrode being left in for 2 min, the next one for 4 min and the final one for 6 min. The weight of copper deposited goes up successively, showing that the longer the charge flows, the more charge will pass to the blue copper in solution and turn it to solid copper metal.

The plenary should collate whichever factors you have shown to show which factors increase the work that electricity does. To secure pupils' understanding of the effect of voltage, current and time, it would be helpful to return to whichever model of electricity you have been using and showing pupils how each of these factors individually would increase the work that the moving charge does and then how they could be combined to give a still greater increase in the work done.

Energy

Energy is a surprisingly difficult concept to define, which is surprising for an idea that is so ubiquitous in scientific thinking. Teachers are quite commonly confused about it, often presenting it as 'magic stuff' that makes things happen and this perpetuates inaccurate ideas about it (Millar, 2005). The name means 'activity' which roughly equates to be able to do work, that is to move things or to heat them or to change them in some other way. This is the way that pupils hear it used in everyday conversation, for example in 'energy drinks' that are supposed to give the consumer the ability to perform better in sports because they can move faster or further. It is a 'quality' or property of objects, not a physical substance that we can have amounts of, though it is often described as flowing from one place to another or being transformed, as if it were a substance. However, it can be recognised easily enough from its effects and is most definitely a useful idea that links apparently very different scientific topics.

The other way of understanding energy is as something that can have a value given to its changes and so (in the midst of much uncertainty) lends itself to a mathematical treatment. This is, however, not an approach that is likely to enhance the understanding of pupils with LD. Although the idea of the total energy being conserved is important, showing this numerically is liable to cause more confusion than it dispels.

One final, practical issue with teaching this topic is that lessons are often a circus of mini-activities or multiple examples. It is important that pupils who may find this approach confusing or overwhelming are given explicit support to see that these examples all relate to common ideas, or an 'integrating framework', so that their experiences contribute to a coherent understanding of energy as something that causes change.

Learning intentions for such a unit might include:

- Energy makes things change, for example get hotter or move.
- Energy is observed and grouped in different ways.
- Energy can be stored or can be moving.
- Energy can be transferred from one place to another.
- Energy naturally travels from a place that has a lot of energy to a place with less energy.
- Energy sources are places that have a high level of energy.
- Energy spreads out in the environment.
- Renewable energy sources often build up energy that is spread out in the environment.

Lesson 1: Deciding what has energy. Classifying energy

Although the classification of energy is not an approach without problems (Millar, 2005), it is a widespread one. The other approach that has been advocated is to focus on the site of energy conversions. In practice, it may be best to use the approach pupils that pupils have encountered at primary school. If this is the classification of energy, pupils will have encountered a list of energy types, typically the seven below, which I have further divided into two sub-groups:

Types of stored (potential) energy

- 'Uphill' (gravitational) energy
- Elastic energy chemical energy

- Chemical energy
- Nuclear energy

Types of moving (kinetic) energy

- Movement energy
- Heat (thermal) energy
- Electrical energy
- Light energy

We should be aware that these are slightly arbitrary, relying on individual judgement and level of relevant knowledge. For example, a hot object would be described as having heat energy using the categories above but the temperature it possesses is attributable to the vibrations of the particles that make up the solid. Does that mean that we should describe a hot object as having movement energy? Moreover, you could make life quite a lot simpler by avoiding the multiple types listed above and simply talk about what actually happens, rather than introducing classes of energy to explain phenomena. However, there is no doubt that pupils find classifying things satisfying and that alone may be justified enough.

A common approach to introducing or revising these types of energy is to have a circus of objects chosen to illustrate them and to ask pupils to match the object to the type(s) of energy they believe it illustrates. These objects might be a battery in a circuit causing a light bulb to light up, a lit candle, a clockwork toy, a kettle heating water and a radio.

Some pupils will struggle with the number of choices and it may be helpful to help them to make a decision by asking them first how they can *tell* the object has energy before asking them to decide what kind. For example, is something moving or changing? Is something being heated up? What do they observe about it that they can connect to one or more of the energy types in the list? Group discussion helps pupils to refine their ideas and explanations; perhaps each group could present their thinking on one item in the circus to the group at the end. It may also help to have the energy types listed in a column with the different items listed with images of the items they have considered in a second column. They can then connect the energy types and items with lines to reduce the burden of writing.

A plenary could usefully focus on how easy it was to decide on the type or types of energy that each of the items exhibited. This helps to reinforce the idea that classification is subjective and imprecise but can nevertheless provide a useful way of handling information.

Lesson 2: Energy changes and the spreading of energy in spontaneous change

If you have started with the energy circus described for lesson 1, you have already encountered one of the difficulties with teaching energy, which aspect of a phenomenon to focus on. If you are looking at the bulb in a circuit, should pupils be considering the chemical energy in the battery, the electricity in the leads, the light (and some heat) from the bulb, or all of these? It may help to look at the energy in an object or system, such as the circuit, at the start and at the end of the change. In the case, the battery has chemical energy at the start, when the circuit is joined there is a current (electrical energy) and light energy. It would be quite appropriate to re-visit the same objects/systems as they looked at in lesson 1 but with the additional refinement of 'before' and 'after'. To extend the analysis, you could ask them to look at what moves the energy, here the electrical current, but in other activities, other forms of movement energy transfer the energy to somewhere else.

This approach may be used to help pupils to see that there is a sequence that often involves stored energy being converted to movement energy and gives additional structure which helps pupils with LD. It also gives additional rehearsal of the terms and ideas used in lesson 1 which will give more secure learning. Pupils might be expected to look at a greater number of items this time, especially any they did not engage with in the previous lesson. This approach provides a useful development of the thinking in lesson 1 but is entirely consistent with it.

By considering where the energy comes from and how it does work, this structure also provides the basis of the idea that energy naturally (or more accurately spontaneously) tends to spread out, from a concentrated store into the environment. This is the basis of subsequent lessons on sources of energy (objects or places which have a high level of energy) and the way this is spread out when we draw on the store. It also prepares pupils for a consideration of the fact that human energy use is causing climate change, including global warming by releasing energy into the environment, and this is exacerbated by the rising levels of carbon dioxide. This analysis also paves the conceptual way to look at things which draw energy in from the environment and concentrate it. These things do not happen spontaneously and humans have to devise special devices to 'unspread' energy and this is the basis of several renewable energy technologies, such as wind power, solar power and ground heat source pumps.

Lesson 3: Where can humans get energy and which sources of energy are best?

Because an analysis of possible energy sources inevitably involves the comparison of multiple sources and so will exceed the cognitive load which pupils with LD can sustain, it is crucial that the number of sources is limited. In making the choice as to which source to consider, key factors will be which systems pupils can have hands-on experience of and which are locally relevant. It always astonishes me when in a former mining area, teachers do not talk about coal as a major energy source, albeit a historical one, because it will doubtless have shaped the social and economic geography of the area hugely. As pupils look at the four energy sources, they can assess what energy is being converted into another form, reinforcing the work of the previous two lessons.

Showing that the movement can be used to generate electric current can be achieved by showing the sources in conjunction with a dynamo. Dynamo kits can be bought but vary hugely in price. Alternatively, mounting a bicycle dynamo and light on a board, with a handle added, is a less expensive way of showing that movement can generate a current. As an alternative, you could make a windmill, of the sort outlined in lesson 4, and use that show how the turning of the blades generates electric current, for example by lighting up bulbs in a circuit.

Likely ways of creating the movement to generate electricity are:

- Carbon-based fuels. Although coal is tricky to ignite in a lab, firelighters are made from mineral oils on a waxy solid, so give an impression of what coal burning would do to the environment. Be sure to give out only a very small piece of firelighter and supervise this activity closely. If they use the fire lighter to heat a small beaker of water, they can then understand that it is the steam that turns the dynamo (called a turbine when it's very big).
- Wind power, which can be modelled using an electric hairdryer on a paper windmill.
- Tidal/wave power. Waves can be made in a ripple tank (or fish tank or glass trough of the sort normally used for showing Group I metals in water. If you are out of a lab, a shallow tray can be made by cutting a large pop bottle lengthways and making sure that the water is shallower that the neck of the half bottle. Make sure you have absorbent towels on hand to mop up spillages and avoid slip hazards.
- In photovoltaic cells, the movement is of charge, so we cannot see it. PV cells can be shown by looking at solar-powered calculators or using a small photo-voltaic panel placed in a circuit on a circuit board.

In terms of class management, it will also help if pupils can have concrete experiences of sources, as far as possible, and to fully focus on one source at a time, rather than being whisked on a lightening tour of all the sources. It may be easier to move groups in this instance and leave the experiments where they are. Key information, such as the cost of generating electricity from each source can be given along with information about the environmental impact, can be placed along with the experiment. (Make sure that the information is in whole but manageable numbers and specifies that this is for a certain amount of electricity. Data go quickly out of date but this is only for comparison purposes, so does not have to be absolutely accurate.)

For example, one report in 2021, the electricity for an average home cost £32 each month if the electricity came from a coal-fired power station. The cost of gas-powered power station went up to £55 for the same amount of electricity. Finally, this electricity was made from tidal power costing £4, from solar panels costing £8 and from wind costing £16.

Pupils can be asked to think about questions such as:

- How long will be able to keep using this energy source without running out?
- How expensive is electricity made this way?
- What would it be like to live in a place where this source was being used to generate electricity?
- What effect would generating electricity this way have on wildlife and the environment?

A table can be a useful way to collate information and, rather than plodding through three or four energy sources, it may be a good idea to get pupils to consider one source in a group, then to 'snowball' with another group who have looked at another energy source and finally to conduct a plenary, during which you note down pupils' thoughts. This group response can then be made available to each pupil to provide them with an accurate summary.

Lesson 4: Comparison of selected energy sources 1: Wind power

Pupils who have travelled in the countryside may have seen wind turbines, if they have not, they are likely to be used to the idea of old grain mills which ground grain to make flour.

Simple model turbines can be made using a small motor and the voltage produced tested, plus materials that can be found in schools. [See: https://www.teachengineering.org//activities/view/cub_earth_lesson04_activity2 and https://www.teachengineering.org//activities/view/cub_energy2_lesson07_activity2]

Pupils can use a hairdryer to turn their turbine and see what voltage they can produce. They can then start with a turbine made using the template given at: https://www.teachengineering.org/content/cub/activities/cub_earth/cub_earth_lesson04_activity2_template_v2_fv.pdf. However, they can then explore one (or more, if time permits) of a range of variables, including:

- The number of sails on their windmill/wind turbine
- The length of the sails
- The speed of the wind
- The direction of the wind, relative to the sails

If pupils measure the voltage, there can be a competition to see who has made the most effective turbine. If they are liable to struggle with measuring voltage, they can look at how brightly the windmill makes two bulbs connected to the windmill and motor light up and see what value of their variable gives the brightest bulbs.

As a plenary, you can collate their results to design a 'super windmill' that uses everything they have found out. The issue of wind speed and direction could be factored to choose suitable sites locally, including what the land is used for and whether maintenance staff will be able to reach it, which offers an authentic bit of inter-disciplinary learning.

Lesson 5: Comparison of selected energy sources 2: Wave power

Wave power is more difficult to demonstrate directly as there is no way to model easily how the rise and fall of the water drive a dynamo. (The previous wind turbine activity showed that a turbine is just a motor which has its spindle turned in order to supply power, rather than needing a power supply to turn the spindle.) However, it is possible to show how the tidal movement can be used to move a floating object up and down. A rod that moves up and down can then turn a crankshaft. The crankshaft (of which there are videos) will turn a second rod in a circle. The second rod can then turn the dynamo. (In real-life situations, a crankshaft is not needed because the flow of water turns the turbine directly but the dynamo or small motor you will have is not able to withstand getting soaked in water.)

If you put a spindle (a piece of thick wire or even the inside of a biro) cork or piece of expanded polystyrene foam into the water, you can show clearly how the water surface is moving up and down as the waves move over its surface. The floating material moves the spindle up and down. This can then be used to turn a crankshaft (of which a video could be shown). Finally, the crankshaft turns a dynamo, which they know will cause a current to flow.

Pupils could then work in groups to think of ways to get the most energy from a stretch of tidal water. Remind them that they can think about the ideas that they explored when trying to get the most powerful windmill; this time it is sea water that is moving rather than wind. They may come up with ideas, including changing the shape of the floating object to make move further when a wave hits it, having more dynamos or choosing areas where the waves are highest. They can then be invited to think about what difference their ideas would make to the people living inland from the site, for marine wildlife and shopping.

A final activity could involve a directed activity relating to text in which pupils look at an article on tidal power and identify the benefits and limitations of it, perhaps by underlining positives in one colour and negatives in a second colour. You could use the account given at: https://www. renewablegreenenergypower.com/tidal-energy/tidal-energy-tidal-power-facts-for-kids which sets out some key advantages and disadvantages of tidal energy.

Lesson 6: Comparison of selected energy sources 3: Solar power

Pupils will probably be familiar with solar-charged portable items, such as calculators or garden lights. There are also solar-powered buggies that can be bought for investigating solar power. These are lots of fun when they work but there have been concerns expressed about how well they charge, and that means that pupils do not see a significant difference in the distance moved by the charged buggy. If you do not have buggies, or have encountered problems with them, you can carry out an investigation using small solar panels, which can be wired together to give a greater surface area to absorb light, in a series circuit. The voltage across the panels can then be measured. This investigation can be carried out in a very similar way to the Elodea bubbler experiment set out in Plants, lesson 5. Using desk lamps as the light source (with care as they get very hot when turned on), pupils can investigate the change in voltage when the lamp is brought nearer to the panels or pulled further away. They can also experiment with the effect of changing the number of panels and even look at the effect of the angle at which the light hits the panels, mimicking how different the capacity for solar generation is in countries in more northerly or southerly parts of the world. As an extension, they could see what happens when they change the colour of the light, by placing a piece of coloured acetate sheet over the lamp before turning it on and it becoming very hot.

The plenary should emphasise that solar panels make a useful contribution to electricity supplies and are clean and silent at the point of use. However, they can only generate during daylight hours. A further consideration is that some of the elements used to make the panels are likely to run out soon, so we cannot expect to keep making more and more panels to meet our energy needs. This sets you up for lesson 7, on reducing the energy we use.

Alternative to lessons 4–6: Getting energy from biomass

If you cannot get all the equipment needed for any of the preceding three lessons, this makes a popular alternative. Burning food to release the stored energy is commonly carried out in a topic that includes digestion but can also be used to consider biomass as a source of heat, both directly (in stoves and boilers) and to create steam that turns turbines in power stations. Different foods can be used to represent common sources of biomass, for example:

- Cocoa pops to present animal manure
- Shredded wheat cereal to represent straw
- Cornflakes to represent food waste
- Crushed up crisps to represent the waste from deep friers/waste from edible oil pressing

This needs to be done in a well-ventilated lab, as it is liable to get very smoky! Check whether any of the pupils are prone to asthma before doing this and discuss whether the activity is liable to trigger an asthma attack. Warn them to have their inhaler handy, just in case, and seat them near to an open window. Measuring how much energy is released by combustion is an activity that commonly overwhelms students with the amount of measuring and calculation. If you have sufficient time, pupils can weigh out a suitable amount of food to burn, for example 10 g. Alternatively, samples could be pre-weighed for them or they could use a kitchen scoop to measure out, say, one level desert spoon (15 ml). The good stuffs burn best with a good air supply, so putting them on a gauze on a trip is ideal. Equally, I have known teachers without a lab to go outside and get pupils to hold solid pieces of food in a pair of tongs, igniting them with a domestic blow torch for making crème brulée.

Measuring the heat released classically relies on pupils measuring the temperature of the water before and after combustion, then using the volume of water to calculate the amount of energy transferred from the burning item to the water. I would suggest that you focus on the same amount of water each time, which can be marked on the inside of a glass beaker or even a clean food tin, with a waterproof pen. Use a generous ration of water to food mass, for example 100 cm³ water for 10 g burning food, to keep the temperature of the heated water at a safe level. Assume that the tap water is always roughly the same temperature and simply measure the final temperature. The beaker of water can be clamped above the gauze and food, rotated away from the food whilst it is being burnt and then quickly rotated back over the lit food. If you are doing this away from a lab, a tin can is a good item to heat the water in and the wall of this can be held with a pair of tongs.

This is a very 'rough and ready' experiment, which is far from accurate. I think it is perfectly OK to simply order the fuels in order of the energy that they released. Even with three or four types of biomass, patterns will be observed around the structure and composition of the fuel. Straw burn well and quickly, as does the shredded wheat cereal, as their structure allows air to move around the fuel. Crisps generate a great deal of heat, due to their high oil content.

The other joy of this experiment is that there is no much wrong with it, and pupils can usually identify all the ways in which it was not an accurate way to measure the heating power of the fuel. I have used an image of a food calorimeter and shown them how energy values can be measured accurately, in comparison to their experiment.

The plenary can focus on the place of biomass incineration in turning waste into a fuel, which provides us with energy is a useful form and reduces disposal in landfill sites.

Lesson 7: Reducing our energy use: Insulation

Although the focus of the previous six lessons has been on how to generate electric current in the least damaging ways, the need to reduce the energy we use is also essential to minimise harm to our planet. This is another hands-on lesson and it is usually very well liked. A plenary at the end is essential if learning is to be secured as pupils may well just want to keep making modifications to their model and lose sight of its purpose. Testing out how to insulate a model 'house' is an engaging and relevant way to explore this, although something like a shoe box or printer paper box is common but presents significant storage challenges if the activity runs over two lessons. Smaller boxes can be prepared in advance from cereal boxes cut into half, which makes the walls and floor of the model house. A cardboard roof can be created from the remaining card of one side of the box, which is folded in half. Pupils may then choose to cut out windows and a door. The heat loss from the house can be explored by putting a beaker of hot water into the house and seeing how much it cools down in 5 min. (It may be useful to poke a hole for a thermometer through the roof to facilitate the measurement.) After that, they can test out the effect of different types of insulation, using a fresh beaker of hot water each time so that the temperature stays roughly the same (hot water cools down much more quickly than warm water). For example, shredded paper taped to the roof and walls, or fabric on the floor to represent carpet, or even taping fabric across the door and windows to represent curtains. They can also stick polythene across the window to model glazing and can add a second and then a third layer to show the effect of double and triple glazing. The results are far from precise but should enable pupils to see that some forms of insulation have a big effect on heat loss, whilst other forms have a smaller effect. It also shows pupils that insulation stops us losing heat from buildings, which reduces the cost of heating and reduces the warming of the atmosphere by the escaping energy.

Lesson 8: Planning a carbon neutral school

If you can access an infrared camera, it is fascinating to take pupils out to survey which parts of the exterior of the school buildings are warmest. The infrared camera lets them clearly visualise the places where heat is being lost. Based on their observations, they can make recommendations on how to reduce the energy lost from these 'hot spots'.

If this activity is not possible, pupils could design a 'school for the future' using everything that they have learnt about energy transfers and energy sources to recommend how a simple school building (a three-room primary school is manageable to plan for) should be built to have minimum running costs and minimum impact on the environment. This lets pupils draw on knowledge from outside the classroom as well as what they have learnt in their lessons and permits very different responses to the same brief. In order to help them to focus on the energy considerations, it may be helpful to give them a framework of self-assessment questions to answer about their design, for instance:

- How is the building going to get electricity for heat and light?
- How locally can the electricity be made?

- Will the source of energy for making electricity be available for a long time, for example for the next 100 years?
- In what ways does the building reduce the amount of energy needed to keep it warm?
- Are there any other features of the building or its contents that will reduce its impact on the environment?

An alternative that many schools use is to plan the energy sources for an imaginary island, using the resources that they are told are present on the island.

Earth and space

Although the explicit curriculum expectation of coverage of this topic is not always significant, I think this topic has much to recommend it in terms of developing scientific literacy. The topic can also be linked to others, such as the living things in which a colony on the moon or another planet in the solar system could be planned, or the likelihood that life exists elsewhere in the solar system can be considered. The topic provides excellent examples of the way that scientific thinking has been informed, including by observations. The other appealing aspect of the topic is that astronomy has been important to many different cultures and so it offers rich opportunities to consider science that does not originate in Europe. Learning intentions for the topic might be:

We can use what we see on Earth to understand more about it.
Scientists have used observations to work out what is in space and how things in space are moving.
In our solar system, each planet is different, depending on how far form the sun it is.
The Earth has conditions that suit living things but scientists think that other planets may once have had life too.

Lesson 1: What do we know about the Earth?

A common approach to this question is to start with old models of the Earth and its atmosphere and to ask pupils to critique these. This is a slightly risky approach because it assumes that pupils are interested in what people 500 years ago thought and that they have enough general knowledge to counter these older models. If the lesson is run in a 'staged' manner, using the very structured development of ideas that is described as 'directed instruction' (see Section 2), it is possible to develop pupils' reasoning incrementally. This can be achieved by considering evidence and then conducting a plenary, the topic of the structure of the Earth can be a great way to help pupils to see how evidence is used to formulate ideas that can then be tested scientifically. There are two possible aspects of the Earth that could be considered here, and which one(s) you opt for depends on your context.

1. How do we know what shape the Earth is?
    This can start with some suggestions as to possible shapes, of which a sphere is likely to be top. If they do not volunteer it, a flat disc is a useful alternative and possibly an egg shape. It is useful to have physical examples of each of these, preferably several sets so that pupils can handle them as they discuss the evidence. If PE colleagues can lend you some footballs and rugby balls, these are ideal and circles of card on the same scale can be cut out. (You can ask at this point, assuming they have not suggested a box shape, why no-one has suggested a cube. You may well get the answer that no-one has ever seen the corners. You could respond by asking whether mountains are not just worn away corners of the box.) Pupils should be asked to talk in groups about which shape they think the Earth is, and what their reasons are for choosing it.
    They can then be presented with evidence, one piece at a time, and asked to say which of the two or three possible shapes the evidence supports or rules out. Suitable pictorial evidence includes:
    a. A picture of a partial solar eclipse, showing the shadow of the Earth as curved. A picture of the sun or of Venus from the Earth, showing that other things in space are spheres.
    b. A view of very flat land (It is probably not a coincidence that the flat land of the fens led to it being the heart of the nineteenth century flat Earth movement.)

  c. A picture of the Voyager aircraft, stating that this flew round the world in 1986 and came non-stop back to where it had started from, it was unfuelled so did not need to stop for fuel. The NASA website has an image of the aircraft.

  d. A picture of ships appearing over the horizon with their masts appearing first and then the rest of the ship coming into view, along with a caption saying that this happens no matter which direction the ships sail from or where the observer is looking at the sea from.

  e. A picture of the Earth taken from space.

    All the pieces of evidence apart from item (b) rule out any non-curved structures (such as the cube) but the equivalence in all directions in item (d) makes the sphere the best way to explain all the observations. The picture on (e) confirms that the Earth is a sphere.

2. Is the Earth just a ball of rock?

  One way to approach this would be to ask pupils to think about what the school site and environs are like. What is the ground like on their way into school? Their memories can be prompted by sharing photos that you have taken. Can they see any rock? If they see soil or plants that are growing in soil (such as grass or trees) that is a marker for rock being broken down to make the compost. They may also, depending on where the school is, see buildings made of stone or brick (made from tiny fragments of rock mixed with water to form clay). This should underline the importance of rocks and how widespread they are in the built environment. But is the rock the only thing that makes Earth what it is? Pupils can then be shown a picture of the moon's surface, with an astronaut on it showing the oxygen cylinders on their back, and asked what is different about the Earth and the moon? They should, with help if necessary, be able to recognise that there is no water, so no plants, and no atmosphere.

  Having established that the surface of the Earth has solid rocks, liquid water and a gas (air), the next part of the session moves on to what is below the surface of the Earth.

  The simplest way to do this is to make a model and ask them what they can tell about it just by looking at it. One way to do this is to get balls of blue tack or plasticine in which are embedded something denser, such as a steel ball bearing to represent the iron core or, as an alternative, a glass marble, along with balls that are the same size but made just of blue tack or plasticine. Give them the opportunity to feel their weight and directly weigh these on a balance if you can. Then establish that they can tell the difference from the weight. Then cut through one of the balls that is uniform throughout and say that we know how heavy the Earth would be if it was the same rock as is on the surface all the way through. But the Earth acts as if it was heavier, for example when we measure the gravity on it. How can we explain that? By now pupils should have been helped to see that the heavier ball must contain something that is not blue tack or plasticene but is 'heavier' (denser). One of the heavier spheres can be cut open to reveal that there is a heavier centre.

  Pupils can be shown a video clip of a volcanic eruption, with the explanation that volcanoes are where what is under the hard rocky surface of the Earth bursts out because there is a weakness in the hard rock (the crust) and the rock is being heated.

  At this point, they are likely to have the idea that the hard surface is something like the solid chocolate round a soft centred filling. (If you have done the activity with plasticine balls, they may think of it like a chocolate with a soft centre and a nut in the middle.) The semi-liquid rock emerges from volcanoes is like the soft centre. This model is quite useful because as you go down deeper, the next rock layer (the mantle) can be described as being semi-solid, like a piece of chocolate that has been warmed but has not completely melted as would happen if the soft centre was hot. (In fact, it is a solid in which the particles rearrange slowly under pressure but that does not merit consideration here and semi-solid can be used as a 'fit for purpose' phrase, even if not accurate.)

  To test the model of a three-layered Earth (solid-semi-liquid-solid), we can observe how the vibrations or 'shudders' from earthquakes travel through it, instead of using an ultrasound to check on an unborn baby. This is because 'shudders' travel differently through solids and liquids. You can show this by letting pupils experiment with blocks of ice in a small plastic box with a lid and a matching box and lid-containing liquid water. If the bottom of the box is tapped with a pencil or spatula and the pupil puts their ear close to the lid, a different sound can be heard.

  Analysing the way that these 'shudders' move through the Earth shows us that there is a solid middle part of the Earth with liquid above it and then a solid outer layer. (The solid middle is the inner core, which is where heat is released by reactions like those in a nuclear power station. It is made of iron metal, which makes the Earth act like a magnet and the very middle part of it is solid, because although it is very hot, the pressure of the rock layers over it cause it solidify.)

The plenary for the lesson should re-visit the evidence that they have seen and then the inferences collated to give a summary description of the structure of the Earth.

[Optionally, the lessons shown in materials section, lessons 6 and 7, could be used here to show how the liquid rock becomes solid and then goes through the rock cycle until it is liquid once more.]

Lesson 2: Are other planets like Earth? Trends in the solar system

Looking at different planets offers an excellent way for pupils to spot patterns and to generate explanations for the trends (incremental changes). It is very useful to have a chart displayed showing the planets in the order they are away from the sun.

The lesson could start with photos of Venus and Mars taken from Earth, and saying that these are Earth's cousins, not the same as but the most similar to our planet. This lesson is going to look at them and the other planets that move around our sun. This may be the point at which to ask whether our moon or any stars should be included? (The answer being that it shouldn't, according to our definition, because the moon moves around the Earth and not around the sun. Similarly, stars are suns for other planets. They look very tiny to us because they are so far away.)

I think comparing planets is also an opportunity for pupils to look at data, albeit in a simplified form. If you think that the number of different planets will overwhelm the learners, focus on the inner four. If numeracy is a major issue, using a simple Likert scale to represent the variables enables pupils to understand the trends in a semi-quantitative manner, for example showing the temperature of the planet on a 5 point 'chilli scale', where 5 chillies is the very hottest planet temperature. Variables that can be considered, although not all, can include the following:

> Name
> Distance from the sun
> Temperature
> Size (diameter or 'distance from side to side')
> How long it takes to move round the sun
> What is it made of?
> What gas is around it?

One way to get them to start looking at the variables is to give them cards (paper squares) and ask them to put the planets in order of closest to the sun to furthest away from the sun. They can then cut the paper longitudinally into two parts, keeping the data part, and stick them together to make a table (Figure 4.10).

Pupils can then be asked to look at one of the features and relate it to the distance from the sun. What pattern do they see? Can they explain them?

They may remark upon the fact that:

- The planets get colder the further they are from the sun because they are further from the place where heat is given out.
- The four planets closest to the sun are similar in size, the next two are much bigger and the outer two are in between the sizes of the small planets and the big planets.
- The time to move around the sun gets longer when planets are further from the sun because the longer the route it takes to move around the sun.
- The first four planets are solid and made of iron and rocks. The outer four are made of metal, rock and ice with a thick layer of liquid hydrogen and helium around them.
- The four outer planets have a thin layer of hydrogen and helium gas. They are very big planets and so can pull even light gases towards itself. The three next closest planets have atmospheres but the inner planet (Mercury) has none (because it is too small to pull the gas towards itself) and any gas is hot so escapes easily. The Earth originally had a carbon dioxide atmosphere but green plants have taken carbon dioxide out of the air and released oxygen. Its two neighbours (Mercury and Venus) never had green plants growing on them, so the carbon dioxide levels remained high.

Planet	Approximate distance from the sun in millions of km	Average temperature on surface in °C	How long to go round the Sun	Atmosphere	Approximate distance from centre to the surface in km	Made of
Mercury	60	Between 425 and − 180 (180 °C less than 0 °C)	88 days	Helium gas	2 400	Mostly iron metal with a thin covering of rock
Venus	110	450		Carbon dioxide gas and clouds of sulphuric acid	6 000	Iron metal with a covering of rock
Earth	150	16	365 days	Nitrogen and oxygen gas, water vapour and a small amount of carbon dioxide gas	6 000	An iron core, with a layer of molten rock above that and plates of solid rock on the surface
Mars	230	−28	687 days	Carbon dioxide	3 400	An iron core, with a layer of molten rock above that and plates of solid rock on the surface.
Jupiter	780	−145	12 Earth years	Mostly hydrogen and helium gases	72 000	Hydrogen and helium liquid and gas
Saturn	1430	−176	12 Earth years	Hydrogen and helium gases	60 00	An iron and nickel core covered by rock and a layer of liquid hydrogen and helium
Uranus	2870	−224	88 Earth Years	Hydrogen and helium gases	25 000	Rock covered in a layer of ice
Neptune	4520	−201	165 Earth Years	Mostly hydrogen and helium gases	25 000	Rock covered in a layer of ice

Figure 4.10 Simplified data on the planets and our sun.

The planary should help pupils to see that the distance from the sun affects the size of the planet (big planets can pull further away from the sun), its temperature, what it is made of and the gases on it.

A modelling activity is a useful and fun way to reinforce the point about the trends. Inflatable solar system models can be bought. Pupils can then be asked to take one (pre-inflated) planet and find how far it is from the inflated sun. It is essential that you have calculated the scale of your model in advance and have pre-inflated the models (the sun in particular takes quite a long time). For example, using a scale of 100 million km being shown as 1 cm gives approximate distances from the sun of:

Mercury	60 cm
Venus	1 m
Earth	1.5 m
Mars	2.2 m
Jupiter	8 m
Saturn	14 m
Uranus	29 m
Neptune	45 m

Lesson 3: Could there be life on other planets?

To build an explicit link back to the previous lesson, pupils can be asked to look at the tables that they created and asked which planet(s) they think would be 'just right' for life? This part of the solar system is sometimes called the 'Goldilocks zone' because it is not too hot, and not too cold, like Goldilocks' porridge. They may say that the Earth is the best place for life but challenge them to look again and see which other planets are nearby and might be possibilities. They will probably nominate Mars and Venus. If asked what the problems might be, they should be able to identify that they are much hotter or colder than Earth and that they have very high levels of carbon dioxide. Might this be used for plants to grow and they would start changing the atmosphere in the way that they did when they first grew on Earth? It's possible if there is water.

Ask pupils to consider the evidence that there may have been water. Each pupil could take one or two statements relating to just one planet and look at them with a partner. What do they think of the evidence? Is it strong or just suggestive of there having been life? They can then 'snowball' with another pair to discuss what they conclude. This can then be repeated for the second planet.

Mars once had seas and rivers that flowed into them. We can tell this because sedimentary ('bitty') rocks form when rivers flow into seas and we have seen sedimentary rocks on Mars.

We have also seen groups of small round lumps of ironstone. The lumps look as if they have been worn smooth as they were carried along in a river and then dropped together where the river slowed down.

Scientists think that as volcanoes erupted on Mars, the liquid rock reacted with the water on the surface and 'locked it up' in the rocks.

Scientists have found chemicals, such as methane (natural gas) in rocks on Mars that are made by living things.

Mars' atmosphere is almost all carbon dioxide gas, which plants need to make food and grow. However, the gas is much more spaced out than on Earth, so plants might find it hard to take up enough carbon dioxide.

Venus has a surface that, like Mars, suggests that there were seas and rivers on it.

Scientists found a gas on Venus that is usually made by living things and is not likely to form naturally on a hot planet like Venus.

The temperature on the surface of Venus is probably too hot for life to exist there but the clouds 50 km above the planet are cool enough for living things to survive in droplet. However, the clouds contain strong acids.

They have also detected something in the clouds that behaves like 'red oil', a mixture of chemicals that can come from living things.

'Red oil' can react with chemicals to make more 'red oil'.

As more red oil forms, it reduces the acidity of the clouds and so makes it easier for living things to grow there.

The discussion can be steered by five key questions, which can be directed to pupils as they discuss the questions:

a. What evidence do you think is most important in knowing whether there was life on Venus or Mars?
b. Do you think there were ever any living things on Venus or Mars?
c. Just because there used to be life somewhere, does that mean that things could live there again?
d. How has the planet changed since there was any life?
e. Would the changes make it more or less likely that something could live there?

The plenary enables different groups to feed back their thoughts and for you to say that this is how science works, people look at evidence and try to make sense of it which is not always easy!

Light and sound

These two topics can be taught independently but it is useful to consider them in tandem, not least because of the conceptual features that they share. Both involve the transfer of energy by waves, both systems carry convey detailed information by having waves which vary in characteristics and both rely on a suitable detector (the eye or the ear). If the two are done one at a time, with reference back to the first example, you avoid the confusion of 'same but different' that happens when two similar things are introduced in the same lesson. It is a topic that is relevant to pupils and blends aspects of biology, which they often find appealing, with physics, which they quite often do not find as instantly appealing. The topic also gives a chance to talk about diversity without it being a contentious or judgement-laden issue, for instance the fact that some people with autism have brains that respond strongly to sounds that other people find comfortable.

Suitable learning intentions might include:

- Sound and light are different sorts of waves.
- Sound and light waves carry information that living things detect.
- Humans sense sound and light through special organs, their eyes and their ears.
- Different sound waves and different light waves have different energies.

Lesson 1: What is sound? How do sounds differ?

An introduction to sound needs to ensure that pupils understand that sound is carried in waves of compressed (squashed) and expanded (spread out) air. The experience of seeing how the vibrations are set up is very helpful. This can be done with stringed or percussion musical instruments, if available, but a home-made guitar made with rubber band of different lengths does the job. What pupils need to be helped to see is that the instrument moves (which is why wind instruments are much less helpful here) and that the movement of the string or surface that is struck, such as the drumhead (the skin that is struck), or the prongs of the tuning fork. The focus at this point is just to see that a moving object that moves to and fro quickly makes a noise.

The next concept is that the moving object pushes the air, squashing it as it moves one way, then leaving a space for the air to spread out into as it moves the other way. A slinky spring is ideal for demonstrating how this happens. The spring should be stretched out straight and then the end moved along the axis of the extended spring, pushing towards the opposite end of the spring. If you keep doing this in a steady rhythm, pupils should see that there are 'squashed up areas' alternating with spread out areas. This shows how the push of string or whatever on the air can cause vibrations to move through the air.

The final activity is to explore how we can change sound, either by making it louder or more quiet, or by changing the 'pitch' how squeaky or deep it sounds. This is traditionally done with a signal generator connected to a speaker and a cathode ray oscilloscope (CRO). The signal generator produces alternating current (AC) and can have the amplitude or the frequency of the output changed. Pupils can see that when the height of the sound wave, visible on the CRO screen, goes up, the sound gets louder but the pitch does not change. This can be explained by saying that the more energy is used to push the air in the speaker cone, the louder the noise is. You can then change the frequency, which is how quickly the cone in the speaker pushes against the air. The faster the pushes, the higher the pitch and the 'squeakier' the noise sounds. If you make the frequency even greater than any of the pupils can hear, you can tell them that a dog could still hear it and this is the sound a dog whistle makes, opening up a discussion about how dogs' ears differ from human ears in having a larger sound detector (cochlea) and how young human ears can hear higher pitched sounds than older human ears. [This experiment is demonstrated at https://www.stem.org.uk/resources/elibrary/resource/28842/signal-generator].

The plenary can be used to re-visit to the slinky spring model and, for pupils, to see that harder pushes of the spring are similar to the higher waves on the CRO and correspond to a louder sound. Gentler pushes are equivalent to a quitter sound. If the pushes on the end of the spring are faster, they correspond to faster waves, seen as being more 'packed together' on the CRO screen, which are higher sounds. Less frequent pushes on the spring correspond to a lower sound.

Lesson 2: How do we hear? The ear

Although the structure of the human ear looks very complicated, it is interesting to many pupils. It offers a chance to talk about the challenges of hearing loss, including why their headphones should not be on at a deafeningly high level! I would suggest that the ear is looked at with a focus on what the ear does in the transmission of sound, ignoring the chemistry of ear wax or how the ear assists with balance.

It is very helpful to look at an anatomical model, if you can, to show the different structures in 3-D before looking at a 2-D diagram.

If you use a simplified diagram, the 'route' into the ear is:

- The outer ear (a sound 'funnel')
- The ear drum, a thin 'skin' which moves when it is pushed by the sound waves
- Three tiny bones which are moved by the eardrum
- Another, smaller thin 'skin' that moves when the third bone pushes it
- A jelly spiral (like a snail shell) that moves when the jelly is pushed by the moving skin
    Either, simply,
- Nerves go from the jelly spiral to the brain and tell it what the sound waves are like.
    Or, in more detail,
- Different parts of the jelly spiral move, depending on how fast the sound wave is hitting the ear
- Nerves touching the jelly spiral send a message to your brain telling it how quickly the sound waves are wobbling the jelly
- The brain knows if it is a high, medium or low sound
    Possible approaches to pupils understanding the sequence of events could include:
- Drawing arrows on a diagram to show where the sound moves and then joining each statement to the correct part of the ear
- Putting the statements above into the correct order (you could group two statements together to reduce the choices pupils have to make)
- Ask pupils to work in groups to role play how the sound gets to your brain
- Give pupils a diagram to cut out and make freeze frame showing the stages in sound perception

A very useful and easy to construct model to illustrate how different parts of the cochlea resonates when different frequency sound hits them is Barton's pendulum, shown in Figure 4.11. Pupils can see that different parts of the 'jelly spiral' are different widths, with the top part of the spiral being much narrower than the lower part. A series of pendulums of different lengths can be strung up from a string 'washing line', for example strung between two retort stands. Each pendulum is set up using a lump of plasticine or paper cone hanging from string of different lengths. These are like the jelly (and sensitive nerve endings) in the different thicknesses of the spiral. The 'driver' bob is a final piece of string with a bob on it that acts like the sound wave. This should be adjustable in length, for instance being secured on with a paper clip so that it can be removed and the length of the string altered. What pupils can see is, firstly, that when the length of the string of the 'sound wave' bob is lengthened it swings to and fro more slowly,

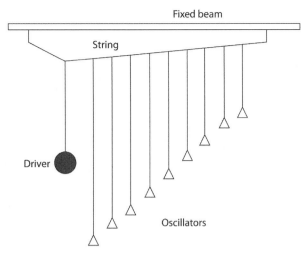

Figure 4.11 Barton's pendulum being used to show how the different parts of the cochlea respond to different sound waves. Adapted from an image created by Amitchell125 and shared on Wikipedia Commons: https://commons.wikimedia.org/wiki/File:Barton's_pendulums.svg under the Creative Commons Attribution-Share Alike 4.0 International license.

like the waves that give deeper sounds. Conversely, a shorter driver string will give a more rapid. Secondly, they should see that only one of the pendulums will be made to swing hard by the 'driver'. As the 'driver' swings more and more quickly, the shorter the pendulum that is made to swing hard (resonate). This shows how low-pitched sounds are detected up by the wider parts at the bottom of the jelly spiral and how the high-pitched sounds are detected by the narrower parts, towards the top of the spiral.

However, you choose to look at how we hear, the plenary should ensure that they see the link between different sound waves/air pushes and how the ear carries the message through to the sound detector, or cochlea. Nerves then take information about the sound waves to our brain.

Lesson 3: What is colour?

(Before teaching the next two lessons, it is worth finding out if any pupils have colour vision impairment. If they are comfortable to talk about it, they can be a great asset to the lesson, sharing what they see compared to those with full colour vision. They will benefit from a colour identification app, which can be downloaded on to a tablet or phone and which says the colour of the object it is pointed at.)

The lesson should start with the concept that light is energy that travels in regular 'pulses', in a similar way to sound. Like sound, it carries energy. Light waves are much more like the pupils' idea of an archetypal wave in being an 'up and down' wave, rather than a 'to and fro' wave. They also move much, much faster than sound waves. A return to the slinky spring model is helpful to show what light is like in a concrete way. The content that they considered under sound can be picked up again here by asking how light waves might be different form each other, remembering what they know about different sound waves. What we would like to establish at this point is that the waves could be:

- Smaller or higher, corresponding, respectively, to dim or bright light
- Closer together or further apart (higher or lower frequency)

This leads us to the idea that different colours have different closeness of waves. The closer the waves, the more energy the light waves bring us. It is interesting to ask pupils which of the colours of the rainbow they think has the most energy, opinions vary with some saying that red is a 'hot colour', whilst blue is a 'cold colour' so red has the most energy.

One way to show the answer to this question is to make a 'rainbow' with a thin beam of light (shining a light through cardboard with a slit, for example) on to a glass or Perspex prism. You can then project the 'rainbow' or spread of coloured light, onto something light sensitive positioned in front of the rainbow. Suitable light sensitive materials include blueprint paper or some photographic film or filter paper that has some silver bromide precipitate on it. (The paper needs to be made in advance, dried and kept in the dark, for instance wrapped in foil until you are ready to use it.) You need to remember (or take a picture, or mark in pencil on the paper, which side of the rainbow is violet and which is red). Once you see a change appears, remove the light-sensitive material and take a photo to capture the difference before longer exposure to daylight produces a uniform change.

At this point, the key points can be recapped, namely that light carries energy and that different colours carry different amounts of energy, violet the most, red the least. Although it is tempting to extend this conversation into the rest of the electro-magnetic spectrum, I would suggest that teachers resist sharing, despite the fact that it could be done. This is a point in inclusive science teaching where 'less is more' and 'enough is as good as a feast'. Further considerations of other examples of electro-magnetic radiation can be held back for future consideration if it is needed or of interest to pupils.

A good conclusion to the lesson is to show pupils that just as white light can be split into different colours, the same colours can be re-combined to make white light. A Newton's wheel, when spun fast enough, shows how colours can be combined to make white light. [See https://www.stem.org.uk/resources/elibrary/resource/28166/newton-wheel].

Lesson 5: Seeing colour: The eye

The eye is more complicated to explain in full than the ear because the eye does several things that contribute to our vision. The eye focuses the light to detect colours, light intensity and shape. Since the focus of the last lesson was on colour, colour vision is a good place to start. This is also justifiable in terms of engagement since the detection of light intensity is unlikely to be of very immediate interest to pupils and the focusing aspect of the eye can be addressed either separately, or secondary to developing an understanding of how the eye detects different colours.

The first stage of the lesson is to establish that although they saw that white light is made of lots of different colours, we are now going to look at what the least number of colours that we need to make white light or could split white light into. These three colours are red, green and blue. You can show this in various ways. If you are in a lab, you will probably have access to microscope or optics lamps and can cover them with coloured film and shine them on to a white screen. Alternatively, you can dust off an ancient overhead projector and displaying overlapping pieces of coloured film. There are digital demonstrations available on-line but it can also be done using three torches with a circle of red, green and blue film, respectively. If you do not have coloured film, you can colour overhead transparency or clear polyethene pockets with permanent markers.

Although this activity is taught with a large amount of content, such as the names of the so-called secondary colours made by mixing two of the three primary colours. However, I do not think that knowing the names of the secondary colours enhances understanding usefully, so it suffices to say that we can make different colours by mixing the colours (in different intensities, that is different number of light waves hitting a certain area) and mixing all three (all of equal intensity) gives us white light.

[Many schemes of work choose to look at the appearance of coloured objects when they are placed in different primary coloured light at this point. However, this is not necessary to explain how the eye detects colour, pupils simply have to understand the relationship between the light beams that come from a coloured object, irrespective of its relationship to the light the object absorbs. That we see the light that is not absorbed is especially challenging because it involves an inverse relationship, we see what is not absorbed, which taxes many pupils' processing capacity. For this reason, I will restrict my use of the primary colours here to being an introduction to the way that the eye detects colours.]

The path that light takes can be traced on a simple diagram, in a way analogous to the path that they traced for sound waves going into the ear. To reinforce the idea that the light travels in straight lines until something causes it to bend, they can use strands of spaghetti to show the path of the light, sapping it off highlights the points at which it bends. They may notice that the curved structures help to bend the ray of light to the centre, as does the liquid in the eye. (This effect is easily shown by putting water into a pop bottle with indents around the bottom, with a light shining down on it. Pupils will see that the shadow around the base of the bottle that the parts that curve out focus the light and give a bright halo, whilst the indents cause the light to scatter and so have a dark shadow. A pop bottle containing water and an identical one

'Amount' (intensity) of red light	'Amount' of green light	'Amount' of blue light	Colour we see
++ (full intensity)	++	++	White
++	0 (light off)	0	Red
++	+ (reduced intensity)	0	Orange
++	0	+	Violet
++	++	0	Yellow
++	0	++	Bright pink
0	++	0	Green
+	++	0	Blue
0	++	+	Acid green
0	++	++	Turquoise
0	0	++	Blue
0	+	++	Grey-blue
+	0	++	Dull purple

Figure 4.12 How the three primary colours can be added to give the colours of the rainbow.

containing air also allow you to show that the liquid in the eye helps to bend the light through the hole and on to the light-detecting part at the back.)

When the light reaches the back of the eye, it hits the lining (the retina) and this can detect colours. It can detect red light, green light and blue light. It does this by having three sort of colour-sensing cells, each one detects a different primary colour. Nerves run from the retina to the back of the eye and take messages to the brain about the amount of blue, green and red light that has hit the retina. Your brain then adds the information on the three colours together to sense what colour it was that came into the eye.

The intensity of each colour will be 'read' as one of the many colours of the spectrum, and this can be tested using the light sources that you used before but experimenting with reducing the intensity of coloured light by moving the source of light further from the screen (shown as + in Figure 4.12) putting or by leaving the colour source off completely (shown as 0). The sorts of results that you can expect are shown in Figure 4.12.

Lesson 6: Making colour blueprinting

Blueprinting (also called cyanotyping) is a fun way of linking and reinforcing the ideas that pupils have encountered about light. It can be done outside a lab, which is inexpensive (which is why it was popular with early women scientists, who often did not have their own incomes. Anna Atkins used blueprints to produce the world's first book to be illustrated with photographs.) It is also low risk to pupils, provided they do not make the solutions, and the results can be very attractive indeed. The reaction is between two iron compounds which react together in light. The light-sensitive paper made from the two iron compounds needs to be prepared in advance and allowed to dry away from direct light. It should then be stored out of direct light, wrapping it in kitchen foil is a good way to store it. [See https://edu.rsc.org//resources/making-and-using-blueprint-paper/1591. article for full details and risk assessment.] Bright sunshine was the original source of light but the chemical reaction will still take place on a dull day or if the light falls through glass, such as on to a window sill, but will occur much more slowly, due to the lower intensity of the light. If you can borrow an ultraviolet light (of the sort used to read security marker for instance), that is ideal, but even microscope or reading lamps with an incandescent bulb (rather than an LED 'energy saving' bulb) will speed the process up.

Its inclusion in this topic is because the production of the blue dye that happens on the paper (or cotton or linen fabric, if you prefer). The reaction happens when light energy hits the chemical mixture on the paper. This is like the reaction that happens when coloured light hits the back of the eye and, like this reaction, it is reversible, but the rods go back to their original form in a few seconds. The blue dye may fade much more slowly, over several months.

Using what they have learnt about light, which colour of light do they think will make the reaction happen the fastest? They may remember that blue is the highest energy light. What coloured light would you want in a room where you were making blueprints? Red, because we can still see it, but it carries less energy and will not affect the paper as quickly.

As this activity is meant to be educational rather than purely entertaining, you need to decide what your learning intention is. If you have different coloured lights, this can be carried out as an investigation of the effect of white light and different coloured lights on the time taken for the paper to turn blue. You could leave paper samples under a light for different lengths of time to see what the minimum time is to get a good blue colour with the light source you are using. It can be used to compare different items that are placed on to see which ones let the most light through (plant materials, such as flowers, give some very artistic results and show the relative thickness of different petals and leaves).

Alternatively, you can use this as synoptic revision activity. Pupils can be asked to show what they have learnt about sound and light on their print. They can draw their image and text in black permanent markers on a piece of acetate or a single piece of clear plastic from a polythene pocket and use this to create their blueprint. (Whatever they have drawn will remain pale yellow whilst the background turns blue.) They can also place objects of their choice on the paper to get a 'shadow prints'.

References

Driver. R. (1988). Theory into practice II: A constructivist approach to curriculum development. In P. Fensham (Ed.), *Development and dilemmas in science education* (pp. 133–149). Falmer Press.

Johnstone, A.H. (1991). Why is science difficult to learn? Things are seldom what they seem. *Journal of Computer Assisted Learning*, 7(2), 75–83.

Millar, R. (2005). *Teaching about energy*. Department of Research Studies Research Paper 2005/11, University of York.

Naylor, S., & Keogh, B. (2000). *Science concept cartoons*. Millgate House Publishers.

Reid, D. J., & Hodson, D. (1987). *Science for all: Teaching science in the secondary school*. Cassell.

Worley, B., & Paterson, D. (2021). *Understanding chemistry through microscale practical work*. Association for Science Education.

5   Conclusion

Whether you have worked systematically through the book or, more probably, dipped into sections that are of most immediate relevance to your practice, you will be aware that it has advanced several key ideas, namely:

- Learning science is beneficial for all pupils, without exception.
- There are numerous good reasons for learning science, of which preparation to be a professional scientist is only one.
- As a subject, science has a history of elitism and exclusion and these are now deeply embedded in all aspects of scientific culture.
- These trappings are not essential for developing secure scientific literacy and acquiring scientific knowledge.
- The science curriculum and its associated pedagogy create many additional barriers for those with learning difficulties.
- There are multiple practical actions that collectively enhance the inclusiveness of science education.

Every part of the book is intended to show that science is a worthwhile area of study for all pupils but only if it is the right sort of science and the pedagogy is flexible and able to respond to diverse needs. In Section 2, I have analysed the barriers that science education typically presents in detail and have considered various practical strategies to improve the accessibility of science. These strategies are not only linked to research evidence and current ideas about thinking and learning but also reflect the experiences of both the author and numerous colleagues. Implementing all these ideas is the work of a professional lifetime, but if you add a few of these ideas each year, you will develop a wide repertoire of ways to enhance inclusion in science. Although teachers are most commonly prompted to revise their inclusive practices by a specific pupil's needs, the strategies described are not intended only to be targeted at those pupils but rather to be available for anyone who may find the approach helpful. In writing this, I am acutely aware that every class teacher is working in a unique context and implementing any of the suggestions depends upon their professional judgement as to their suitability. What I hope is that you now feel both motivated to enhance inclusivity of your teaching and that you have a 'toolkit' of changes that you can consider implementing. This should enable you to make an informed choice about how you might respond to the support needs in your science classroom. Section 3 illustrates the issue of how the assessment that is usually used is considered and the way on which it can create further barriers to inclusion has been reflected upon. I drew the reader's attention to the numerous ways in which success in science can be described and captured. Section 4 illustrates how the principles and strategies described in Section 2 might be enacted in the teaching of some exemplar science topics. Again, this is illustrative, and only the teacher who has a detailed knowledge of their setting and pupils will be able to decide whether the suggestions are likely to be successful for them. Similar considerations apply when teachers consider which sources of further support listed in Section 6 might be helpful in their setting.

The book is intended to offer a counter-narrative to the widely held beliefs that science is inevitably non-inclusive and is only really suitable for some learners. I have been privileged to see pupils with very complex support needs engaging enthusiastically with science learning and hope that teachers will find in the book encouragement to explore further what can be done when such prejudices are set aside. There is a huge gap in the evidence on science education that is intentionally inclusive of those with learning disabilities and every effort to map this gap helps to reduce our collective unknowing. The contents of the book are intended to serve as the first conversation in a renewed discussion on genuinely inclusive science that retains the characteristic of science as discipline, rather than a 'watered down' version of it. This is a topic which

DOI: 10.4324/9781003167815-6

last had a book dedicated to it nearly 40 years ago, when Reid and Hodson (1987) wrote their book with its aspirational title, *'Science for all'*, so this debate is long overdue. I hope that what you have read stirs you both to practical action in your classroom and to contribute to a wider conversation about what science education is, could be and should be for.

Reference

Reid, D. J., & Hodson, D. (1987). *Science for all: Teaching science in the secondary school*. Cassell.

6 Further sources of support and ideas

Unfortunately, there is very little available that explicitly addresses pupils with additional/special needs who are learning science. Teachers either have to use materials from bodies with a focus on science education or apply ideas that are associated with a particular need to science resources. The science organisations that teachers work with are often sympathetic to the plight of science teachers who work with pupils with learning disabilities (LD) or other additional/special needs but most choose for strategic reasons to focus on neuro-typical pupils. The reasons for this focus on a group who are seen as the source of future science professionals have been considered in Section 2 and do not need repeating here. However, it is worth pointing out that there is an alignment of focus of the science professional bodies, the curriculum and exam boards and publishers, on typically achieving pupils. The apparent near invisibility to the science education community of these exceptional learners perpetuates outdated stereotypes and continues to fuel low aspirations. At the time of writing this book (late 2022), I have been endeavouring for over five years to find a host website where inclusive and accessible science resources could be shared by teachers and have not succeeded, yet.

Professional bodies who have been actively engaged in inclusive science teaching

Having said that, many of the science organisations are sympathetic to the needs of diverse learners and those who teach them science. Amongst those organisations who have shown an active interest in them are:

- **Association for Science Education (ASE)** (www.ase.org.uk) is a cross-disciplinary organisation, which has a very active primary education membership and consciously includes technicians in its work. This means that it is a valuable umbrella organisation that can facilitate professional development of those working with pupils whose learning is significantly different to their chronological age and support staff who wish to become involved. An on-line ASE Inclusive Science Education group meets six times a year and is open to members and non-members who wish to discuss inclusive science teaching and learning. The group often invites a speaker who has been identified by members as having something to share that may be useful; beyond that the group offers a forum to ask questions, share experiences and talk to like-minded educators. To register, please go to www.ase.org.uk/inclusive-science-education-special-interest-group
- **Royal Society of Chemistry (RSC)** (www.rsc.org): The RSC offers a vast range of on-line resources on the Teach Chemistry area of its website and regional support in the UK and Ireland via its area education co-ordinators. The focus for secondary resources is chemistry and materials science but the primary resources address science more generally. The RSC also offers funding (shown under the Awards and funding tab on the home page) that can be used to enhance science/chemistry provision in schools and is not difficult to bid for. Currently, money available includes a chemistry teaching empowerment fund that enables teachers to organise a collaborative venture (such as a cross-phase meeting). The Outreach Fund provides money to enable people and organisations to run outreach and engagement events in schools or with the public. The Inclusion and Diversity Fund offers money up to £5,000 for innovative projects that can enhance inclusion in the chemical sciences. There is also a £1,000 accessibility grant to pay for adjustments to make a science event accessible for someone with a disability or health condition, for instance additional support staff to support a pupil on science-related trip.

DOI: 10.4324/9781003167815-7

The RSC's Biological and Medicinal Chemistry Section (https://www.rscbmcs.org/) offers educational grants that currently have three areas of focus: enhanced equipment, chemistry clubs and partnerships of three, which funds work undertaken by three partners, such as a school, college and university.

The RSC also has local sections (regional groups) who can be asked for funding to support initiatives in their geographical area.

- **Royal Society** (https://www.royalsociety.org) describes itself as the oldest learned society and is primarily focused on supporting professional scientists. However, they do offer a Partnership Grant Partnership Grants | Royal Society which is intended to promote partnerships on STEM projects between schools and industrial or academic partners. It is encouraging to see that one of the links on the web page for this scheme is headed 'special educational needs and disabilities' and I know of one special school who have successfully applied for funding. Although universities and industries make (understandably) a lot of use of outreach and partnership as a way to recruit future specialist staff, many are very open to requests from groups of pupils with additional/special support needs. Aside from the cynical thought that working with you enables them to 'tick their inclusion box', remember that your pupils offer them an opportunity to work with a much more diverse group of pupils than they may be accustomed to. My experience of involving academics and industrial partners in inclusive science or STEM initiatives suggests that, far from finding it a difficult duty, they view it as a very enlightening piece of professional development. The partners report that it greatly improves their understanding of science communication and enhances their professional practice.
- **Lightyear Foundation (**https://www.lightyearfoundation.org) is a charity which sets out to *break down the barriers to disabled children taking part in STEM*. They offer a range of activities and resources which broadly correspond to wider STEM provision but with an intentional focus on making it suitable for learners with additional/special support needs. Teachers are welcome to join the free SEN in STEM Network, which has many teacher members as well as other parties interested in this area, such as professional bodies and education officers from visitor centres. Teachers are also able to access Network resources and connect with other members with a shared interest in inclusive science through their LinkedIn group. Lightyear offers Making STEM Accessible CPD (continuing professional development) sessions plus a consultancy service for a fee to provide help on a specific topic/issue. Lightyear also offers 'Making STEM Accessible' sessions which can be paid for on a session-by-session basis. Lastly, Lightyear hosts a web page of diverse STEM role models who are STEM professionals with various types of disability. The organisation runs work inspiration trips for pupils with additional/special support needs which correspond to some of the career information work done by other bodies such as the STEM Ambassador network.

There are numerous science- and STEM-promoting organisations that do not focus explicitly on inclusion and I would encourage the reader to take the initiative and ask these bodies how they can support pupils with LD or other additional/special needs. They may want to get involved but simply not know how to, so your request for specific help with science may initiate fruitful conversations about what support is needed and how the organisations might help. The same applies to local places of interest, visitor centres, museums and the like.

One of my key pieces of advice to teachers is to, 'Make your professional body work for **you**'. Writing this section, it has been very encouraging to see the rapid shift in the attitude of professional organisations to diversity and inclusion. What was seen as a nice 'optional extra' has now become core business and the offers by the different bodies reflect this transformation. If you have a discipline-specific request, I would strongly recommend that you should approach the relevant professional body to discuss this.

In the area of employment, you will notice that a number of organisations promote interaction with employers. This is of value to all learners, as it helps them to see that what they are learning has 'real world' relevance but there is a common assumption that science/STEM workplaces are only for the academic high achievers. This focus of many employers on attracting this level of staff disguises the fact that technical and scientific workplaces need staff of a range of skills, aptitudes and qualifications to function. People who enter support roles in a STEM environment because they enjoy STEM are still very much part of a STEM community, and an important one. Apprenticeships, supported internships and courses at Further Education Colleges provide very suitable routes for those who thrive with different learning and assessment routes to those that most of their teachers have succeeded on. Only if pupils can see the range of opportunities that the STEM workplace offers, they can make an informed decision about whether it is a workplace they would like to be in.

Below are some organisations that I have interacted with, or which have been recommended by colleagues with an interest in the area of inclusive science. They are grouped according to their subject focus.

General science

- **National STEM Learning Centre** (https://www.stem.org.uk/): The centre offers continuing professional development, it also hosts the UK STEM Ambassador website. Through 17 regional hubs, the STEM Ambassador network brings STEM professionals and school or community groups together.
- Dr Susie Nyman is a curriculum manager who has written extensively about approaches to multi-sensory (multi-modal) education to enhance learning, especially literacy. Her website is drnymanconsultancy.co.uk
- WISE (Web-based Inquiry Science Environment) (https://wise.berkeley.edu): Virtual experiments linked to scientific explanations. These digital representations of experiments are very well liked by teachers working with diverse learners. Whilst they can be used as an alternative to hands-on experimentation, they can also make a powerful adjunct to learning through hands on, as they offer the opportunity for repeat runs of the experiment and at the same time offer clear scientific explanations. They can either be used as preparation for doing an experiment or to re-visit the experiment after it has been conducted and so offer useful reinforcement. Because they are digital, those who suffer quickly from cognitive or sensory overload are able to control the rate at which ideas and observations are displayed.
- The **CREST Awards** (https://www.crestawards.org) are a series of awards offered by the British Science Association at different levels (Discovery, bronze, silver and gold) aimed at different age groups of primary and secondary pupils and requiring them to run a STEM investigation. The Discovery award is given for a series of one-day investigations, the other levels for more extended investigations of increasing level of complexity and challenge. There is a minimal charge for schools other than those in Wales but this provides a way to recognise and reward engagement with STEM.
- **Young STEM Leader Programme** (https://www.youngstemleader.scot) is a recent initiative that is already being taken up enthusiastically by teachers working with pupils with additional/special support needs. It is free to schools in Scotland whilst schools in England pay a subscription to undertake the award. The programme offers both informal and formal awards, the latter being credit rated by the Scottish Qualifications Authority. There are a total of six possible awards and schools can choose which level and route would suit their pupils. The informal awards are internally assessed whilst the external awards are verified.

  All the awards are given on the basis of a portfolio, which has been deliberately left very flexible in terms of evidence that is accepted. Pupils need to show (and they can have help with the record-keeping) that they have run a STEM activity or activities and delivered these to an audience. This could be a STEM club for pupils younger than themselves or a community group or at a public event. This could not only involve doing experiments in the style of a 'science fair' but has also involved things as diverse as setting up a 'Facebook for grannies' and teaching older people how to use social media or running a pop up beauty salon in school. The versatility of the scheme is one of its strengths, the other is that it positions the pupils as STEM leaders, rather than passive recipients of STEM.
- **Earth Learning Ideas** (https://www.earthlearningidea.com/): Earth science is a very versatile topic that can be linked to many different topics and can be studied meaningfully with very little equipment. The activities on the website make extensive use of models to make events accessible that take place in dangerous places or over very long timescales, so could be used as a vehicle to consider how and why scientists use models.
- **Council for Learning Outside the Classroom** (https://www.lotc.org.uk) provides practical guidance and professional development for teachers wanting to enhance pupils' learning outside the classroom. This can offer valuable enrichment and does not need to involve travel to remote places but can simply involve making better use of the school environment.

Practical science

- **CLEAPSS** (https://www.cleapss.org.uk) is a consultancy body that offers advice on practical work, including on the safety of practical work, to its members in England, Northern Ireland and Wales. They offer advice to support staff and teachers in primary, special and secondary schools and FE colleges in the curriculum areas of science and technology. Most local authorities subscribe to it, and if you work in a subscribing authority (or academy trust in England), you will be able to access its resources. Independent schools and colleges subscribe on an individual basis. In addition to holding an extensive searchable database on equipment, reagents and experiments, which is updated in line with the latest evidence and legislation, they offer training for staff. They can also offer advice on the design of laboratory and workshop spaces. CLEAPSS staff are all experienced teachers or technicians and they can answer individual queries if they are not covered by the general documentation, for example if you have a specific safety concern relating to the support needs of a pupil doing a specific experiment.
- **SSERC** (https://www.SSERC.org.uk) is the equivalent of CLEAPSS in Scotland and offers a similar service to that provided by CLEAPSS but linked to the Scottish curriculum.

Biology and field work

- **The Royal Society of Biology** offers a similar programme of CPD and professional recognition for teachers and technicians as its sister organisations in chemistry and physics. One distinctive offering is a competition for specimen drawing, the Nancy Rothwell Award, which would appeal to students who enjoy drawing living things. There is also a photography competition with an under 18s category. This is a theme each year and the competition could be used to encourage pupils to capture photos of the living world that represent the theme.
- The **Linnean Society** is a learned society that advances work in 'Natural History'. It offers grants of up to £1,000 for project that see young people projects that let young people 'take the lead on projects that involve their local nature and natural spaces, to aid young people in realising their influence, to have their voices heard, and see their ideas come to life'.
- **Our-local-nature-grants** (https://www.linnean.org/the-society/medals-awards-prizes-grants/)
- **Royal Microscopical Society** (https://www.rms.org.uk) offers an outreach programme, provides financial help for primary or secondary schools wishing to buy microscopes and sends out loan microscopy activity kits to primary schools.
- **Science and Plants for Schools (SAPS)** (https://www.saps.org.uk): This website and the associated professional development support are intended to help to enhance the teaching of plant science. Experiments with plants can be straightforward to manage, interesting and accessible. The 'science club' resources, see at https://www.saps.org.uk/teaching-resources, suggest interesting activities that are suitable for pupils with LD.

Chemistry, material science

- The **Royce Institute** (www.royce.ac.uk/outreach/) supports learning about materials science and has an active outreach team. They lend, free of charge, 'kit boxes' with a set of interesting and interactive investigations into materials and their properties. To promote outreach work and enrichment activities, they offer an outreach bursary of up to £500.
- The **Salters' Institute** (https://saltersinstitute.org/) aims to 'make chemistry matter for all' and offer a series of activities, including public programmes, on-line lectures and chemistry festivals on university campuses, plus an on-line chemistry club that offers activities such as on-line quizzes and videos that pupils can engage with independently. There are some hands-on activities listed under the Resources tab, many of which are possible outside a lab. The previous Chemistry Club handbooks numbers 1 and 2 offer more ideas for hands-on activities, graded according to degree of difficulty and, again, many of them being achievable outside a lab. The former hard copy handbooks are now available on-line via: https://allaboutstem.co.uk/resources/download-the-salters-chemistry-club-handbooks

Physics

- **Institute of Physics** (https://www.iop.org/) of special interest is their Limit Less project (https://www.iop.org/strategy/limit-less) which aims to gather evidence on damaging stereotyping and to provide guidance on how to change such views. The focus is currently on gender and ethnicity but since all under-represented groups face equivalent barriers of low expectation, lack of role models and a narrow, inflexible view of what physics is and who can do it, I think the work is of wider value and would encourage teachers to engage with it.
- The **Ogden Trust** (www.ogdentrust.com) aims to increase 'engagement for all young people (4-18), particularly those in under-represented groups'. It offers a range of programmes under two headings, 'Supporting teachers' and 'School partnerships'. The teacher support programme works with those teaching physics (whether or not they have a teaching specialism in physics), or physical processes at primary level, to support the development of their subject knowledge. Since understanding whatever you are, teaching enables teachers to identify what is conceptually essential and what can be adjusted or omitted, I think secure subject knowledge is important for all teachers. I absolutely reject the notion that good subject knowledge is only needed for those teaching future science specialists.

    The schools' partnership provision focuses on increasing what is referred to as the 'science capital' of the school community. It aims to enhance the wider learning environment, including by working with support staff (both technicians and teaching assistants), and investing in learning spaces and resources. The schools' partnership also supports enrichment activities through engaging families and the wider community. They also assist with networking with local employers so pupils can have relevant physics experiences.
- **National Aeronautics and Space Administration** (https://www.nasa.gov): As noted in the Earth and Space topic, this has a variable presence in the curriculum but is popular with pupils and can serve as the basis of observational work that requires minimal apparatus. NASA has a host of educational resources (categorised by American grade bands), many of which do not require specialist lab equipment. These could be used to enrich topic such as energy, living things or to show examples of designer materials in a chemistry topic.

Organisations that work with specific groups of people according to the nature of their support needs are listed below and are grouped according to the type of need that they cater for.

Special educational needs support

To meet the practical needs of individual pupils, the first port of call should be local provision, such as the psychological service, the hearing impairment inclusion support service. Individual authorities or academy trusts will have policy documents relating to pupils with additional/special support needs and these are likely to give further information about local support and specialist service.

- National Association for Special Educational Needs (nasen) (www.nasen.org.uk): NASEN describes itself as existing to *'support and champion those working with, and for, children and young people with SEND and learning differences'*. Membership is free for educators working in a UK educational institution and that will enable you to access their library of resources and receive newsletters and updates. NASEN organises conferences and regional events at which those working with diverse learners can meet and share ideas.

Specific learning difficulties

Many people with LD have functional difficulties that are associated with specific learning difficulties (SLD), even if they do not have an SLD diagnosis. True to my belief that inclusion should benefit everyone and impede no-one's learning, the following group offer advice that may be beneficial to a number of pupils, irrespective of the cause of their difficulties.

- **The National Autistic Society (**NAS) (National Autistic Society [autism.org.uk]) is a UK wide charity that supports people with autism and those who work with them. They provide information and training on the condition.
- **Scottish Autism** (www.scottishautism.org): In addition to the NAS, Scotland has an additional group, which undertakes similar work but only within Scotland.
- **British Dyslexia Association** (https://www.bdadyslexia.org.uk) provides information and professional development for teachers working with pupils with dyslexia and dyscalculia. They also administer the award of 'Dyslexia friendly' status to schools and other organisations.
- **Dyslexia Scotland** (https://dyslexiascotland.org.uk/) offers support and training to teachers, and others working with people with dyslexia or affected by the condition, in Scotland.
- **Dysgraphia,** and how to support pupils with it, is described at: https://www.structural-learning.com/post/dysgraphia

Sensory impairment

- **The Royal National Institute of Blind People** (https://rnib.org.uk) supports those with sight loss and their page on 'Getting the right support' (https://rnib.org.uk/living-with-sight-loss/education-andlearning/getting-the-right-support-sen-and-inclusion) is a helpful summary of how educational settings should operate to support a learner with additional/special support needs. Although the focus here is on visual impairment, much of the information is more widely applicable.
- **Scottish Sensory Centre** (www.ssc.education.ed.ac.uk): In addition to specialist training for those working with deaf, visually impaired and deaf-blind people, they provide specialist resources. Under the British Sign Language (BSL) glossary tab, you will find BSL glossaries of curriculum terms. This can be used to provide multi-modal support for the development of a technical vocabulary as well as with deaf or hearing-impaired pupils. (The glossaries are also available as an app for phones and tablets).
- **The National Deaf Children's Society** (http://ndcs.org.uk) provides information packs about how to be a deaf-friendly primary or secondary school, and guidance on managing remote learning and school trips so that pupils with hearing impairments can participate fully. Similar adjustments will be needed for other pupils with social and communication difficulties, so this is a useful checklist.

Index

Note: Page numbers in *italics* refer to figures.

Printed in Great Britain
by Amazon

25224217R00082